An Unjust God?

An Unjust God?

A Christian Theology of Israel in Light of Romans 9–11

Jacques Ellul

Translated by Anne-Marie Andreasson-Hogg

 CASCADE *Books* · Eugene, Oregon

AN UNJUST GOD?
A Christian Theology of Israel in Light of Romans 9–11

Previously published in french as *Ce Dieu injuste? Théologie chrétienne pour le peuple d'Israël.* Paris: Arléa, 1991.

Cascade Books
An Imprint of Wipf and Stock Publishers
199 W. 8th Ave., Suite 3
Eugene, OR 97401
www.wipfandstock.com

ISBN 13: 978-1-62032-361-8

Cataloging-in-Publication data:

Ellul, Jacques.

    An unjust God? : a Christian theology of Israel in light of Romans 9–11 / Jacques Ellul, translated by Anne-Marie Andreasson-Hogg.

    xxii + 112 p. ; cm. Includes bibliographical references.

    ISBN 13: 978-1-62032-361-8

    1. Bible, N.T. Romans IX–XI—Criticism, interpretation, etc. 2. Judaism (Christian theology). I. Title.

BS2665.3 E49 2012

Manufactured in the U.S.A.

Contents

Foreword

THE STANDARD OUTLINE OF PAUL'S GREAT LETTER TO THE ROMANS SEES chs. 1–8 as a foundational "systematic theology" describing God, the problem of human sinfulness, and the solution in Jesus Christ. Then chs. 9–11 constitute a kind of part two, an excursus answering the question: "If all this is true, how then does it relate to what God was doing in Israel before Jesus arrived?" Part three, then, chs. 12–13, builds a comprehensive account of the ethics and discipleship implications of this grand theology. The first impact of this new work from Jacques Ellul, *An Unjust God?*, is to elevate the importance of Romans 9–11. They are no minor excursus but a dramatic step beyond part one. Now, the "therefore" that opens ch. 12 is tightly linked to the message of chs. 9–11, not just to chs. 1–8.

The title of this work, first published in French in 1991, three years before Ellul's death, comes from Romans 9:14: "What shall we say, therefore? Is there some injustice in God?" And the emphatic answer: "Far from it!" Why, we might ask, would this question even come up? Perhaps it is because it appears that God has transferred his promises and affection from Israel to the Church. Perhaps it is because God's choices sometimes seem arbitrary (e.g., Jacob have I loved; Esau have I hated). Perhaps it is because the evil and faithlessness that take place among people are attributable to God's action in hardening their hearts.

Jacques Ellul's careful reading of Romans 9–11 is an astounding exercise in careful listening. Unfazed by the deeply rutted and now predictable interpretive pathways established through this material, Ellul is massively open to a fresh direction in hearing what God might actually be saying. He draws on linguistic studies and on two of his favorite biblical commentators, Wilhelm Vischer (1895–1988) and Alphonse Maillot (1920–2003), along with other classic and contemporary thinkers; but, Ellul is always his own man as he grapples with the text in fresh ways. It is hard not to think that Ellul's intense relationships with the Jewish people during the Nazi Occupation of France affected his views. Seeing their suffering, living alongside them, and learning from them—the great rabbinic teachers as well as the ordinary people—Ellul has been a staunch, lifelong advocate for the Jewish people and for the state of Israel. Still, this is not an argument based on sentiment or sympathy, but on a careful study of the text of Scripture.

For Ellul, there is no question of Israel and the Jewish people losing their identity, importance, or salvation with the coming of Christ, despite their general failure to recognize and affirm Jesus as the Messiah. What changes is their election to carry the Gospel of redemption and freedom to the "pagans," to the ends of the earth. Israel had turned in on itself; the Jews attempted to build their own righteousness by their (mis-)understanding of the law, rather than fulfilling their mission to be a blessing to all the nations. With Jesus Christ, the Church—made up of Jews and pagans—is given that election by God to proclaim and live out God's freedom, forgiveness, and welcome to the ends of the earth. Few Christian authors have ever captured the anguish over the Jewish people expressed by Paul at the beginning of Romans 9 as Ellul does in this work. And few writers have ever seen the suffering of Israel over the centuries so profoundly linked to the cross and suffering of Jesus in the way that Ellul has.

This side of the New Testament, Ellul sees a sad betrayal by the Church of its own election to be a blessing to the whole earth! Not at all unlike what Israel experienced, the church's self-justifying doctrinal legalism and exclusionary practices (not the least of which has been its anti-Semitism) replaced their calling to be the heralds of freedom before God. Why haven't the Jewish people accepted Jesus as the Messiah? For Ellul, the fault lies in large part at the feet of a Christian Church that has failed to be the faithful Body of Christ in continuity with the Jewish Savior of the world, Jesus.

Ellul has powerful insights into Paul's ongoing Jewishness, into the shifting role of Israel throughout history and its future end in God's purposes. His views on salvation, predestination, condemnation, and election are challenging and will not always be persuasive to all readers. No matter! In the end, as after reading any biblical meditation by Ellul, we are drawn into the scriptural text anew, with expectation and excitement. Ellul often said, "You can ask any question of the biblical text—except for the Serpent's question 'Yea, hath God said?'" Ellul also insisted that God's questions for humanity were far more important than humanity's questions for God. In Ellul's *An Unjust God?* we are treated to a veritable intellectual/spiritual feast of inviting God to question us about Israel and the Church.

May 2012

David W. Gill, PhD
President, International Jacques Ellul Society
Mockler-Phillips Professor of Workplace Ethics
Gordon-Conwell Theological Seminary

Preface

Labyrinth and Ariadne's Thread

IN ORDER TO HELP THE READER UNDERSTAND WHAT FOLLOWS AND WHAT might appear to be a labyrinth—or, depending on one's mood, a series of sophisms—I will attempt to summarize the argument and show both the contradictions that Paul faces and the way in which he chooses to solve them. It is true that many of these contradictions arise from our own conceptions, our own preconceived ideas, and from the simplification that we have brought to the complex tangle of God's work, the work that God ties to the work of man. We are too accustomed to our elementary "either . . . or," whereas God's action—*when he acts*, which is not always, for God is not Providence—is never as simplistic as we imagine it to be.

Here then, first of all, are our contradictions:

1. God decides everything. He is absolutely free in his decision and never has to account for any of it. How could man then be responsible, how could he be "condemned," if he has merely followed, as his fate, what God has freely decided?

2. God is merciful to those who believe in Jesus Christ. At the same time, however, God is absolutely faithful and never withdraws his grace from a person on whom he has bestowed it. The people of Israel still benefit from the first promise and from the first covenant. Yes, but . . . the same people of Israel did not acknowledge Jesus as Savior. So then, either man is saved in Jesus Christ and Israel is condemned, or Israel remains the people of God and man is not saved by grace in Jesus Christ.

3. God creates people for various destinies: some to bear witness to his love, others to bear witness to his wrath. Why should the latter be "punished" since they were made in advance to reveal this wrath?

4. God "saves" some and "rejects" others, but what is the purpose of this salvation or rejection given that man cannot do anything about it? How can one accept that those people, while not responsible, should be damned for all eternity? What aim is God pursuing with such arbitrary decisions?

5. If Israel is still God's people, what then is the use of the church? And, reciprocally, if the church is now God's new people, then Israel is no longer anything. Is that not obvious?

6. If everything is by grace, if God only saves by grace, what then is the use of the Old Testament, and in particular what is the use of the Law? Conversely, if the Law still applies, if it is still necessary, if one still needs to obey the commandments, then God no longer saves by grace but by the excellence of human obedience.

7. Everything gets even more complicated if we take into account the fact that in this long history of Israel there is always a called one and a rejected one who come in pairs: Isaac and Ishmael, then Jacob and Esau, then Moses and Pharaoh, and so forth. And it is obviously not by accident that we are told these successive stories with these inseparable pairs.

Paul approaches these logical impossibilities by following two rigorous paths: First, while absolutely free, God is also absolutely faithful. He never reneges and will keep his promises regardless of what man does. Secondly, God is the Liberator: he frees man and never forces him, neither through a pre-established "destiny" for his life nor through any constraint in the moment. Man remains free to choose his path, but in the end, through a meandering and roundabout way, it is always God's will that is accomplished.

Such then is the simplified course of the theology that we will describe in detail as we go along:

The chosen people remains the chosen people. This choice is a free act of God, but it has no connection (as we too often imagine) with eternal salvation. It is only the choice of a servant destined to carry the witness of God (the covenant) into the world. Given that the chosen people did not completely fulfill this mission, it is replaced, *for this mission*, by those who are called in Jesus Christ and who will proclaim the love of God to all people. Moreover, the Jews are part of this new witnessing people because some of them (a remnant) have believed and because the remnant includes the whole (*pars pro toto*). If the majority of the people of Israel *made this error*, it is *in order that* all men may know grace and election. Pagans who converted to Christ must be grateful to the Jews. And, to the extent that the church is indeed charged with the same promise for the world, it is not the replacement for the Jewish people but its heir. To the extent that this people still exists as the chosen people—the first one—Christians and the church are a shoot growing out from this root and ancient trunk. Thus the people of *Israel become a witness to the faithfulness of God, and to the permanence of the promise. The church, in turn, becomes a witness to its universality and its freedom.*

Such is the outline developed by Paul to solve the contradictions mentioned above. We shall now enter into the details of his demonstration without losing the guiding thread I have outlined, which is of course a simplification.

Epistle to the Romans 9–11

The Unique People

9:1–5[1]

1. Through the Christ, I declare that I am speaking the truth, I do not lie; through the Holy Spirit, my conscience renders me this testimony.
2. I have great sorrow and in the deepest part of my being, I feel ceaseless grief.
3. I would even wish to be anathema (cursed), separated from Christ, in favor of my brothers, my relatives in the flesh.
4. They are the Israelites, theirs is the condition of sons, the glory, the covenants, the gift of the Torah, worship and the promises.
5. Theirs are the patriarchs, and it is from them that the Christ came as man. May he, who is God over all be blessed forever, amen!

This Unjust God

9:6–29

6. It is not that the Word of God has failed! But all those who come from Israel do not constitute Israel.
7. Neither are all of Abraham's descendants members of the family. It was said to Abraham: "In Isaac you will called a posterity."
8. Thus, the natural family is not God's family, only the family of the promise is considered to be Abraham's descendants.
9. Indeed, here is the word of the promise: "At that time I will come and there will be a son for Sarah."

1. This is the translation provided by Alphonse Maillot in his *Commentary on The Epistle to the Romans.*

10. And this is not all: it was after one and the same conjugal act of Rebecca and our father Isaac,

11. (As the children had not yet been born, and had done neither good nor evil, so that God's project might remain free,

12. a project which does not depend on human works but only on the One who calls) that it was said to Rebecca "the older will be subject to the younger."

13. As the Scriptures say: "I loved Jacob, but I pushed away Esau."

14. What should we then say? Is there not some injustice on the part of God? Impossible!

15. For He said to Moses: "I will have pity on whom I want to have pity and I will show mercy to whom I want to show mercy."

16. So there is no question of wanting, or striving, only the mercy of God counts.

17. For Scripture said to Pharaoh: "This is why I raised you up, that I might show my power through you, and that my name might be known all over the earth."

18. So then He pities whom He want and He hardens whom He wants.

19. You will object: "What is he complaining about? Who can oppose his will?"

20. But rather, who are you, a human being to challenge God? Can the work say to the worker: "Why did you make me like this?"

21. Does not the potter forming the clay have the right to use his clay to make a luxurious vase as well as a worthless vase?

22. And if God wanting to show His anger and reveal (all) that is possible for Him, endured with much patience the vases of burning, ready for destruction

23. and if wanting to make known all the resources of His glory towards the vases of glory, He prepared them ahead of time for glory, what fault would we find with that?

24. We who have been called not only among the Jews but also among pagans?

25. This is indeed what he said in Hosea: "I will call my people, those who were not my people and I will call beloved, she who was not beloved.

26. And in the very same place where they heard: "You are not my people! They will be called Sons of the living God."

27. Isaiah for his part, cries about Israel: "Even if the number of the children of Israel is like the sand of the sea, only a remnant will be saved.

28. For the Lord will fully and promptly accomplish His word on the earth."

29. And as Isaiah was saying in advance: "If the Lord Sabbaoth had not left us a few descendants we would all have become like Sodom and we would have resembled Gomorrah.

How Will They Believe?

9:30–33

30. What more can we say? Simply that pagans who did not pursue righteousness have obtained the righteousness that comes from faith.

31. As for Israel, who was pursuing a righteousness that comes from the Torah, did not even attain the Torah!

32. And why? Because it thought that this righteousness did not come from faith but that it could come from works. It stumbled over the stumbling stone.

33 As Scripture says: "See I lay in Zion a stumbling block, a rock on which one stumbles: but whoever trusts in him (believes in him) will not be ashamed."

10:1–21

1. Brothers, my dearest wish and my prayer to God for the Jews is that they may follow the road to salvation.

2. I testify that they have zeal for God but this zeal is without discernment.

3. Because they did not know God's righteousness and were trying to establish their own, they did not submit to the righteousness of God.

4. For the Christ who makes all believers attain righteousness is the end of the Torah.

5. For Moses wrote about the righteousness that comes from the Torah: "He who practices it will live from this righteousness."

6. But the righteousness that comes from faith says this: "Do not say: Who will go up to heaven? It would make Christ come down again!"

7. Nor should you say: Who will descend into the abyss? It would bring Christ back from the dead!"

8. Actually, what does it say? "The word is close to you, in your mouth and in your heart." This is the word of faith, the word we are proclaiming.

9. For if you confess with your mouth that Jesus is the Lord and if you believe from the bottom of your heart that God raised him from the dead, you will be saved.

10. For belief from the bottom of the heart leads to righteousness, confession of the mouth leads to salvation.

11. For Scripture says: "All those who put their trust in Him we not be ashamed!"

12. Thus there is no difference between Jews and Greeks, for all have the same Lord, who is generous to all who call upon Him.

13. For all those who call upon the name of the Lord will be saved.

14. But how will they call upon Him in whom they have not believed? And how will they believe in the One they have not heard of? And how will they hear if no one proclaims?

15. And how will it be proclaimed if God does not send anyone as it is written: "How the feet of those who proclaim good news come on time!"

16. But all have not listened to the Good News! In fact, Isaiah says: "Lord, who believed what we heard?"

17. For faith comes from what one hears and what one hears comes from the word of Christ.

18. I say it again: "Have they really not heard? Yes, they have! Their voice was heard over all the earth, their words unto the ends of the world."

19. I will add: "Did Israel really not understand?" Moses was the first to say: "I will make you jealous of a nation which is not a nation, I will make you angry about a nation of fools!

20. Late, Isaiah will even dare to say: "I was found by those who did not search for me, I revealed myself to those who were not questioning me."

21. And about Israel he says: "All day long I stretched out my hand toward a disobedient and stubborn people."

The Grafted Olive Tree

11:1–24

1. Then, I will say: "Has God then rejected his people?" Impossible! In fact, I am a Jew by birth myself, of the family of Abraham, of the tribe of Benjamin!

2. So then God has not rejected his people whom he knew before all others! Or else, you must be ignorant of what Scripture says in the story of Elijah, when Elijah complained thus to God against Israel:

3. "Lord they have killed your prophets and they have destroyed your altars, I alone am left, and now they want to take my life."

4. What answer did he receive? "I have kept for myself seven thousand men, those who have not bent the knee before Baal!"

5. It is also so in the present time: there is a remnant which comes from the free choice of grace.

6. And if it is by grace, it is not from works, or grace is no longer grace!

7. What does it mean? Israel did not find what it was searching for, but those who are chosen, found it, the others were hardened.

8. as it is written: "God gave them a spirit of stupor, eyes that could not see and ears that could not hear" until today!

9. David said: "May their altar be a snare, may they be its prey, may they fall and may it be their retribution!

10. May their eyes be darkened so that they cannot see! Make them bend their backs forever?

11. I will say again: "Did they stumble and fall without recourse?" Impossible! For thanks to their stumbling, the salvation of pagans occurs, which will arouse their jealousy.

12. and if their stumbling made the world rich and their humbling made the pagans rich, what will not their completion bring (How much more their fulfillment?)

13. I am telling you, who are pagans from the beginning: I am all the more the apostle to the pagans (and I glory in this ministry)

14. when I arouse the jealousy of those of my race this way, to bring some of them to salvation.

15. for is their rejection means the reconciliation of the world, what will their inclusion mean, if not life from the dead?

16. If the first fruit is holy then the whole dough must also be so, if the root is holy so are the branches,

17. and if certain branches are broken and you, the wild olive tree have been grafted among the other branches, and if you share in the rich sap of root of the tree with the other branches

18. do not despise the (broken) branches. If you were to despise them, remember that you do not bear the root, but that the root bears you.

19. You will say: "Branches were broken so that I could be grafted."

20. Yes, but they were broken because of this unbelief. Whereas you, *you are holding on by faith.* So do not look down on others! Rather fear!

21. For if God did not spare the original branches, he will not spare you either!

22. Rather consider the generosity and the strictness of God: strictness towards those who fell, but generosity towards you. As long as you remain in this generosity, otherwise you too will be cut off!

23. As for the Jews, if they do not remain in unbelief they will be grafted! For God has the power to graft them again.

24. For if you, who naturally belonged to the wild olive tree, have been cut, and then been grafted onto the cultivated olive tree, contrary to nature, how more naturally (according to their nature) will they be grafted onto their own olive tree!

Mystery and Renewal

11:25–36

25. Brothers, I do not want to leave you in ignorance of this mystery so that you may not think yourselves the sole bearers of good sense. There is a hardening of part of Israel until the full number of the pagans has come in.

26. And thus all Israel will be saved as it is written. "From Zion will the liberator come, and he will remove Jacob's iniquities far from him

27. and this will be my covenant with them: then will I remove all their iniquities."

28. As far as the gospel is concerned, they became enemies (for God), but as far as God's free choice is concerned, they remain his beloved because of their fathers.

29. For the grace and the calling of God are irreversible.

30. Just as in the past you were unfaithful to God, now through their unfaithfulness you are shown mercy,

31. in the same way, now, they are unfaithful because of the mercy that is shown to you so that now mercy might also be shown to them.

32. for God locked all men together in unfaithfulness so that he might have mercy on all.

33. How deep are the riches, the wisdom, and the knowledge of God! How undecipherable are his decrees and unsearchable his ways!

34. For who indeed has ever known the mind of the Lord? Who has been his counselor?

35. Who has ever been the first to give to God and should be repaid?

36. For from Him, through Him and for Him are all things! To Him be the glory for ever and ever! Amen.

12:1–2

1. Therefore I exhort you brothers, by the compassion of God to offer your bodies as a living sacrifice, holy and pleasing to God. This will be your reasonable worship (or: conforming to the Word).

2. Do not conform to your age but be transformed by the renewal of your intelligence (or: your way of understanding) so that you may discern what the will of God is, what pleases Him and what is well done (or that you may discern that the will of God is good, perfect and pleasant).

Introduction

I WILL NOT TALK ABOUT "THINGS HIDDEN FROM THE BEGINNING OF THE world," and there will be few inventions on my part; I will limit myself to drawing from sound sources. I only claim to breathe new life and relevance into sources, which now are ignored and left aside, whether it be the commentary on *The Epistle to the Romans* by Karl Barth (which I will not actually follow to any great extent) or especially the admirable articles by Wilhelm Vischer, published in the journal *Foi et Vie*, which I will follow closely, while attempting not to plagiarize. For it is actually Vischer who should be credited with infusing new life into the three fundamental chapters (9, 10, and 11 of Paul's Epistle to the Romans). We will come back to this point. I have to emphasize that these publications by Vischer are voluntarily or involuntarily neglected today. One piece of evidence for this will suffice: Father Pierre Grelot, in his *Introduction to the Bible*, gives an enormous bibliography on the Epistle to the Romans, yet does not include Vischer' s articles. I will say again that these articles are unique: no one else before Vischer and hardly anyone after him has taken up the question that Paul raises and done so with such rigor and clarity. Obviously, I have also made use of recent commentaries on the Epistle to the Romans, but what led me to this study was mostly the effort to set straight and clarify Christian thought with regard to the Jewish people, which, in a time such as ours, seems to me to be of primary importance.[1] Yet, only these three chapters by Paul specify with

---

1. As I was beginning to write these Bible studies for our church in Pessac, I was asking myself whether such a study was opportune and relevant. It seemed to me that the attitude of Christians towards Jews was much more tolerant, and that except for some limited movements there was not much hostility towards them anymore. Was a "theological study" really necessary then? All of a sudden I was astounded to hear the declarations of Pope John Paul II in his weekly "general audiences," in Saint Peter's Square in Rome, during the month of August 1989. Three sessions of this public teaching (catechesis) were about the infidelities of the Jewish people! The general theme of the

cogency what a Christian theology of the people of Israel should be. It is astonishing to note that Christians (and sometimes church authorities and theologians) have accumulated a frightening numbers of judgments and accusations against the Jewish people without referring to the only indisputable and *comprehensive* source. Of course, the Gospels can give us indications, but only concerning individuals or certain groups belonging to the Jewish people, not anything about the people as a whole. In the Gospels, we meet scribes who are too legalistic, Pharisees who are too purist, and priests who are "too much the theologian" (their great scandal is the one Jesus caused in the theological realm), but this does not tell us anything about the people of Israel. Furthermore, contrary to what has been too universally asserted, the Gospels show us good and understanding Pharisees and scribes who are open to the message of Jesus. There is Nicodemus, Jairus (a chief in the synagogue), Joseph of Arimathea, Simon the Pharisee, as well as so many others! Jesus never refused to dine at a Pharisee's house and what he proclaimed with his "*Woe unto you . . .*" is nothing more than what so many prophets over the course of centuries have also proclaimed.

The Gospels show us the existence of political parties (the Herodians) and/or resistance parties against the Romans (the Zealots) in halftone; Jesus does not participate in them but he does not reject them either. Among his disciples are two zealots, but also one tax collector (that is, a person who collaborated with the Romans). There is no overall judgment of the Jews. Jesus never rejects his origins. And if there is a crowd that clamors for his death, there is also a crowd that acclaimed him as Messiah when he entered into Jerusalem. Thus, in all of this one

---

teaching was about "the covenant with God." The pope proclaimed, *on three occasions,* the faithlessness of the Jewish people to its covenant with God. He declared that these infidelities had already been denounced by the prophets (as long as one reads them only partially!) and that, since this covenant had been broken by the Jews, God has replaced it with a new and eternal covenant in Jesus Christ. "In the old covenant, God had chosen Israel to be his chosen people, but Israel was supposed to reflect its consecration to God in the holiness of its way of life." Israel has been replaced by Christians, "at the end of the *new* covenant, Christians are consecrated as members of the chosen race, a royal priesthood, a holy nation." The pope clearly repeats in full the most traditional and oldest Christian "theology" (if we may say so) against the Jews. The *old* covenant is outdate and *cancelled* by the new covenant . . . ! Admittedly, the pope said that the Jews were "in a certain way" our older brothers, contrary to the precise declarations of this "teaching"! Let us not forget that the pope received Yasser Arafat with great honor and that, except for Arab leaders, he is the *only* head of state who has never recognized the legitimacy of Israel . . .

cannot draw anything that might be of help in understanding where the Jewish people are to be situated in a Christian perspective or what its continued existence means. Yet, we have an exact and precise answer to that question in these three chapters of the Epistle to the Romans—there, and nowhere else in the New Testament. However, for almost two thousand years these three chapters have either been completely ignored or else their meaning has been distorted. In any case, with regard to the Jews, they have not been of any use in "Christian" thought and "Christian" theology as a whole. It seems that the obliteration of this Pauline theology can be ascribed to the anti-Semitism that arose early in the church. It is distressing to make note of this, but it is a fact! I will not dwell on the origin of this Christian anti-Semitism, but it is nevertheless necessary to remember a few elementary points, because it is rare for a group of New Testament texts to be so thoroughly ignored or distorted.

I think that one may emphasize that from the beginning there was a social opposition between Jews and Christians. In the first century, the Jews were scattered all over the Roman Empire and they often had high-ranking jobs; many of them were wealthy, whereas Christians mostly sought their converts among the poor, the slaves, etc. There *might have been* a reaction against the high and the mighty (I am not saying that all Jews were among those—certainly not, especially those who still lived in "Palestine"[2]). Sometimes Christians felt despised, even if we do see in Acts that rich Jews became Christians.

Furthermore, it is certain that in some cities, the Jews were hostile to Christians. It has even been said that Jews who sought to avoid conflicts with the authorities or who wanted to keep the sect from increasing its influence informed on Christians. Indeed, in the eyes of the Roman authorities, Christians were nothing more than a Jewish sect. However, from 70 B.C. onward, when Roman hostility against the Jews manifested itself, with Christians obviously included, they were the ones who tried to distance themselves and openly declare themselves not only non-Jewish but, moreover, against the Jews. And the New Testament writings subsequent to this date are marked with this anti-Semitism. One needed to escape Roman repression of Jews throughout the whole Empire.

It is only much later that the accusations against the Jews that have now become typical will arise: they are a people rejected by God because

2. It might be interesting to remember that the word "Palestine" was given to this region *by the Romans*.

they did not believe in Christ, and are therefore a "lost" people. (The pagans, for their part, do not yet believe, so they are "innocent," but the Jews are guilty because they refused to acknowledge that Jesus was the Son of God, and because one can only be saved by grace, this people is damned.) It must be noted that this condemnation, this rejection (along with all the accusations that will follow), is not the result of an honest reading of the texts, but rather the result of an argumentation, a "theological" deduction. And later, in the fourth and fifth centuries, this very harsh hostile and accusatory stand on the issue will harden when the Empire becomes "Christian." An abundance of *Tractatus adversus Judaeos* can be found among the writings of the church fathers. It is a question of power: it was not possible for the Jewish people to make any claim, however little, to the role of "chosen people." Commentators will talk about the *Old* Testament, the *old* covenant (which means the same thing) not in the sense of "first" or "venerable," but in the sense of "over," "finished," "outdated."

The New Testament fulfills and goes beyond the Old Testament, which finds itself consigned to a minor role—that of announcing and prophesying about what was to be the absolute work of God: his Son. Everything else, including the Hebrew language, will become suspicious. Next, by continuing with "deductions," the Jewish people will be accused of deicide because Jesus was God; they will be accused of being solely responsible for the death of Christ (thus making a gigantic mistake as to the meaning of the sacrifice of Jesus, actual heresy!). Thenceforth this label will be used to justify all the horrors of anti-Semitism. All sorts of associations will follow; for example, the wandering Jew: until the end of time, the Jewish people will be identified with Cain, the murder of his own brother . . .

Obviously, throughout this catastrophic journey through Christian beliefs no one ever took our three chapters from The Epistle to the Romans into consideration. Most of the time, these were actually blotted out, and sometime their meaning was completely distorted. This went on throughout Christendom. Even John Calvin, who was so careful to give an exact reading of the Bible, wrote a stunning commentary on them. He analyses those chapters by developing an argument against the Jews following four themes.

First of all, Paul is writing to continue the debate again the Jews that attempts to prove Jesus is indeed the Messiah of Israel, and that the denial by the Jews is unfounded. Then, he goes on to affirm that the Jews' disbelief is "a monstrous thing." Although he never uses the term, the understanding is truly a "sin against the Holy Spirit." Of course, with the appearance of reason, Calvin uses all of these texts to prove his doctrine of double predestination. One can certainly see this theology in these chapters; and we will reflect on this at length. But Paul, he says, argues in this debate "without any maliciousness" so that they might not be "put off" but rather be led to convert. It is clear then that nothing in Calvin's commentary addresses what seems to me to be the question raised by Paul, namely: What is the Jewish people to become *now*? Is it really "rejected" in a final way and, if so, what does this rejection mean? Last, what place does the Jewish people have with respect to the church in this seventeenth-century society, which one may still call Christendom?

One of the first commentators who read these chapters in a different way was Barth; at the same time Franz Rosenzweig also took up Paul's question in his admirable book *The Star of Redemption*. Yet, in Barth's commentary on the Epistle to the Romans (the Big one), it is again the church that he is mostly interested in as he reads these three chapters. I will not analyze Barth's complex thought but will only quote the titles of the chapters he gives to this commentary on the epistle. Chapter 9 is entitled "The Tribulation of the Church" and comprises three main points: solidarity (between Jews and Christians), the God of Jacob, and, finally, the God of Esau. Here, the people of Israel is not damned. Barth shows that it is part of God's salvation plan and that it belongs (the God of Esau) to what Luther called the work of God's "left hand."

Chapter 10 is entitled "The Guilt of the Church" and has two parts: "Krisis of Knowledge" and "The Light in the Darkness." What is very characteristic of Barth is that he is actually more interested in the church than in the Jewish people and will use texts that are directly related to the latter and then apply them to the former. This is no doubt legitimate: for all the criticism that Paul directs at the Jewish people, Barth applies to the church to show that it is in the dark and in danger of condemnation as well. Fortunately, chapter 11 is "the chapter of hope." But here again it is the "Hope *of the Church*" and the main themes are unity, freedom, and the faithfulness of God. Where however, is the Word addressed to non-Jews and linked to the *temporary* rejection of the Jewish people? Barth is certainly the first one to affirm that this rejection was temporary. He affirmed that hatred and persecution of Jews was proof of the demonization of Hitlerism and that the great difference between Hitlerism and Soviet communism was precisely that Stalinism was not anti-Semitic (and it is true that in the era between the two World Wars, the actual attitude of Stalinism towards the Jews was still unknown!). Yet we can see how the opinion about the Jewish people was fixed and established when such a theologian as Barth, one so favorable to the Jews, could not see that these three chapters are a true theological treatise on the Jewish people.[3]

I have said before that the change took place with Vischer. His little book of *Bible Study* on these three chapters was published in German in 1940 and then in the journal *Foi et Vie* in French in 1948. Vischer reminds the reader that when Paul wrote the Epistle to the Romans he had apparently completed his work in the East, and was getting ready to bring the gospel to the West, and that he was sending his letter to Rome as a "sum total," a "synthesis" of his theology, and as such it is not only an intellectual construct, but also a spiritual message, a sermon, and an exhortation. He sent the letter as an introduction prior to his ar-

---

3. Michel Remaud is of course right when he emphasizes that, on the one hand, "if it is true, as we believe, that the Scriptures are accomplished in Jesus Christ, we may be willing to assent as well to the proposition that Christ represents a sort of crystalliza- tion of the destiny of his people." This has been completely concealed for two thousand years. Jewish hermeneutics and the Christian hermeneutics of the Suffering Servant are mutually exclusive. Such is also the case of the situation of the Jews after Christ. But one must acknowledge that in this respect one cannot give any special authority to the church fathers. Remaud is not sure that we can "step over nineteen centuries of history to return to *scriptura sola*," but as far as I am concerned, I would say yes without hesitation! One might wonder how the church fathers could be so wrong on the subject of the Jewish people! The Shoah opened the eyes of many Christians and gave us a new perspective on the Jewish people. I would like to add one quotation from Barth (found in Franz Lovsky, *Antisémistisme et mystère d' Israël*, lecture given on July 23, 1944: "The insane and frenzied persecution of the Jewish people is . . . for us, the picture of this 'Servant of the Lord' which the book of Isaiah shows us as being punished and sacri- ficed for others. Is it not our Lord Jesus Christ that we see vaguely, as in a mirror behind all of these Jews who in Germany, France, and Poland are shot, buried alive, crammed and smothered in cattle cars or gassed? Are these facts not a revelation, a letter, a word, a proof of God? Is it possible that the Christian community is unable to see what this is all about? Is it possible that Christians fail to fall to their knees and cry: 'You have carried the sins of the world, Lord, have mercy on us! *You* are there in the shadow of the persecuted *Jew*, and *you* are the one who, once again is being rejected. It is indeed your solitary death that these events show us once more. And just as God gave up his Son for us, two thousand years ago, the Christ is once again struck with the tragic destiny of his brothers and sisters in the flesh . . ." Whether one likes it or not, this is indeed one of the great turning points in Christian theology, and it does indeed start with Barth!

rival in order to prepare the work that he intended to accomplish among the pagans (but there were also many Jews in Rome). I will not delve into the historical debate about the date and the occasion of this epistle but I will confine myself to the current opinion. Moreover, details on these historical-critical problems would hardly change what I have to say about the text. Be that as it may, in order to understand these three chapters, one needs to place them back into the sequence of the epistle. This is, of course, well known, but it probably bears repeating!

In chapters 1 and 2, Paul attests that the gospel, the good news proclaimed by God, is that God is mighty *to save* anyone who believes, the Jew or the Greek, without any distinction, as long as a person *believes* in this saving power. This is not might in itself, nor self-satisfied might; it is the power of God oriented towards the salvation of man. Therefore one cannot can claim to "accomplish one's own salvation" by oneself. There is no saving work, for man has no power to justify himself *by his own means*, whether by good works (for pagans) or strict and exact obedience to the Law (for Jews). So the great message, the great "reversal" follows: God gives salvation freely (salvation by grace) to whoever believes in Jesus Christ. There is no question of merit, no question either of disobedience or sin forgiven in Christ. This free salvation cannot be destroyed by anyone, and no one can take it away from whoever has received it by grace (chapters 3 to 7). Consequently, the Law does not play the same role as before: it has become a spiritual law, and it corresponds to the promise given by the Prophets (*I will put my Law in your heart*). There is therefore no more condemnation to fear from the Mosaic Law "for those who are in Christ," and we have the assurance that nothing can separate us from the love of God manifested in Jesus Christ (chapter 8). Then Paul links chapters 9 to 11 to the Jews. Finally, we have the last part, chapters 12 to 15, where Paul draws from this salvation by grace, ethics and a vision for the church. Everything is by grace, yet we must not forget what consequences might follow in practice. For example, Paul shows how a church should organize itself from this starting point: what the gifts of the Holy Spirit are, what functions are necessary in the church, and what the role of civil authorities is. There must be tolerance among brothers and the manifestation of this salvation by grace in relationships will be the love that orders the life of the church.

This brief overview shows us that everything is perfectly connected in this epistle, yet our three chapters do not seem indispensable! Indeed, it is perfectly possible to go from chapter 8 (the Law has become spiritual) to chapter 12 (what are the ethical consequences of this spirituality?). Nothing essential is missing if chapters 9 to 11 are removed, and certain exegetes thus interpret them as some sort of parenthesis. "But why then are they included at all?" Well, it is only "a little salute" to the brothers of Jewish origin. Other exegetes go further and believe it is an "an erratic block" that was probably added to the text at a later date (Oscar, Cullmann). I believe such a position is a serious mistake. First of all, this view relies on a misinterpretation of chapter 8. In reality, the question addressed in this chapter is basic. If salvation is given by grace through faith, what becomes of the Law revealed to Moses and confirmed by the Prophets? Yet, this Law was a revelation from God. God only revealed himself to Israel and did so through these commands. How then, could these be considered null and void? From then on, Paul studies the question of the Jewish Law and shows that it remains. It has become spiritual, but it is indeed the same Law. Therefore, logically the question "What becomes of the Law in an economy of grace?" is inevitably followed by the question "What becomes of the chosen people (its exact complement) when election is achieved by grace and no longer through lineage from Abraham?" These chapters are rigorously coherent with the rest of the epistle. And if the rest (starting with chapter 12) is centered on love, it is clear that in Paul's thought this love should first of all be for the Jews (then for authorities, for the "brothers" etc.)! So, far from being a parenthesis, I would, with Vischer and Alphonse Maillot, say that these chapters are a critical point in Paul's theology and are connected to a set of fundamental questions, the main ones being: the question of the very truth of the message of the gospel; Paul proclaims that "the gospel is the power of God for the salvation of everyone who believes." Yes, but the Jews (that is not Judeo-Christians, but those who refused) do not "believe." Consequently, the Jews are not saved by the gospel! If the Jews are not saved, how can one say that God saves *any* person through the gospel! Insisting on the fact that the Jews do not believe raises a tremendous theological question (which at times caused terrible conflicts in the church). Indeed, if the refusal of this faith by the Jewish people leads to their rejection, it means that everything depends on man, and the will to be merciful, which is God's, becomes ineffective. Simply put, God offers and man decides by himself to accept or refuse. In other words, it is the opposite of the famous proverb "man proposes and God disposes." Here

"God proposes and man disposes!" In addition, this choice made by man corresponds to a moral or religious power, so that man is endowed with a free will before God; yet where in the Bible (but also in daily life!) do we see that man has such a free will? This would mean that after Adam's break with God, after the will to decide good and evil, man would still possess the power *to do good according to God's will* (because he would be choosing this salvation!). This also goes against the liberating omnipotence of God. We know that the God of Abraham, of Isaac, and of Jesus is first of all the God who liberates, who liberates from all types of slavery. He does thus, as the text often says, "by a mighty hand and an outstretched arm," that is, with matchless power. How could we believe that it would be enough for a "No" uttered by man to crush this power and reduce the liberating will of God to nothing! I am well aware of the opposite argument, namely, would God "accomplish the salvation" of man against the latter's will? How many times do we see this situation in the history of Israel: God speaks, man refuses. But nothing stops there. Quite the contrary, everything begins at that point! Man is not saved in spite of himself. Man does not obey God by constraint, like a machine. This is where the story begins, the story of "God-with-man." God will resort to a hundred means to lead man to finally say "Yes." Without any constraint, but through slow persuasion!

Thus, whether God's will is going to be accomplished in and through him does not depend on man. But God never forces! This is what Barth calls the freedom of man within the freedom of God! Now this question also presents another side in these chapters. Indeed, the refusal of the Jews should be all the heavier since it is to the Hebrews that God linked his promise: he chose that very people. So if everything were to be cancelled, could we say that some men can, by their refusal, destroy God's promise? Actually, we know (and we see it time and again) that God's promise is never eliminated by men, whatever they may want, think, or do! When Jesus reminds us that not all the descendants of Abraham are heirs to the promise, he is not going against the Torah! Right from the start, after Abraham we see clearly that not all carry the blessing. Paired with Israel is Ishmael and paired with Jacob is Esau: they are equally sons and equally descendants, yet not equally bearers of the promise and of the covenant. Only those chosen by God are, and this election is also by grace (Israel has no prior merit); it affirms the sovereign liberty of God's omnipotence.

We must look more closely at the concept of a "remnant." When Israel disobeys there is always a "remnant" that faithfully carries the promise and grace (Benjamin and Judah for example). This "remnant" carries the whole weight of the covenant and passes it on. The others, the "Jews" who want to do good on their own, through their works, through their apparent faithfulness to God's commandments, claim to be the true descendants of Abraham and therefore the true holders of the covenant, but in reality, the error lies in the phrase "on their own." They claim (without being aware of it of course) to be holders of grace and to "own" it (just like Christians who have the absurd audacity to say "I have faith"!). This fact on its own shows that they do not understand God's "politics"; they have not understood God's intention. They take the covenant for granted, and from then on, they need to lead a life of corresponding works. In the Torah and in the Prophets, however, the covenant is never taken for granted; it is always supposed to be received anew through a surprising miracle of grace. One might possibly compare them to the older son in the parable of the Prodigal Son; the younger son comes home, bows down and asks for forgiveness—and he is the one who receives pardon—whereas the older brother is dissatisfied and remains *outside*. He remains outside but the father tells him, "You are always with me." And this is important. For the promise of God was given to *all* of Israel. It is not restricted like election and we will have to return to this "all Israel"! Thus, the refusal of the Jews to accept grace in Jesus Christ does not cancel their election as "the chosen people," but because *they* refuse this grace, it must be taken over by others. From now on, the pagans will receive this grace. Therefore, the Jews are still experiencing election, but grace in Jesus Christ is received by others who are now the ones to proclaim it. From this point of view, one can say that this people is rejected, but it certainly does not become a cursed people!

The present "rejection" of the Jews attests to the total seriousness as well as the severity of grace, which is in no way an easy solution to the problems of life or an undemanding guarantee of salvation! However, by the grace of God, a greater good came from this refusal by Israel: the extension of election to the pagan peoples. Moreover, this extension had already been announced in the Psalms and by the Prophets! "Here is Philistia and Tyre, along with Ethiopia—'in Zion they were born.' Indeed of Zion it is said, 'They were *all* born there! And the Most High establishes her'" (Ps 87:4–5).[4] We are now entering a movement that we might call dialectic; it remains incomprehensible in formal logic and yet fits with the complete story of God and his people and with Paul's teaching. Faith is not man's work; no one can decide "to have faith," no one can, by his own will, place himself within faith. It is God's free gift: "We have been saved by grace through faith" (Eph 2:8). Similarly, no one can save himself through his own works, so no one can be saved if he refuses this grace (that is, if he does not take and adopt the means that God has determined for him). No one may eliminate the grace that is granted to him either. One may temporarily decide not to obey, but this is only for a time, and God is both faithful and patient. This refusal in no way eliminates the grace that is offered to you, and it does not precisely because this grace does not depend on you: it is founded solely on the free will of God. In the end, Israel will inevitably receive the grace that is offered, the grace to be the people of God, the people that, far from being deicidal, was the bearer of God in Jesus.

One essential issue remains: it seems to me that these words about covenant, election, and grace have suffered a certain amount of distortion in all our theologies.[5] What I will propose will seem to be—and I am well aware of it—both scandalous and unacceptable, but it seems to me to be what stands out about the history of the Jewish people and its God. We have traditionally interpreted these words by applying them to our own personal salvation. "The only thing that matters to me is that I might be saved." Already here, we forget "You shall love your neighbor as yourself." Thus, my salvation cannot be my only aim; I can only conceive of it in the context of the salvation of all my neighbors, and in truth, the salvation of anyone. Furthermore, we have interpreted the word "salvation" in the sense of escaping eternal damnation, entering into God's paradise, not being condemned by God to . . . infernal suffering or nothingness. Even though I do not want to shrug off that idea, since the word "grace" includes *also* that meaning (in addition to the equally fundamental idea of being free of charge), I believe it is wrong to confuse the meaning of all the words I have listed. In other words, election is not in my view an arbitrary choice made by God in order to grant

---

4. This is the English translation of the text found in the French Bible translated by Louis Segond.

5. A very beautiful critique of these distortions can be found in G. Vahanian, *Anonymous God*.

salvation, to forgive our sins by grace. There are actually two "lines." On the one hand, yes there is this forgiveness, which God grants us and through which we escape his wrath (and this is the line of "humanity reconciled to God through Jesus Christ"); and on the other hand, election has a completely different meaning: God chooses a person, a group of individuals, a people, not for the purpose of saving them, but so that they may fulfill a certain role *on earth*, that they may accomplish a certain task, that they might serve God. The elect of God are not those who after being saved are singing hymns but those who have been given the responsibility by God to represent him on earth in order to do his work. That is the meaning of "chosen people": not "saved people," but people entrusted with a mission. And justification implies both meanings: one is justified for salvation, and in preparation for the work of God and for God, which is sanctification. "Saint" does not mean beatified; saint means set aside, on earth, for this work among men. The covenant covers both meanings but with a preeminent place given to covenant for *the purpose of* . . . for the purpose of assuring the presence of God among men, and for the purpose of testifying to the accomplished work of God (in Jesus Christ for Christians). If we benefit from the covenant with God, it is certainly not for our own personal benefit, for our happiness (in the modern sense of the word), but for the purpose of this work that God entrusts to a person (prophet, apostle) or a group of people (Israel, the church). When the latter do not fulfill their role, God does not reject but chooses, in a "second degree" within that chosen people, the "remnant," that is, those who will ultimately take up the work and the action of God.

I believe this explanation (although it is much too brief) was necessary to avoid any confusion in the reading of the three fundamental chapters concerning the people of Israel within the perspective of Christian theology, which for so many centuries has been obsessed only with individual salvation in Jesus Christ and has, unfortunately, neglected the meaning of election and covenant. We have forgotten, for example, that if God delivered his people from slavery and from Egypt, it was not to please them, not to insure that they would already enjoy angelic happiness on earth that would one day end harmoniously "in heaven." No, it was indeed so that this people would testify that YHWH is the one and only God, that this God is the master of history, that the love of this God is the only truth, and that God testifies through his reconciliation with that particular people, to his will to be reconciled to all of humanity. This is the mission of Israel, a mission that has not been cancelled by Jesus Christ. This is why our three chapters are fundamental: They are exactly in the middle of the epistle, between the proclamation of grace and the concrete consequences it entails. They are the turning point of Paul's thought, or as Maillot said: "It is an Epistle to the Romans squared." In these three chapters, there is no mention of any no particular maliciousness on the part of the Jews, no mention of their being deicidal! Quite the contrary, these texts bring a large portion of hope for the Jews and require cooperation between Jews and Christians!

1

The Unique People

RIGHT FROM THE BEGINNING OF THE NINTH CHAPTER OF THE EPISTLE
to the Romans, Paul strongly and clearly affirms his solidarity with this
people. It is very important to emphasize this fact (and we will encounter the same assertion at the beginning of chapter 10) because Paul has
traditionally been declared an enemy of the Jews, and his whole theology has been seen to condemn the Jews. As chapter 8 ends in the great
joyous proclamation of the love God has shown us in Christ and from
which nothing can separate us, Paul says he is full of grief for the sake of
his brothers. This may seem very curious, indeed, coming after the assertion that salvation is by grace outside of the Law (which leads Maillot
to maintain that the Torah is completely abolished). Paul explains, "I
am telling the truth . . . I do not lie . . . ," and "it is not only 'my opinion'
that I am here presenting (my conscience is a witness to this); it is the
Holy Spirit himself." In a way he maintains that the following argument
is completely vouched for by the Holy Spirit! The Spirit who causes us to
address God as Father guarantees that Paul's grief is sincere and that his
great concern is Israel! This grief is at the core of his being. Paul could
not have been an "anti-Semite." Vischer says that it is the very grief of
Jesus that is transferred to his apostle, the grief of Jesus weeping over
Jerusalem (Luke 19:41–42). Paul maintains that if any further sacrifice
is necessary for God's people to acknowledge Jesus as the Messiah, he is
willing to sacrifice himself, to become "anathema," which means loathed
in the strong and religious meaning of the term, rejected from the company of the elect, subject to a *herem*. He is even ready to be "separated
from Christ" (even though a few lines earlier he stated that nothing can
separate us from the love of God manifested in Jesus Christ), which is no

doubt the utmost limit to which he would go if it could help his people in any way. He, who became obedient by grace, can in no way come to terms with the refusal and rejection of Israel.

If he states such things, it is not to add anything to the sacrifice of Christ or to give himself up for the salvation of his brothers, but he does so in order to affirm that his own obedience must be part of the obedience of his people, almost that it is dependent on the fact that those who did not believe (and have therefore "disobeyed") must not remain in a state of disobedience! His sense of membership in the people of Israel is so strong and his faithfulness to the election of Israel is so unquestionable that, were they to persevere in this disobedience, then he also would accept his own exclusion from the gospel. And when he claims the Holy Spirit as his witness, it is indeed to affirm that he is not referring to human faithfulness but to this special tie between all Jews as the people of God, which nothing, not even faith in Christ, can sever. It is essential to emphasize this in our time when many Jews, following the spirit of the age, are no longer believers! However, declaring that the Jew who has become a Christian does not cease to be united to his Jewish people also means affirming that the gospel, if it is wholly true, requires complete and wholehearted solidarity between those who disobey and all those who obey! This is a crucial truth in our world! Not only does this prohibit any judgment of non-Christians by Christians, it is, moreover, a question of solidarity: all Christians should feel and declare themselves to be in solidarity with non-Christians! If I am saved, I cannot bear the thought that one single individual might be "damned" and excluded from God's love. Before God I declare that I am in solidarity with that individual. I do not want to be separated from him on judgment day. No matter what he might do or say, he is my neighbor, and Jesus commanded me to love him as he loved unbelievers . . . The Christian should say with Paul, "I would rather be anathema than see people damned." We also have the example of Abraham arguing with God to save the sinful people in Sodom (yet finally obeying God and stopping when God told him to)!

The first verses thus have a far-reaching impact[1] and are still terribly relevant today. For as Paul proclaims his anguish, he does not make this a personal affair or a family affair (my brothers in the flesh . . .); what

---

1. In the early church, this was of course also valid with respect to the relationship between Christians coming from Judaism and Christians coming from paganism; the first constituted the link between the people of Israel and the pagan world.

he wants to state is "the truth in Christ." He sees his people in Christ and sees the role and the future of this people in relationship to Christ. Paul does not insist on this nor does he explain it at length for the purpose of presenting us with a gratuitous theological construct. Do not forget that this letter is addressed to the Christians in Rome, who were not well acquainted with the Jewish *people* and were not converted Jews; therefore, they need complete instruction. In this prophetic role, Paul is not expressing patriotism or ethnic solidarity. Paul is working to unite the church and to explain God's plan.

Now that he has declared his love for the people of Israel and his faithfulness as an Israelite, Paul will explain *who those Jews are*. They are not just any people; they have not been excluded since Jesus came. Not at all! First of all, Paul generally speaks of "Jews" but calls them "Israelites" here. With this name, he begins listing their gifts and their uniqueness. Let us remember that at the beginning of this same letter (3:2) he already said that the Israelites were given "the oracles" of God. The oracles are, in practical terms, the words of the promise and of the Law. In our text, he now continues to list the things that make Israel, God's people unique in the world.

They are called "Israelites" from the wonderful name that was given to Jacob by God and that was passed on to the whole people: this name is their divine qualifier. Once and for all, God tied all the display of his unique divinity to their historical existence (Vischer), and this has not in any way been cancelled. This is their real name, given by God—and we know the importance of naming in Jewish thought. This name designates the whole Being and is the statement of its truth. It shows that in them and with them, God made a covenant with mankind. They have been *adopted*, says Paul; this does not come from their will or from flesh and blood. Because of their adoption, they are children of grace and not natural children. Their name, their being, their relationship to God have nothing to do with the fact that all men are, in a sense, children of God since all descend from Adam. This does not refer to the "general relationship" between God and men. By insisting on this term "adopted," Paul means that grace makes them sons of God, for Israel was called "first born of God" (Exod 4:22). Paul means that the only son Jesus did not cancel this divine filial adoption of Israel.

To these adopted sons belongs the glory, the *kabod* YHWH, which accompanied Israel in its journey through the desert and which filled the Ark of the covenant.

The assertion that the glory of God belongs to them is doubly important. First, let us remember what Paul said at the beginning of his epistle: "All have sinned and fall short of the glory of God." Unlike all other men, the Jews, although they have sinned, have received this glory and are not deprived of it! I have often put forward one meaning for this glory of God (a bold assertion, one that may be wrong, but I insist on it): I believe the glory means revelation. When Jesus says he glorifies the Father, it means that he reveals him, and when the Father glorifies Jesus, he reveals who this Jesus is. I believe that all other explanations are either meaningless or weak. Consequently, in my opinion, to say that the glory belongs to the Jews means that they are the ones among men who can still reveal the presence of God. Before the revelation of Jesus this was unquestionable, since then it seems impossible. Yet, it is so and the explanation will come later. Furthermore, says Paul, they are the trustees of the covenant, of both the successive covenants and the provisions of the covenant in the most precise and integral sense. The covenant is thus the act by which God forms an alliance with man-the-sinner, not to condemn him according to his justice, but in order to save him according to his mercy. Even if they do not know it, the Israelites are also the first bearers and witnesses of this covenant, which God establishes with all of humanity in Jesus Christ and through which men are reconciled to God. This universal covenant was already written in their election because they have been chosen to bear witness to God's love and God's revelation to all men.

As a consequence of his covenant, God states his Law—and we often need to repeat this—which is not a gloomy and sterile legal code but the positive, good, and saving expression of his will. And if God reveals his Law, it is not to place man under a yoke but to reveal to him how he should live so that it is at all possible for him to live. (The commandments are, according to Barth, the boundary between life and death: on this side you live, on the other side you enter into the realm of death by transgressing). When God gives his Law on Mount Sinai, it is right before entering the desert, but also, right when the Jews become free and need a law so that their freedom might not be incoherent, might not be a case of "one thing being as good as another."[2]

2. Ellul, *Ethics of Freedom.*

The Israelites are also the holders of the cult (that is, service and worship). They are the example of what a real act of worship should be (recitation and meditation on the Word of God). Furthermore, they have "the promises and the patriarchs" (this of course refers to all the promises God made to the patriarchs and especially the promise of the Messiah), and they are the authentic descendants of the patriarchs: Abraham, Isaac, and Jacob (see especially Gen 12:2ff. and 17:16ff.). This seems to me to be radically important in our era and very different from the importance that Paul gave to it. Indeed, in the past fifteen years, the argument that the Jews of today have no historical claim to the land of Israel because they are not in any way the descendants of the ancient Hebrews regularly comes up in anti-Zionist propaganda. This is pure usurpation on their part and they cannot claim ancestry going back to the patriarchs! Here is Paul, however, maintaining that the Jews of his time were without any doubt descendants of these patriarchs; and there cannot be much doubt as to the identity between the Jews of today and their ancestors in the Roman Empire . . . This Paul maintains the legitimacy of the people of Israel as descendants of the patriarchs for us today too. Moreover, the fact that Paul uses a verb in the present tense shows that the privileges of Israel are not only gifts of the past, formerly granted by God to Israel, but permanent gifts still existing today.

We must therefore clearly reject the view that these privileges have passed from Israel to the church (which we are often told). This is precisely what Paul *does not say!* I have the feeling that the purpose of this list is to establish that Israel has not been dispossessed of any of the rights, privileges, and mercies that God has granted. On the contrary, what is admirable is the fact that Christians are by grace now also called to share in these privileges (we will see this again in chapter 11). Christians can only give thanks to God for the gift that is given to them and consider with respect and gratitude the privileges of Israel, which they now share! This brings us to the greatest of these privileges. Paul concludes this passage by reminding us that, in the flesh, the Christ comes from this people. What would Paul use as a more decisive and important argument to certify the present relevance of these privileges of Israel? This people has been the bearer of the ultimate mercy of God toward all of humanity! Moreover, Franz Mussner sees another argument to affirm the relevance of these privileges in the present: As far as Paul is concerned, Christ is not dead. The living Christ is still bound to his people. If the Christ is still alive, accepting his people, he has never separated himself from that people, and he has never contested those privileges granted by his Father. Consequently, these are still relevant.

One can never repeat enough that Jesus is Jewish, that he never denied it (he proclaimed, for instance, that he came for the lost sheep of Israel—that Israel is the people who are the children of the house . . .). On the contrary, he fulfilled and fortified the promises and he lifts the first covenant higher. He restores to Israel's worship its former strength and truth (outside of intellectual discussion), and he is a reflection of the divine glory in the midst of his people.

All of this is merely the development of the fundamental confession of faith according to which "salvation is of the Jews," a statement attributed to Jesus himself (John 4:22) and which clearly means that Jesus does not separate himself from this very people, that he is only a representative of this people, which the first generations of Christians fully acknowledged. Paul strongly insists on this fact: "For from him and through him and to him are all things. To him be the glory forever!" (Rom 11:36), and "For us there is but one God, the Father, from whom all things came and for whom we live; and there is but one Lord, Jesus Christ, through whom all things came and through whom we live" (1 Cor 8:6). The fact that Jesus was born of Israel reinforces the privileges of Israel and makes them more relevant, even if these Jews do not believe it. After all, how many times do we not read that in the face of prophets sent by God, the people revolted and rejected the messengers. But . . . after the necessary time, this same people finally accepted them as true prophets and included their prophecies in the Book.

The question that Jesus raises is harder, and the answer is more inacceptable, all the more given that Paul does not scale down the scandal. After affirming the persistence of this chosen people, he concludes with a doxology that could only appall the Jews and that still appalls them today. Indeed, he declares that Jesus is above all and that he is blessed forever. This is the breaking point with monotheism conceived in Israel. Is there really a break, however? This same Paul says (Rom 11:36) that God is not removed nor supplanted by the Christ, but only that God makes himself known and reveals himself fully only in Jesus. All the gifts belonging to the Jews are more understandable, more luminous, more assured in Jesus, so that Jesus appears as the one who brings all Israel to its culmination. To the Jews, this is inevitably blasphemy. The summit of the gifts that God has given them becomes for them a scandal because they interpreted these privileges as belonging to them, as being their unique relationship with God, which neither needs to be confirmed nor brought to a culmination point. They descend from Abraham (according to the flesh) and it is impossible for these privileges to be given to anyone else. Later, we will return to this idea of the appropriation of privileges, which is one of the keys to Paul's theology. Be that as it may, Paul affirms, "All these gifts, these privileges were the action of Grace and Jesus is the last gift of grace for Israel."

In this list of graces granted to Israel that Paul proclaims as still being valid, and still relevant, we need to note in passing that this theology of Paul concerning Israel, while it totally breaks with Christian practice against the Jews, also breaks with Islam. Mohammed does not discuss the question of the salvation of the Jews. He cuts any discussion short by saying, "The Jews are in any case condemned, whether they believe or not" (Sura 18). Finally, I would like to show that in this introduction to theology the list of Jewish privileges is certainly not accidental. It is necessary to consider these verses in parallel with Paul's statement about the "pagans" in the Epistle to the Ephesians (2:11–12): "You were separate from Christ, excluded from citizenship in Israel and foreigners to the covenants of the promise, without hope and without God [*atheoi*] in the world." It is the exact counterpart of what we have seen for Israel: Israel does have the hope of the Messiah; it constitutes a city (*politeia*). The Jews do have the covenants, the promises, and they do have a true hope. Israel lives in relationship with God and knows God in this world. In other words, through the coming of Christ, by his consecration through the Jews, but also through his proclamation of a universal Word of God, the old pagans receive by faith the same privileges as Israel. The parallelism of the two passages is striking, and it is obviously not by accident that Paul begins his theology of Israel in this way. All the more given that the text to the Ephesians goes on to say, "But now in Christ Jesus you who once were far away have been brought near . . . [he] . . . *has made the two one* and has destroyed the barrier, the dividing wall of hostility." This is a fantastic proclamation: Jews and pagans are now *one*. And if we take such a vision seriously, we as Christians must be astounded that we lived in hatred of the Jews for so many centuries! The only possible conclusion is that "this is a mystery of iniquity."

2

This "Unjust" God

WE ARE NOW APPROACHING ONE OF THE MOST DEMANDING QUESTIONS, and these statements by Paul can only scandalize us, unless we accept the theology of double predestination: from the beginning of the world, and forever, God has established the salvation or perdition of each individual regardless of the kind of life that person leads on earth. We are then scandalized by God's arbitrariness, which seems to us an injustice. On this point, it is important to remember that we cannot judge God on the basis of *our* criteria and *our* values, etc. *We* have a certain understanding of "justice," and from that starting point, we claim that we can judge God and declare him just or unjust. That would mean that *above* God there are certain values (justice, good, etc.), which *we* know and which would allow us to pass this judgment. If there are values above God, then we must relentlessly affirm that God is not God! He may be whatever we decide: a representation, a fiction, etc., but not God. If God is God, then there is nothing above him, nothing that enables us to judge him. The Bible constantly reiterates that good is what God does; justice is what God decides, and so forth. Indeed, without referring to what theologians have called God's "attributes" (as if we could know these in themselves, as if we could analyze them!), we can know—through the example of the presence of God in Scripture—that on the one hand, God is absolutely free, there are absolutely no limits to his will (he is the one Kierkegaard called "the unconditioned one," that is, neither his being nor his decisions are conditioned or caused by any outside reality and that he does not enter into the realm of cause and effect), but on the other hand, one must always remember that God is love (not love is God!).

One cannot say that he is *arbitrary* in what he decides, for such an assessment would mean that, in our eyes, there is a rule that God should follow in order not to be *arbitrary*. I know full well, however, that these facts cannot help us from being indignant and scandalized when we are faced with such an action on the part of God. In any case, with or without indignation, the key to these twenty-three verses is, on the one hand, this absolute freedom of God in his sovereignty, and on the other hand, the total inability and powerlessness of man to "bring about his own salvation," to have, on his own, good and just works that will be accepted as such by God. On the contrary—and Jesus confirmed this on several occasions—it is when man claims to do just works that he is the most culpable. This is the meaning of the invective against the hypocritical Pharisee . . . Paul's whole argument about the Jewish people rests on this double theological foundation. Therefore, in the presence of a reality that we cannot understand, we have to choose between indignation and *sacrificium intellectus*. But the direct relevance of this presentation of the will of God in the text is the fact that it tends to affirm that there is no *fault* in the disbelief of the Jews regarding Jesus. For even though there is responsibility, the disbelief of the majority of the Jews comes from God, so does the belief in Jesus by other Jews. Let us repeat again that we are not to judge God, for in doing this, he is pursuing a purpose that Paul will describe to us; pursuing it not in an arbitrary way but in accordance with what the Hebrew Bible reveals as God's mode of action in the history of mankind.

The Word of God has not remained without effect nor is it powerless: it is not rendered obsolete or void by the choice made by the majority of Israel. For this Word of God is Jesus, who himself fulfills everything that God had declared. Let us repeat again: The teaching of Jesus is not what is new (he only repeats what we find in the "Old" Testament). It is the *life* of Jesus that is new. The fact is that in the course of this life, and all the way to the cross, he *fulfills* what until he came had only been promise and proclamation. In particular, he fulfills all the things that had been declared about Israel: he gave his life and became accursed on behalf of his brothers. "Christ redeemed us from the curse of the Law by becoming a curse for us, for it is written: 'Cursed is everyone who is hung on a tree.' He redeemed us in order that the blessing given to Abraham might come to the Gentiles through Christ Jesus" (Gal 3:13).

Jesus thus bore all God's condemnations, rejections, and exclusions,[1] including those of today, those that we believe concerning the people of Israel. If Israel is rejected, it is in fact Jesus who is rejected! If all of Israel's history is condensed in Jesus (although the history does not stop there but continues with all of Israel), then in him is found that which we have such a hard time understanding: the "Yes" of God and the "No" of God at the same time. For it is a fundamental truth that there is no division or separation between the "Yes" and the "No." One only needs to read the Prophets to discover that the terrible "No" that they often pronounce does not end there; there is always a "Yes" that closes and ends the prophecy.[2] In God's work, there are no things or people that are totally under "No" and others totally under "Yes." In the saintliest of humans there is still a "No" from God ("a thorn in my flesh . . ." and "a messenger of Satan to harass me," says Paul) and in the worst of people there is always a "Yes" from God—profoundly hidden—which will be revealed at the end of time.

As far as God is concerned, no one is completely white or completely black. Luther understood this perfectly with his *Semper peccator et semper justus*. If the Jews refuse to believe in the Christ crucified, their "No" which appears to be exclusive does not render the "Yes" that God pronounced on the Christ and on them powerless. Despite their "No," they are still under the "Yes" of God. All the more since their refusal to believe is in accordance with the prophecies spoken by Isaiah and so many others ("I have held out my hands to an obstinate people . . ."). Just as Jesus fulfills the word of revelation, so Israel prepared through successive acts of disobedience all through its history (which caused the election of a "remnant") the decisive moment when it would refuse to believe in this Messiah. In its eyes he was not a Messiah because, as we know, for Israel the coming of the Messiah was to usher in God's kingdom and result in the new creation. This was constructed theologically in a very subtle way (based on certain texts only), but it was an intellectual construct. We must admit, as is the case with many Christian theologies, "that knowledge puffs up and only love builds up." The tragedy is that a

---

1. See my short essay "L'Homme de douleurs, souffrance et tentations de Jésus."

2. That is why it is disastrous to only read fragments of the Prophets, a few verses. . . . In reality, a prophetic book is something that must be read *in its entirety,* with the understanding that the apparent contradiction is the key to the revelation given by the prophet.

majority of Israel did not see the love that was in Jesus and did not see that it was the very love of God that was manifested in him.

However, this specific election of a remnant is already manifested in the fact that God changed Jacob's name to Israel: henceforth all of Abraham's descendants are not necessarily Israel. Only a few of them carry the "seed" of Israel. In biblical thought, the "seed" is the heir who takes on the inheritance. It refers to Abraham and Israel's call to represent God on earth, to announce to all the will of God, and to live according to the will of God. Since everything in God's action is by grace, the three aspects of Israel's calling are aspects of grace, a quality coming from grace.

In Abraham's family, the specific inheritance is the seal of grace. As we have already seen in verses 6 to 9, this seal is not given to *all* of Abraham's heirs according to the flesh: "Despite the fact that they are Abraham's posterity, they are not all his children," and "The children of the flesh are not God's children; the children of the promise are the true posterity." Ishmael is certainly a son . . . but according to the flesh.

We are faced with a significant judgment here, a judgment we will come back to later. Why is Ishmael not the posterity of Abraham although he is a son? Is it because he is not the son of the lawful wife but the son of a concubine? In reality, this is not a question of morality—and thus no one was paying much attention to it! Let us remember the incident that happened as Abraham came to Egypt: He was young and Sarah was beautiful. In order to avoid any trouble, Abraham says that Sarah is his sister and Pharaoh can sleep with her . . . God will not hold it against Abraham! No, as is usual in biblical revelation, everything is placed in the relationship to God. Abraham received the promise of posterity. Sarah, who was old, did not believe it and laughed . . . Abraham believed most certainly, but the fulfillment of this promise took a long time! Abraham is tired of waiting and decides that he is going to accomplish, to carry out, and to achieve the promise of God himself, by his own means. He chooses a woman likely to have a child and he does have this child. But it is precisely because this child is the result of a human decision that he is not the gift of God. Because the child is the result of a voluntary and autonomous act of the man who received the promise, God does not acknowledge him as the child of the promise. This is a fundamental and decisive point, namely, when God makes a promise, then he, and only he, must at the time he chooses fulfill the promise! Yes, Ishmael is born of the flesh. But the son of the promise was to be born of grace! And Abraham should have had the patience to wait for the granting of this grace! This is a lesson we all need to learn in our lives. Only the one born of the miracle accomplished by God will be heir to all the blessings. This was intensely "unjust." First of all, according to the code of law at the time the oldest son usually received the inheritance. God chooses the younger, however, and thus from the legal standpoint, God is "unjust."

God often makes this kind of choice and prefers the one who has no right or legitimate power. Only the one born of a miracle of God will be considered by God as the heir of the promise. Let us notice, however, that Ishmael is nevertheless blessed by God; the difference, the only difference, is found in the inheritance of *the promise of God*, which points out the person who will bear the truth of *this* Word of God from generation to generation. At each stage, God chooses a new bearer by grace. As Paul says, God chooses "when as yet the children were not born, and had done neither good nor evil, so that the purpose according to God's free choice might stand independently of any works and might be the free expression of the free will of him who calls." The situation will be the same later when God announces to Rebecca that her older son will be subject to her younger son, but "subject" does not mean submitting, vanquished, or weakened; no, it only marks the bearer of the promise. This is not a human inheritance that is handed down. The drama of Abraham will in fact be repeated throughout all of Israel's history and culminate in Jesus. In fact, this people of Israel wants to be faithful, wants to accomplish God's Word, and obeys this God scrupulously, but it wants (just like Abraham) to do all of God's will by itself, and by so doing it holds God in this obedience: God cannot reject because his will is scrupulously done. And, at each great stage, God sets aside (I do not say "abandons," and even less "condemns") so many good works, so much good will, so much obedience, to choose among the people the one who will be "the real bearer of the promise," and who does not deserve anything more than the rest. It is precisely because he does not claim to be doing anything of himself that he will be totally free for the unexpected and surprising service required by God.

Let us notice that the exact same drama occurs in Christian churches: excessive organization, moralism, obedience to "the Word of God," faithful ritualism—in summary, the excessive will to comply perfectly with revelation blocks the action of the Holy Spirit and destroys the freedom acquired in Jesus Christ.

Here in our text, the point is the pursuit of the promise, that which fundamentally was for the purpose of God. What, however, is the content of the word "promise," which we have constantly been using? What is the promise? It is the promise of the covenant (which must remain a *gift* of God), the promise of the Messiah, and the promise of the kingdom to come. Israel's role is to affirm, to announce to all people the existence of that *future*. It is the declaration that all may participate in this joyous gift contained in the promise. That is, it opens up a hope. Who will carry this promise to the world? God remains free to choose the individual, and from generation to generation, God chooses. Not everyone is called to that particular service, to become an ambassador of God on earth. The promise does not automatically go from one to the other (and I would like to say: not any more than the notorious "original sin" is transmitted hereditarily)! The beginning of this "selection" by the grace of God is striking. God chose Jacob: he chose him concretely to fulfill a certain mission that he entrusted him. The principle of election is God's pleasure (in the sense of joy). So God is arbitrary then? *Yes*, just as love is arbitrary! Why do this man and this woman love each other (in truth)? No one has ever been able to explain it. Since the subject is love, I do not think the famous translation "Esau have I hated" can account for the thought of Isaiah or Paul. God does not know hatred! There is no place for it in God's immense love. This phrase from Isaiah, which is taken up by Paul in verse 13, is very worrisome because it is in contradiction with all of the revelation on the God of Abraham, Isaac, and Jacob and because it seems to confirm the judgment of anti-Semites on this cruel and unjust God. We have already explained the "injustice" of God and his "arbitrariness." But with this verse we are coming up against a difficulty. As Maillot showed, there is probably, if not a misinterpretation, at least a misunderstanding about verbs such as "love" and "hate," which explains our reaction. For us, these verbs are words that express feelings and a general disposition toward such and such a person. In Hebrew, these verbs are very concrete.

We will have to come back to the practical, active, and concrete character of Hebrew vocabulary and thought. Just as *dabar*, the "Word," also means "action," so the verbs "love" and "hate" express a certain way of acting rather than a feeling. "I have chosen Jacob" is the same as "I have loved Jacob." So although literally the Hebrew and Greek verbs mean "hate," we should no doubt understand this in a concrete manner: "I have not chosen Esau" or "I pushed away." God chooses whom he wants . . . but that choice is not about eternal salvation; it is not about the promise of life, no. God chooses whom he wants for his service and to fulfill the role he wants men to take up.

In all these texts, there is no talk of eternal salvation or eternal damnation. What happens to those who are rejected? We see them in biblical history as they become successful men who live well. Ishmael does receive a blessing and he also receives a promise: he also will become a great nation. He is not damned. It would be easy to make the same mistake that was made in the case of Cain, who became the image of the wandering Jew, eternally condemned, carrying the mark of damnation ("The eye was in the grave and it stared at Cain"[3]). The text, however, is very clear. The sign that God put on Cain is not a sign of damnation, rather it is the sign of the protection that God guarantees to Cain: he is wandering the earth, but is under the protection of God! Esau will become rich and powerful, and Jacob is afraid of him, but finally the two brothers are reconciled. God does not pursue Esau with his hatred; he does not entrust him with any mission, that is, an election. What the text reminds us of is the fact that election to fulfill a mission is not based on any "reasons" that would appear to be convincing! God's purpose is not based on good works completed beforehand by man, on any morality that is well respected, or on the validity of human laws. The choice has no other reason than the very will of him who chose. We maintain that God is just by creating this relationship of justice between himself and a man based on *his* free commitment: "I am yours and you are mine"; it is a justice "outside of the Law" (Rom 3:21). The other men . . . well, they are living without a mission, without responsibility before God, without the heavy burden of being the bearers of truth in the midst of a humanity without truth, without being witnesses to God's peace in a humanity without peace, and without being witnesses to God's justice, which surpasses all our ideas about justice because it contradicts our constructions and our philosophies! God chooses counter to any human plausibility.

---

3. Translator's note: this is the last line of a famous poem by Victor Hugo, "Conscience."

There is that absurd story about Isaac: God's plan is to choose the one who from a human standpoint *could not be born* of a hundred-year-old man and woman! (And whether we like it or not, it does remind us of the miraculous birth of Jesus. Which one is more miraculous: that a child would be born of hundred-year-old parents or that a child would be born of a virgin? In both cases, it is an *act of creation* on the part of God). And then there is the incredible story of the choice of Jacob; he is born second, and thus in human thought, he *has no right* to his father's inheritance. Humanly seen, the other one should inherit the promise. But no, he is without any rights! Is it the case that he is more worthy of being entrusted with this heavy duty? Certainly not! His name, Jacob, already shows what he must be, the Liar. He strips his brother of his rights by a trick and obtains his father's blessing in a fraudulent manner. From a moral standpoint, he is reprehensible no matter what! But God's choice does not correspond to any morality or any virtue! Yet we see this Jacob who in the final analysis only takes one reality seriously: God! If he deceives, it is only because, as far as he is concerned, the only fundamental that is given is the blessing from God, inheriting the covenant! When he receives a visit from three men he is able to discern that they are angels sent from God. When he is assaulted by the ford, he knows that he is wrestling with God himself, and he asks for only one thing: the blessing.

The only important thing about this Jacob is precisely the fact that he is able to discern what is the most important! This does not, however, explain God's free and unconditional decision, made from all eternity, to choose this person. We have talked about the freedom of God, his good pleasure, yes, but we also have a small clue—which we should retain since it is given to us in Scripture—not a clue about God's motivation, not a clue about any unavoidable correlation, but a certain guideline that God chooses and that he lets us see as a scarlet thread in the weft. He chooses the son of the hundred-year-old parents, and we know that *the sons of old people . . .* ! He chooses the person condemned to death and he saves him at the last minute. He chooses the person without any right, any morals, and any "human respect"! Just as he choose the *stutterer* to carry his Word, the representative "of the smallest tribe of Israel" (1 Sam 9:21) as the first king, and the youngest of Jesse's sons as the second king. And he chooses the young David against the giant Goliath.

So each time, God chooses the smallest, the weakest, as the bearer of his grace and of his covenant, and it is to him that he entrusts the heavy task of representing him among men.

Exactly the same proclamation is given when we come to the people of Israel: "For you are a people holy to the Lord your God," and "The Lord your God has chosen you out of all the peoples of the earth to be his people, his treasured possession," and "The Lord did not set his affection on you and choose you because you were more powerful than other peoples, for you were fewest of all peoples" (Deut 7:6–7).[4] This declaration occurs so many times!

And here Paul is confirming and generalizing when he explains to the Corinthians that God chooses the weak things of the world to confound the strong and the foolish things in the world to confound the wise, and even the things that have no existence to confound those that "are."

Why this strange politics on the part of God! He does it this way so that there may be no confusion, so that man may not attribute to his own wisdom, his own strength, or his own skill that which comes from God alone. This does not mean that God condemns and damns what is strong, powerful, or rich! Only that there should be no confusion! For the wisdom of God knows very well how quick man is to attribute to himself that which is an act of God or a success of God! Therefore, God accomplishes his works through the one who, humanly, has no means, no chance of succeeding! "So that no flesh may glorify itself before the Lord." The work of God is *God's* work. It has to be recognized as such. So Israel is not chosen for its distinguished virtues but for its weakness. There is a constant inadequacy between the purpose of God and the means that he chooses to achieve it! But God acts by, and through . . . this man, this people because God never acts directly in the world: God uses human beings, but he does not make them into robots. And so the weakest of men is the best instrument of the power of God that will show through as such, and God will be given thanks for having done such great things with almost nothing. In these very verses, Paul emphasizes the freedom of divine election, which depends on the one who calls and not on works.

"The God who determines the course of history, of which Israel is an integral part, acts according to his sovereign choice, which no man

---

4. This is Ellul's own translation of Deut 7.

can influence (Franz Mussner), and, by choosing among the weak and the disinherited, God has an immense choice. In this wicked humanity alienated from God, he chooses freely whom he wants. In the people of Israel, God also chooses whom he wants: the aforementioned "remnant," those who not only do not follow other gods, but most of all those who do not trust in their own virtue, their own religion, their own sacrifices, their own faithfulness, or their own morality. . . . Such are the bearers of the promise that Jesus chose. But could we then believe that "all Israel" would be evil and excluded from grace? Not at all! We will come back to this at length.

However, we must interrupt this development, for as far as Israel is concerned, we are faced here with an extremely difficult question: is evil, the refusal to do God's will, and opposition to God the expression of a power outside of God? In other words, once again we find ourselves facing the following dilemma: if God is good, he cannot do evil; if he does evil (or lets evil be done), he is not good! From this comes the ever-renewed invention of two gods, a god of good and a god of evil (and the absurd idea that the god of evil is the God of the Old Testament, etc.). Certainly, in the mouths of prophets we see the biblical God bring about wars, punishments, and disasters . . . and this hurts our feelings,[5] which makes the God of Jesus the "all good"; that is, the one who is all kindness, all indulgence . . . the "good God." But this is not true. "I am the Lord and there is no other. I form the light and create darkness. I bring prosperity and create disaster" (Isa 45:6–7). "Who can speak and have it happen if the Lord has not decreed it? Is it not from the mouth of the Most High that both calamities and good things come?" (Lam 3:37–38).[6]

We are therefore led to acknowledge not that evil is done and willed by God but rather that it is not outside of God's power. The refusal to obey his will is therefore also included in God's power. . . . Jacob was

5. I recently experienced this. In an article published in the journal *Réformes*, I had written that, after all, AIDS could be the expression of a divine judgment in the face of the unbelievable perversions of our society. I had taken every precaution by making it clear that the guiltiest party is not the person who is sick, but what a scandal the statement created! Everyone was unanimously against me.

6. We must note two things here: First of all, to the evil that comes from God, and which he has decided, man adds the evil he does himself and which God condemns. Secondly, right before the text I have just quoted, we find the following verses: "For men are not cast off by the Lord forever. Though he brings grief, he will show compassion, so great is his unfailing love. For he does not willingly bring affliction or grief to the children of men."

chosen, our text tells us again, "before the twins were born or had done anything good or bad so that God's purpose in election might stand, not by works, but by him who calls."[7] Thus, the very opposition to God's will, far from making God's power ineffectual, is itself founded on the sovereign freedom of the Creator! We have said so before: man's freedom to refuse God's order or action cannot limit or paralyze the freedom of God and his decision. Quite the contrary: it is the omnipotence of the Creator—who is also at the same time the Savior—that makes the *negative freedom* of man *possible*. God's purpose, as we see it in the long course of Israel's history, is manifest, if we are willing to abandon the preconceived ideas that we cling to in order to make belief easier.

The opponents whom God stirs up in the course of history appear in the end to show that God, in his omnipotence, *can* also save them, these disobedient and contradicting ones; and in his love, he does! This is fundamental if we want to understand that the opposition of Israel to Jesus Christ is not the cause of an eternal rejection but the assurance that in Jesus Christ, the God of Israel saves also those who did not want to be saved!

Let us now consider another aspect of this same revelation. In these verses, we looked at the pair Jacob-Esau at length. A little further in the text, we encounter the pair Moses-Pharaoh; Paul will present a generalization by using the image of the potter who makes some pottery for noble purposes and some for common use. We are here faced with Barth's great idea according to which in biblical history and in history in general, there is always before God a pair: one person who accepts the will of God, the mission that God entrusts, and who listens to God's call, and another person who refuses election. However, they are not, as has been believed, two contradictory images, one of a man manifesting the love of God and the other of a man—destined to eternal perdition—manifesting God's justice. That interpretation fails to take into consideration the fact that all of God's justice—the very justice that brings condemnation—was fulfilled by Jesus Christ, and that his condemnation is enough. There is no need for another condemnation of the wicked, because "I came to save *sinners*" and "I will draw *all men* unto me." God's salvation project has always been accompanied by its

---

7. Moreover, this is only the normal consequence of the great proclamation that salvation is by grace without the works of faith. It is difficult to understand how Protestants insisted on the existence of the damned for so long!

shadow, its negative, which is not simply rejected, because in its very
negativity it serves God's purpose. It serves God's sovereign will, not in
manifesting God's justice again and again but in showing that this God
uses human contradiction to draw out an ever greater manifestation of
grace. "Where sin increased, grace increased all the more." If God shows
mercy to the rebel, his grace is manifestedly truer, more powerful and
greater than if he only called the nice little lambs: it would then no longer be grace! In every situation in which the Word of God is proclaimed,
there is always the person who hears and accepts, and the person who
refuses but will also be the object of grace![8] Everything comes in pairs.
And these pairs are inseparable.

Such is the case of Moses and Pharaoh. "I raised you up for this
very purpose, that I may display my power in you and that my name
might be proclaimed in all the earth." If Pharaoh had not opposed God's
will, if he had obeyed, the Hebrews would not have been *freed* by a
miracle; they would not have come out of slavery and anguish solely
because of the Lord's act, and he would not have been proclaimed to be,
above all, *the Liberator*. Pharaoh serves the purpose and will of God. He
hardens the heart of Pharaoh to make manifest that God is more powerful than the most powerful king. (He makes manifest his *power* and not,
as we too often hear, his *justice*.) He will be proclaimed the Liberator,
and moreover, God shows all men that no human power can triumph
over the free will of God's grace. In this story, Pharaoh plays his positive
role: he makes obvious that the most powerful king who decides everything, who dominates everything, will involuntarily bring out the brutal
fact that nothing can stop God's grace from coming through. Pharaoh
plays his role in the history of salvation (just as Judas played his). In fact,
his refusal made him obey God's very plan, as Martin Luther said: "He
published the name of God over all the earth by saying *no*." We do not
need anything else in order to say, "Hallelujah." But once again, let us
make no mistake: in this story of salvation, one would not understand
anything if one considered the Hebrews "good" and Pharaoh "evil." It is
not a question of morals! Only the Lord is good! And he shows mercy
to scoundrels and sinners! So as God's grace works throughout history,
there is always an inseparable pair, which brilliantly throws light on the
condition of Israel, which is *always* both *the elected and the rejected* people (for after all, "Yes" is inseparable from "No," and vice versa; we might

8. I will not repeat Barth's long argument about Judas!

also refer to the "modern" idea of positivity and negativity). As we have said before, Israel is constantly being reduced to a "remnant." "Though your people, O Israel, be like the sand by the sea, only a remnant will return . . . the remnant of Israel, the survivors of the house of Jacob will no longer rely on him who struck them down but will truly rely on the Lord, the Holy One of Israel" (Isa 10:20–23). One might argue that this passage is historically about the remnant that returned after the Babylonian captivity, but in reality the true question is: In whom does Israel put its faith? Does it put its faith in human powers (and lean on the one who strikes!—the majority of the people do this), or does it put its faith in the power of the Lord alone? That is the work of the remnant. Israel remains the chosen people but is so diminished in number and in quality because of its disobedience. This is the experience of Samuel and of Elijah too ("I alone am left . . ."). And so in any disobedience on the part of Israel, there is a remnant, a *feeble* remnant (Isa 1:9), which is a *sprout* as well as the heir and bearer of the blessing.

Is it the bearer of the blessing and of the promise? Yes, but not for itself or for its own profit. This bearer, this sprout, still belongs to the chosen people, it carries election into the midst of the people (perhaps it does that alone, but that is not important), and through *this bearer of the promise* all Israel is saved. This casts an extraordinary light on the condition of Israel in its refusal to accept Jesus. If Jesus is indeed, according to our faith, the son of Israel, and descendant of David, he is the sprout that remains for Israel. The refusal of the Jews does not change this in any way. If the grace of God has always manifested itself through a contradictory pair (both being in the same grace but not having the same role), then the refusal of Israel (on the one hand) is coupled (on the other hand) with the faith of the pagans who have become the church. Thus, if we have understood how inseparable "Yes" is from "No," and how "No" is the very condition of "Yes," this means that Israel is inseparable from the church. Israel does not exist in itself (it has never existed "in itself") but neither does the church. The church does not exist "in itself"—it exists in relation with, according to, and for Israel!

Of course, I am well aware that all I have said—and will further explain—cannot, even if we believe it, really convince us. There is necessarily a feeling of injustice. Paul knows perfectly well the weakness of his "demonstration," for human common sense is expressed in the criticism that man addresses to God: "One of you will say to me: 'Then why does

God still blame us? For who resists his will?'" I will add two remarks before going on to Paul's answer. First of all, our criticism comes implicitly from the fact that we believe that in the end those whom God rejects did not "deserve" this and that those who are chosen did "deserve" it! This again shows, however, that we have gone back to the understanding that we can deserve or not deserve grace. Yet our text, and almost the entire Bible, tells us exactly the opposite. Those who are chosen, called by God, did not deserve anything. Even more, we must understand that all "deserved" wrath and rejection, "For there is not one righteous, not even one." We must endeavor to eradicate the conviction that works have any value.

Yet, there is a reciprocal point that must be considered. Christians often want to "prove" that God is just. They want to demonstrate, by offering various justifications, that God does not commit any injustices. I will not repeat what I said earlier about the "value" of justice, but I want to emphasize the error in wanting to "defend" God's honor (an error we find in all systems of apologetics). Here we are, undertaking the task of "justifying" God, when—let us not forget—it is *he* who justifies us! "But who are you, O man, to talk back to God?" The man who wants to argue with God has nothing to say simply because God is God! However, when we acknowledge God for who he is—sovereignly free love—then our silence is not that of a man downcast by fate, crushed under a mountain of determinisms! For God's freedom is exactly the anti-fate. There is no more fate (*fatum*), no more *ananke*. Free grace restores to man a future that is to be made, not a future already established. The grace and freedom of the God of the Bible are in exact opposition to Allah; there is no longer any *mektoub* or *inch'Allah!* The man who keeps quiet is then like Job, a man who argued indefinitely, who lined up all his questions and all his rebellion but who, once God had spoken, kept his peace: "I know that you can do all things . . ." and covered his mouth with his hand. It is the silence of the person who in truth has acknowledged who God is and who now can do nothing but worship: the silence of respect and thankfulness. All discussions (whether theological or not) presuppose a complete misunderstanding of the Lord and of the work he is pursuing generation after generation.

After this comes the passage about the two kinds of pottery: those made to be "vessels of wrath" (or of "burning") for common use and those made for honorable use. The first will be destroyed in the end, whereas the latter will be glorified. Does this text not contradict everything we have developed so far? God has made these vessels of wrath (or of burning) for the purpose of destroying them. Through this judgment, he shows his power and his wrath. We are here faced with the traditional thesis. It calls for several caveats, however. First, we should note that both kinds of vessels are *useful* to God. He made some to reveal his glory, others to reveal his wrath and his justice. There is a disparity between the terms "the glory" on the one hand and "the wrath" on the other. Neither the wrath nor the justice is the glory of God! They are events and decisions that in no way glorify God. Furthermore, the glory is explained by the *mercy*: it is his grace and his mercy that reveal the glory of God. But what grace and what mercy would there be in saving and honoring the one who in himself is *worthy* of this mercy and who receives it simply as the reward for what he has done? There is no mercy in this! If God gives this gift to the one who paid for it and if he loves the one who is worthy of love, then there is no grace and no mercy! In *that* case, God would have been manifesting *his justice*: he would be just in giving what should be given to the one who did what was done. The employer was just in that he paid the workers of the first hour (who did all the work) the wages that had been agreed upon. It is just that upon returning from his journey he would tell the workers who have worked, "Well done, and now serve me my dinner." Consequently, when the text says that God shows mercy to certain people, he does so to those who do not deserve it! The vessels of honor are not so by nature but rather because the potter made them to manifest his honor and mercy: we should not think of these as being worthy people who have spent their lives doing what God requested. In the same way, the vessels "of wrath" need mercy if these words are a reference to people who have behaved badly, disobeyed, rebelled, and been enemies of God and the gospel! In reality, these vessels are only vessels of wrath because God wants to use them to show his wrath.

Secondly, Paul says that the one case manifests and reveals his mercy and the other his justice. Manifesting? Revealing? To whom and for whom? If this is about the last judgment, about eternal salvation and eternal life, then this does not manifest or reveal anything, since no one on earth can say who is "damned" and who is saved. That is God's secret and it does not show or teach men living on earth *anything*! This can only be about manifesting and reveal something to living human beings! But then we are not talking about salvation! This is about a reality that man can see and note. So in both cases this is about an act of God taking place on earth, in the midst of men, an act that is perfectly visible and comprehensible! Furthermore, the case of Pharaoh is characteristic: his heart is hardened by God so that he may be vanquished (not that he may be damned), so that it might be dazzling and clear that the God of Abraham and of Moses is more powerful than Pharaoh and that he is able to overcome slavery and anguish! This is a *historical* punishment perfectly clear during a man's life. Should we then accept this simplistic conclusion that has so often been believed: he who is rich and successful is blessed by God and therefore saved? Not at all. Pharaoh was rich and powerful, and the wrath of God fell on him. Conversely, the poor are not cursed by God! Here again we must disassociate human success and failure from mercy and wrath. The person who piles up human powers is like a lightning rod that attracts lightning—that is God's justice. It is the very success that makes that person a vessel of burning, of common use. And reciprocally, the person who has failed, who has nothing to present to God, and who is "poor" is a vessel of mercy, and in the course of his life on earth among men he receives glory and mercy! Does that mean that we should declare that all poor people are blessed?[9] Certainly not! There is no authoritarianism here. It is not automatically that a "poor" person—one who is sick or afflicted or destitute or a victim or a punching bag—becomes a vessel of honor. He becomes one, not when God in his sovereign liberty . . . makes him rich or heals him, but when God reveals through him *who* this God is—the God who saves and loves. This *can* only be seen in a life that has been stripped of everything else. And this is why these vessels (made from the *same clay* as the others) are "vessels *of* mercy." That is, they are useful to God for manifesting his mercy, which gives everything and expects nothing from man in return. This is a historical adventure; it is not mystical or metaphysical, and it is part and parcel of the fabric of life. How? Simply this: Who will, among men, fulfill God's service? Who will carry the promise to all people? Who will be the witness? That is all, and it is enough.

Some are useful to God to demonstrate what he can be in the manifestation of his wrath so that men may understand that it is a terrible thing to fall into the hands of the living God; others serve to attest,

9. As a matter of form, I will repeat what has been said a million times, namely: "Happy are the poor" does not in any way justify those who make others poor or who do nothing to raise them out of poverty: such people are typical "vessels of wrath"!

through their concrete example, what the immensity of God's free love can be. The first are not instantaneously and automatically struck down. Throughout the course of their history God *bears with* them, tolerates them, and lets them run their course. He bears with what they do, and this double character brings us back to Job, whose (purely earthly) adversity, contrary to what his friends say, must not be assimilated to eternal judgment. Quite the contrary, Job was powerful and he was struck in his power, but in reality he knows that his avenger lives and that the Lord saves him. In this text—and this will be essential to remember when we get back to the Jewish people—the question is only about glory or wrath manifested among men. We know that the eternal truth of this judgment is completely summarized in Jesus Christ. Only he can bear the full wrath of God, only he can bear damnation. God achieves his double power of justice and of love in only one person, and for all people: in Jesus Christ, who is at the same time chosen and rejected, cursed and blessed. Even more, for us—for all of us—he became curse and blessing. ("Christ has redeemed us from the curse of the Law by becoming a curse for us," Gal 3:13.) So that Paul is able to say with boldness that until Jesus Christ, the last judgment—salvation or damnation—had not been pronounced on any man! "For *all have sinned* and come short of the glory of God and are *justified* freely by his grace in Jesus Christ through the *redemption* that came by Jesus Christ."

We need to weigh each one of the terms of this central theological affirmation, and because I do not believe that Paul would contradict himself within a few pages, I have to admit that the "vessels of wrath" are also saved by grace in Jesus Christ. Condemnation is thus purely earthly and historical. The "rejection" of Israel sets it apart for a time, but it is in no sense an exclusion from salvation. In the people of Israel, there is always a "remnant" that bears the covenant, a posterity that transmits the promises from age to age (see the texts from Isaiah that Paul cites in verses 27–29). In order that his gospel—his covenant—might henceforth be spread universally, however, God calls others, who were not part of the chosen people and who will now receive the same vocation and carry the same promise to the world. "I will call them my people who are not my people; and I will call her my 'loved one' who is not my loved one, and it will happen that in the very place where it was said to them 'You are not my people,' they will be called 'sons of the living God'" (vv. 24–25). This is the only way in which we should understand the parable of the two categories of vessels and the rejection of human arguments. God chooses vessels to carry his gospel (we carry this truth in jars of clay . . .) not because they are more worthy: they are worthy because God chose them! This is all about election for service not for any benefit, as we have already emphasized.

So in the end we can see that there are three movements in this "demonstration": God chooses the bearer of the promise so that the promise might be carried to the universe and so that the covenant might be announced to all. Because the bearer disobeyed, God chose a remnant, and this is repeated in almost every generation. Those who do not fulfill the role for which God chose them are rejected (as "instruments"), and he hardens their heart to show his power. He can choose and he can also reject the one he had chosen (the most tragic "type" being Saul), but this rejection never means exclusion from the love of God, and as such the end of Saul is characteristic: the inhabitants of Jabesh in Galead gave him a burial after his death (1 Sam 31:11–12) and David still calls Saul "the Lord's anointed" (2 Sam 1:13–16); the rejection of Saul did not cancel his anointing as King Saul and David composed in his honor the admirable lament that is included in the "Book of the Righteous" (2 Sam 1:17–27). Finally, the third movement: from reduction to reduction, by choosing a remnant from within the remnant, we are left with only a unique remnant: Jesus Christ himself. From then on, all will be called to become members of God's people, the Jews—just as in each of the prophets who proclaimed a remnant, the role of the remnant was to call all brethren to return to faithfulness to the God of Israel; all Jews, but also all those who throughout the world will hear the proclamation of the love of God! This is what is announced in the message of the text we quoted earlier: "I will call them 'my people' who are not my people" (v. 25). This movement was studied and brought to light by Vischer, who illustrated it thus:

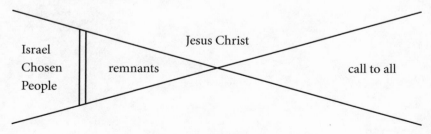

The freedom of God in this "politic" unveiled by Paul is thus a liberty that comes from God's love, which ends in the universal and free mercy of God. The divine "arbitrariness" has nothing in common with a whim. We must always keep our attention fixed on the fact that all of God's "policy" is connected to the aim he is pursuing: *show mercy to all.* If one wants the world to be saved, one must accept and adore God's free and sovereign project which implies that men in this world are not saved by an unknown miracle that would take place in the clouds, but that God would never act without man. Therefore, men must be associated with this salvation project, and they must be for others the witnesses of grace and the bearers of the covenant and of the promise.

3

How Will They Believe?

THREE GENERAL REMARKS THAT WILL ENLIGHTEN AND GUIDE OUR RE-flection must be made before we actually begin our study of the texts. The first remark has to do with the fact that chapter 10 is "off center" with respect to chapter 9. The latter, as we have seen is completely focused on the project of God, the freedom of God, the "arbitrary" choice that he makes, and everything Paul says is a revelation about this God of Abraham, of Isaac, and of Jacob, who is also the God of Jesus Christ. On the other hand, chapter 10 is completely focused on man, on the righteousness that he may (or may not) acquire, on listening to the call, and of course on the Jews. Here we find that the actions and reactions of man, his obligations and his attitude towards God, are placed at the center.

The second remark is that chapter 10, exactly like chapter 9, starts with Paul himself questioning his belonging to the Jewish people and his love for it: "Brothers, my heart's desire and prayer to God for the Israelites is that they may be saved." . . . On the one hand, the idea of making a vow is not frequent in Paul's writings (or in the New Testament as a whole). The vow is not a simple wish, and it is not the same as what we find in the pagan world. Nor is it what a vow has become in Catholicism (I make a vow promising to go on a pilgrimage if God grants me such benefit or grants my request). Here the vow has retained its votive force, I agree to devote myself to the service of this God by presenting a request that commits my whole person and makes me totally committed to him. Paul vows to give his heart (that is, his whole person—let us remember that the "heart" is not sentimental in Hebrew thought) to his beloved people. Moreover, he *prays* for them; it is an "ardent prayer" for the salvation of the Jews. And this mention of a prayer is very important because it shows that a "future" is possible! The "destiny" of the Jews is not set, even if one believes that today they have been rejected; there is no "fate" that is fixed once and for all, and the question of Israel is not closed and finished. Once more, we are presented with the fundamental truth that there are no situations determined in advance. The liberating God, whose work and witness is Israel, is indeed an anti-destiny. This was wholly confirmed in Jesus Christ.

Finally the third preliminary remark that can be made is that at the end of chapter 9 and in this chapter 10, there are an astonishing number of quotations from the Hebrew Bible: ten quotations in twenty-two verses! Why is Paul (who obviously knew the Scriptures perfectly) so keen on including these citations? Assuredly this means that he is claiming to speak not on his own authority but first of all on the authority of the Scriptures: he is saying in effect "I am not making anything up, this is the source of my teaching." Aside from his own problem, he also intends to signify that what is happening to the Jews is neither a surprising nor an unexpected adventure; quite the contrary, it is the fulfillment of a number of texts which had already been revealed to the people of Israel. Their present history is continuing, says Paul, under the sign of the "Old" Testament! This was not obvious to everyone. First of all, these texts had to be understood and received either as a prophecy of what would happen or as a warning to Israel so that it would pay careful attention! To a modern Western reader the interpretations that Paul offers seem rather "far-fetched"! But his method follows the rabbinic hermeneutics of his time perfectly, and we should not forget that he was fully trained in this method! Anyway, it seems that the interpretation of these texts was not a matter of course! They could only be understood "in truth" . . . after the fact! This was often the case with prophetic announcements; their real meaning could only be understood after the fulfillment had taken place.

In Paul's view, the same holds true of these texts, which only become clear after the "rejection" of Israel; or at least, that "rejection" is what makes it possible to understand these prophecies in a new way (because they had obviously all been explained already). By carefully reading this long demonstration, one could say that in fact God is "hedging his bets." Moreover, this brings an extraordinary light on the subject of the famous "freedom of man within the freedom of God" and on the idea that while God predicts everything and knows everything, man is not determined. I believe that just like an infinitely skillful chess player,

God predicts all the possible outcomes of all the decisions coming from all the possible choices made by man, and for each one of these possibilities, God prepares in advance his special answer and his special revelation. In the present case: Israel can either be completely obedient to the plan of God—and let us not forget that God's plan is universal salvation, that is, that all people may know and acknowledge this unique God, this God of love and salvation. In that case, it is indeed Israel that has been chosen to carry this gospel to the world. Then God allows Israel, the faithful servant to do its work. But is it possible that Israel, with all its virtues, all its care to be strictly faithful to the Torah, and with its perpetual adoration of its Lord, may leave aside the essential part of its vocation—namely the proclamation of this gospel of liberation—and may actually close the door to the "nations" by fixating too narrowly on the Law and its own election? Yet, this has often been proclaimed (Ps 87:4ff.) "It is in Zion that I have loved Egypt and Babylon. . . ."[1] In that case, there must be another runner in the relay, another bearer of the universality of God's love to the world. And God has already seen this possibility and he has already predicted the transformation that would occur. Israel is certainly not condemned by God, but it is no longer the instrument used to carry forth this revelation, this gospel. And since the beloved and chosen people of Israel did not do what God expected of it, then none other than God himself, in the person of his Son, came to accomplish the work. Of course, this possibility had to be announced in the revelation to Israel. That is, the texts that are now "open" also *had* to contain God's resolution given this hypothesis! This is why Paul wants to base everything that he says on these texts, which are there to help us understand that the revelation to Israel (which is unique) nevertheless encompasses all the actions and decisions that man might freely choose!

ISRAEL'S MISTAKE: 9:30—10:13

Finally, for what reasons is Israel (temporarily) set aside by God? Its fundamental error concerns first of all, "righteousness." What is this righteousness? When we think of this word and when we want to understand its biblical meaning in God's revelation, we need to take out what we usually mean in Western thought! This is not about judicial justice (conformity to laws and to the sentences of judges), nor is it about politi-

---

1. This is Ellul's own translation of verse 4.

cal and social justice (that which we are used to), which is about equality among men. Finally, it is not a justice "value," neither in a philosophical nor a metaphysical sense. Biblically, righteousness is not a certain behavior that chooses what is right and equitable. Contrary to the precept of the Roman jurist Ulpian, it is not an *ars aequi et boni*. . . . I believe that biblical righteousness corresponds well to what Job says of "Wisdom" (Job 28). "But where can wisdom be found? Where does understanding dwell? Man does not comprehend its worth. It cannot be found in the land of the living. . . . It cannot be bought with the finest gold. . . . Where then does wisdom come from? Where does understanding dwell? God understands the way to it."

All of this could be said of righteousness when the Bible speaks of it! We cannot *in truth* know what righteousness is. We cannot even approximate it. Only God is the Righteous One. Only his will is righteous. We have said so before: there is no criterion of justice by which we could measure God's righteousness! Only God declares what is righteous. What we call by that name will be a human cultural convention (judicial or social justice) or a construction built by human intelligence based on presuppositions established by man (criterion of justice). Having received the Torah from God, Israel interpreted it as being *in itself*, the righteousness of God. That is, Israel claimed to seal righteousness and, in a sense, lock God within the revelation of his justice. To fulfill the Torah scrupulously and in every detail was to be righteous oneself and to be of the righteousness of God. It became then (because we perfectly understand this Torah) a "self-righteousness," a kind of appropriation of the righteousness of God.

Thus, Israel's first mistake was to confuse the revealed Torah with a text that could be appropriated by scrupulously executing what it said. This would be all there was to righteousness, and consequently a righteousness coming from works, a righteousness of strict obedience, and which, because of this, could only belong to the person who knows the Torah, who has received it, meditates on it without ceasing, and a righteousness that could belong to no one else. Of course, it is sure that dozens of texts assimilate righteousness to the exact obedience to the commandments. Yet, in this same Scripture, there were rare though significant warnings! "I *also* gave [your fathers] over to statutes that were not good, and laws they could not live by. *I* made them become defiled through their gifts . . . that I might fill them with horror [by leading them into unrighteousness myself!] so they would know that I am the Lord!" (Ezek 20:25ff.). "As for you house of Israel, *go* and serve your idols . . . !" They should not have made the Torah into a net that would imprison man—because the God of Israel is the Liberator—and they should not have kept it for themselves. If one misinterprets this, one will come up against "a stumbling stone that makes one fall." For "the Lord Almighty is the one you are to regard as holy, he is the one you are to fear, he is the one you are to dread, and he will be a sanctuary, but for both houses of Israel he will be a stone that causes men to stumble and a rock that makes them fall. And for the people of Jerusalem he will be a trap and a snare. Many of them will stumble; they will fall and be broken . . ." (Isa 8:13–15).

What is terrible is that God himself then becomes a "stumbling stone"! Israel is coming up against God; he is the one who makes them fall. Why Paul asks is precisely because Israel wanted to fulfill the Torah "too well." Israel wanted to obtain righteousness through the Law, through strict obedience, through works. In spite of the Prophets, Israel no longer received the Torah as a living Word always in movement, always *new*. *Yet*, whoever *believes* in this God who is a stumbling stone, whoever simply has faith in him, will not perish! (Ps 2:12). A relationship with this God can only be one of love and faith, not a relationship of strict obedience and works. God is not locked inside his Torah. His righteousness is not an exact retribution for works. We are therefore in the presence of a fundamental opposition about the truth and righteousness of God. Practically, for the Jews, justice consisted in giving the other his exact due. This same understanding of justice also prevailed in the relationship with the Lord. However, what has been revealed to us in Jesus Christ is that righteousness actually is the gift given to the person to whom one does not *owe* anything! God *gives* everything. And of course, Israel knew this, because it had received freedom, the covenant, the Torah . . . these absolutely free gifts; and that was God's *righteousness*. He gave righteousness in favor of Israel.

In Jesus Christ, God's justice continues first of all to justify the unjust! So those who were not looking for this righteousness, says Paul, are the ones to receive it! In reality, neither Abraham nor the Hebrew people were looking for this righteousness, and yet they received it. The only thing that God is expecting from man is simply that he should believe; that he should believe in this righteousness that God gives, that he should believe the promise, and that he should believe that God makes him just in spite of his sins and his wanderings. This is an absolutely extraordinary reality which goes beyond our understanding: For God, the person who becomes just is precisely the one who acknowledges that he is a sinner and that he is incapable of filling the gigantic distance that separates him from God's justice, gives up trying, and presents himself as an unworthy sinner. "Woe unto me" said Isaiah, "for my lips are impure." In the same way, the parable of the workers hired at the eleventh hour reveals what God's justice is. For Jesus, justice is not fulfilled when the master gives the workers of the first hour what had been decided; rather it is when he gives the same thing to the latecomers—those who did not deserve anything. There is his justice, and it merges with love.

How can I say that they merge? There is a simple "theological" reason for this: God is *one*. He does not have several faces; he is not like us, divided between contradictory feelings. There is *in us*, because of our weakness as humans, sometimes anger, sometimes love, sometimes a spirit of vengeance, sometimes a spirit of reconciliation. To posit God in our image would be an unacceptable anthropomorphism. He is one! He does not have feelings that change over time and he is not different according to circumstances, according to people, according to times. He is not a "two-faced Janus," with one loving face and one angry face. His love is a jealous love; it implies demand and "wrath," just as his righteousness is the *gift* of love! It could not be any other way because God is perfectly *one* in himself! And when we are told, for example, that "God repented of the evil he had wanted to do," it does not mean that he changes in himself or moves from one feeling to another, it simply means that *in his relationship to man* he changes . . . his pedagogy. Jesus tells us that the Pharisee who came before God very self-assured because he had fulfilled all the Torah, having followed the smallest commandments, would no doubt keep his own self-righteousness but that it did not in any way impress God! On the contrary, the publican who acknowledged that he was a sinner, and that it was all he was (even if he had done some "good works"), left "justified," rather than the Pharisee. For he possessed the righteousness that comes from the Law, and still needed to be justified! Why? He needed to be justified precisely because he had changed the Torah into a Law and had divided it up into "commandments," instead of understanding its meaning, which is a call to obedience, to trust and, to faith. From then on, those who sought justice through the exact fulfillment of this Law did not obtain this justification—the only "measure" that God uses is the measure of faith: "See, I lay in Zion a stone that causes men to stumble and a rock that makes them fall, and the one who trusts in him will never be put to shame."

I believe that the fall mentioned here is the kind that Jews might experience when they realize that their God is now talking to others, and that he is *also* calling those who do not belong to the chosen people! For now God is calling foreigners, those who received neither the covenants nor the promises, so that they may receive this righteousness that he gives purely and simply. The only thing asked of those foreigners is faith; they simply need *to believe* in the gift that is given to them. They simply need to trust the one who announces and proclaims this righteousness in the form of a justification granted by God to whoever puts his trust in him. (And whoever puts his trust in me will not be put to shame!) This is a completely different understanding of righteousness. One might say that the people of Israel is for a time set aside, because in a way, it did follow and scrutinize this Torah *too well* and identified it with God's will: by fulfilling everything that was revealed in the Torah, the Jews were certain that they had fulfilled *all* of God's will. And this is not a moral error, it is a "theological" error! It is obviously impossible to know *all* of God's will. It is even impossible for us to receive it all as a revelation. What is remarkable is the fact that many texts from the revelation to Israel say so! But instead of listening to those, Israel preferred identifying (and thus limiting) this will of God to what it knew in the Torah, and having fulfilled all of this, it had done everything and was therefore righteous.

We can only know part of that will—the part that God decides to reveal to us—and when we have done *everything* that was asked of us, we can only say, "We are useless servants." And it seems that many faithful and pious people in Israel were not ready to say so. Paul acknowledges that these people had a great zeal (fervor, piety, and courage) in fulfilling the Torah, but he is cruel when he says that they lacked intelligence! And especially the intelligence of the Torah! They examined all its letters; they counted everything minutely; their exegesis is multiple and perfect. They knew this Torah with their whole intelligence *and* their whole heart. But Vischer says that their zeal was "a religious and moral idealism striving towards perfection." This perfection has no possible hereafter because it assures a strict righteousness that allows judgment of others. This is not God's zeal, as we see it in many prophets and fulfilled in Jesus Christ—a zeal which then is "a love without reservation, turned toward the other." Thus, because of their narrow understanding of righteousness, the Jews who were in charge of the proclamation coming from this liberating God to all people excluded those very people! They did not understand the heart of the revelation (although it is found in the revelation that was given to *them*), which is the love of God for all without exclusion.

The Torah was not righteousness, but I would say that it was the necessary exercise, the obedience that was required in order to become the bearers of the promise for all. Just as for the first generations of Christians, martyrdom became the great school for witnessing, and for offering righteousness through the unrighteousness of men. By scrupulously obeying the Law, however, the Jews made God's revelation into some kind of privilege because the goyim were excluded—and that means from truth as well as from justice. We know how little interest the Jews had in proselytizing and making converts to Judaism, a fact that was considered a great merit and a positive value by agnostics and unbelievers (and in a sense, it is indeed a positive value if one compares this dignified attitude to the excesses and the means used by Christian "converters"!)

This movement is absolutely conformed to "nature" because Christians repeated it exactly for centuries: they too throughout centuries made "their faith," "their" New Testament, a privilege (only they were saved, only they were loved by God!) and made it even more their property. How many times have we heard this mystic exclamation: "My Jesus!" (even written by a Christian author of a certain renown!). Jesus "our property"! If I say this it is to make clear that I do not in any way judge the Jews for going this way. This zeal—just like many commandments, whether they be Jewish or Christian, which Paul will call commandments from me—is purely human even though it is devoted to God. Israel appropriated the Torah, the message of the promise. The Jews wanted to be worthy of it by following it faithfully; but strangely, they forgot that the Torah is the Word of the unique, universal God. Yet, so many times it was proclaimed that "there is no other God besides me." So Israel should have announced this as good news for other peoples (the God who liberates from all kinds of slavery) and not as a threat to the others who were worshipping other gods! Again, however, we Christians did exactly the same thing when, for centuries, Christian preaching was all about hell and condemnation, instead of being about the gospel! So this is a temptation that we are familiar with, that we recognize, and that we can condemn in Israel. What then is the difference? The difference is that the foundation of Israel was the Torah. But this Torah could not act on its own: it was given to the people of Israel so that, founded upon it, the people could speak the Word of God to all.

The difference with the Christian faith is that the latter is founded on a person, a person in whose name we may say and do many silly things. It is a person that we only know through writings, but also a person in whom we have faith—and also the certainty—that, as the risen one, he is presently alive and is able to miraculously repair the errors, the lies, the contempt, and the laziness of those who should be doing his work and announcing his grace. The only relationship one can have with this person is one of love (which certainly was not lacking in the Torah and Zion) and of faith—simply faith—which summarizes all of God's righteousness, since this righteousness was fulfilled by Jesus Christ to whom this faith unites us! Thus Israel, because it disappointed God's plan to transmit his liberating will to all, is replaced by Jesus, the ultimate remnant of Israel—but still Israel!

This is doubly fundamental: *the church is not replacing Israel*,[2] as we so often believe. The church is the servant of Jesus; it carries the message of the gospel, and it is not Israel. The one who takes the place of Israel is Jesus, the true servant. The other significant truth of this idea of a "remnant" was very greatly elucidated by Vischer: in all of Israel's history, "the remnant" chosen by God to bear his promise was *representative* of all Israel! It is *the pars pro toto* to which Vischer rightly gives great importance. Then, Jesus too, the ultimate "remnant," must be received and accepted as *pars pro toto*; that is to say, all of Israel is included, summarized, synthesized, and represented in the person of Jesus! Therefore, we must not only say, "Let us not forget that Jesus was Jewish," but also, "All

2. I know that this statement will give rise to some discussion based on 1 Peter 2: "But you are a chosen people, a royal priesthood, a holy nation, a people belonging to God. . . . Once you were not a people, but know you are the people of God; once you had not received mercy, but now you have received mercy." I will say that in speaking thus Peter is not addressing the church, or one church, but all those who have been dispersed in Pontus, Galatia, etc. Furthermore, he announces that we now are *one* people, *one* holy nation. The unity is fundamental here and consequently this has *nothing* to do with the church, which is first of all characterized by separations and exclusions! Finally, all of this rests on the authenticity of faith and has little to do with our mediocre beliefs! We will come back to this point later on.

of Israel is in Jesus." Not so that it may be replaced and pushed aside, but it is rather the case that in Jesus *all* Israel suffered, was put to death, etc. Israel is eternally present in this Jesus. Jesus is a gift for all men, as opposed to the Torah, which was I would say the framework, the weapon, and the armor of the Jewish people alone: the first Witness.

So Jesus is "the end of the Torah," as Paul says. This end has two meanings: It is the end in the most obvious sense in that it has no more reason for being to express the good and just will of God, which is his righteousness—it has been completely incarnated in Jesus, so the Torah has no more meaning. It is also the end in that it has been completely fulfilled by Jesus Christ. And once it has been fulfilled, it loses its value because when we see Jesus the person, watch his actions, and listen to what he says, we have a completed Torah. Should we then disdain it, leave it aside, or as Christians, take no more interest in it? Quite the contrary: for we will never know how to contemplate Jesus *well*. We brag when we think that we understand all his words, but we are incapable of really discerning God's righteousness in Jesus.

So then the Torah is a remarkable help in learning *who* Jesus is! It reveals itself to be an announcement, a precedent, and a prophecy. As Paul shows in our epistle, the texts taken from the "Old" Testament are those that let him best show how the righteousness of God, manifested in Jesus Christ, goes beyond and puts an end to the righteousness that man could acquire through the Law! Thus, *the Torah teaches us who Jesus is* in truth, and he puts an end to this Torah as a *Law* of righteousness, a *nomos*. For only Jesus fulfilled the smallest of the commandments, so that after him they are no longer commandments, a law that constrains; but they remain prophecy, and as such they are an opening towards a future instead of being a withdrawal to the duty of the present. This Law that always abides no longer allows us to claim we are doing "works of righteousness" through which we could be righteous before God, but it serves as a guide and a reference point so that we may properly use the freedom we have in Christ. Everything must then be seen in the perspective of Deuteronomy: "See I have set before you Good and Life, Evil and Death. Choose Good so that you may live."[3] We are faced with the choice that marks the freedom we have acquired in Christ, and the good is not only "the Law of righteousness" that allows us to do "works."

---

3. This is Ellul's own rendering of Deut 30:19. It is slightly different from the French Louis Segond translation of the Bible and the NIV.

The first good is to *believe* this word and, in particular, to *believe* what God says when he declares, "choose the Good." In this way, God tells us that he is on our side, that he is expecting our choice, and that he hopes it will be the choice of faith, of good, of his freedom, and of his love. In this perspective, it is necessary for a new ethics to be born, an ethics that is no longer the ethics of the Law and works, no longer the will to obey scrupulously *in order to* obtain righteousness. This *in order to* is the great difference! Righteousness is now given through grace in Jesus Christ, that is, in him we are justified and no longer need to seek anything beyond. His righteousness is given.

Paul pushes the paradox very far: "The Gentiles who did not pursue righteousness have obtained it, a righteousness that is by faith." This is incredible. First of all, it is not true. There were many pagans who pursued righteousness through religious or philosophical means and who were aware of the fact that they were not getting anywhere. So Paul proclaims: when they are reached by the gospel and assent, they are justified and then need to discover what must be done to follow God's will. They do not need to scrutinize a Law already given, but they do need to invent an ethics following the justification! They must take a double risk: the risk of faith on the one hand and the risk of freedom on the other. They must do this without any guarantees, without any revealed objective text. Each one must do so alone before God—but within the fellowship of all those who are loved by God.

The opposition in verses 5–8 shows this dichotomy very well: "Moses," says Paul, "describes in this way the righteousness that is by law: The man who does these things will live by them." The righteousness that comes by faith speaks in this way: "Do not say in your heart: Who will ascend into heaven (in order to find righteousness there!)? That would be to make Christ descend, or who will descend into the abyss? That would be to make Christ come back from the dead! What does it say? The word is close to you in your heart and in your mouth." This is an impressive text: It is useless to try finding righteousness in heaven! Christ was in heaven, and he came down precisely to bring this righteousness to men! All you need to do is believe this, to believe that righteousness did indeed come from heaven with Jesus Christ! There is no need to descend into the abyss (and into death).[4] Jesus already

---

4. We have already said that this formula summarizes exactly what Proverbs and Job say about wisdom

went into the abyss and into death—and came back! His righteousness consists in overcoming the abyss and death! No righteousness is found there, and Paul attacks on multiple fronts, taking on legalists who want to confine themselves to the Law of Moses, mystics who claim to be able to ascend into heaven to find righteousness there, as well as nihilists who think that righteousness (and truth) can be found in death.[5] No, all righteousness (the one from the Law, the one from on high, and the one from below) is acquired by and in Jesus Christ. This discovery is deeply moving and at the same time disappointing. We were prepared to undertake heroic meritorious works, and what is asked of us is . . . hardly anything, hardly anything at all: believe, trust, give our faith, entrust ourselves, and cease to strive by ourselves! And to show that in reality there is no difference between the revelation of God to the people of Israel and his revelation in Jesus Christ, Paul quotes Deuteronomy 30:11–14 (once more!). This means that although in our understanding there may be an opposition between these two kinds of righteousness (Moses says . . . and righteousness by faith says . . .), there is no contradiction and, in the end, from now on the word of Moses must be understood from the starting point of the word of faith! Of course, it could not be any other way. One must have faith that Moses did indeed speak under the inspiration of God and have faith that these words are still God's words. If they are, they cannot be reduced to a scrupulous practice of "these things," for "these things" cannot contain all of God's righteousness! Following these commandments cannot *be* life in itself, but rather, as Barth exactly says: Here are the commandments that constitute the boundary between life and death! If you remain on this side (in a life defined by the commandments—but free within), you can live! But if you do not respect the commandments, if you break them, then you will find yourself handed over to the adventure of the world, a faithless and lawless world, a lost world, which is the domain of death. And Jesus confirmed this: "Whoever uses the sword will die by the sword."

5. So does the poet Charles Baudelaire:

O, death, old captain, it is time! Anchors aweigh!
This country bores us, o Death! Let us cast off!
If the sky and the earth are black as ink
Our hearts you know are filled with rays!
What the poet is looking for is neither Goodness nor Righteousness, only Novelty!

We are now left to our own devices! The word is *close to you*—I am with you always until the end of the world. There is no need to go to the other end of the world! It is in your mouth—so from now on, you will be speaking this word of God! And God will give it to you as you go along. It is in your heart, so look not to yourself but look to the change that God, by faith, is making in your being. This is where righteousness is. But from this starting point, you must live.[6] That is, you must invent the behavior of a freed man who lives out freedom in Christ without expecting any miraculous impetus (although that may happen) and without following the commandments meticulously, but by carefully and respectfully considering them, for they are models and lessons. Let us not forget this major point: nothing is indifferent to God. If we think that in this "Mosaic" Law there are a number of commandments that appear simplistic or seem to be about details or unimportant matters, we are greatly mistaken. They are there to tell us that, *for God, everything is important in a person's life.* The way one dresses or eats . . . everything is important for God, because he is not indifferent to anything that concerns man! Paul confirms this: "Whether you eat or drink, do everything to the glory of God." This rather dramatically limits what we can do, for if we are not hypocrites, we cannot behave in just any which way or do just anything *to the glory of God!* Righteousness must be expressed through faith in Jesus Christ, and in freedom we will have to make the difficult choice of doing what will be most truthful for God among men. We will have to do so by looking at the distress of the world while following the promise of life! This is confirmed by the fact that both of these kinds of righteousness meet at the cross, where on one side the righteous dies for the unrighteous (Rom 5:6–11) but where the Torah is also present, for we have already meditated on . . . the man hanging on the cross. All has been fulfilled. The blood of the cross acquires righteousness for man. We are all called, pagans and Jews—and alas now Christians also—first to believe with all our heart in the triumph of life over death, of God over nothingness, which takes place in the resurrection; and then, as a consequence of this inner faith, we are called to proclaim it to all. Faith makes us partakers of the righteousness and of the Proclamation of salvation. If there is only one Lord, there is only one Father, and all Jews, Greeks, pagans, Christians—all together—are loved. Nevertheless, he is rich "towards those who call on him." And "whoever calls on the

6. See my study *The Ethics of Freedom.*

name of the Lord shall be saved." This promise from Joel 2:32 is taken up by Paul and quoted word for word. Here again, Paul cites the biblical prophecy by applying it to Jesus, but he does not in any way cancel the same promise given to the Jews! Thus, because they call on the "Name," all are saved. Yet, in the end, they are saved through the righteousness acquired for all in Jesus Christ. However, there still remains this drama of Israel, which refuses to accept the identity of the Lord, the "Eternal," and the righteousness of Jesus Christ. What more can we say?

VERSES 14–21

Is there any excuse for Israel in its refusal of righteousness that comes by faith? It has not heard the good news! (v. 18). Salvation and righteousness, which are gifts from God, respond to faith, to the particular faith that one receives and gives to God the Father and the Lord. Before answering this question, Paul gives us this extraordinary chain: "How can they call on the one in whom they have not believed? How can they believe in the one of whom they have not heard? How can they hear without someone preaching (proclaiming) to them? How can they preach unless they are sent? Consequently faith comes from hearing the message, and the message is heard through the word of Christ!"

These verses call for three preliminary remarks: The first and fundamental one is that "faith comes from *hearing the message.*" This is a particularly difficult theme in a society of sight and images.[7] Faith comes from what one hears and only from that! First of all, sight and images are excluded as possibilities for transmitting the truth of revelation and awakening faith. This is radical: no television program, no painting or photograph, can transmit anything of the revealed truth. This is vexing in times such as ours, but I would certainly link the decline of faith to the excess of images and to the fact that information has been reduced to images. There is no doubt in my mind that the present failure of the church is due to the fact that it is enmired in images. I know that this is all the more scandalous for the Orthodox, with their "cult" of icons. Yet, the truth compels us. The icon is very beautiful. It serves as a support for a certain kind of piety. However, it has nothing to do with revealed truth and the call to faith in the risen Christ. Afterwards, when faith has been born by the Word, it is possible that the image could be in an ancillary

---

7. See my book on the subject, *The Humiliation of the Word.*

way a facilitator, a support, but nothing more. Faith comes from what one *hears*; an image or what one *reads* cannot create faith.

We need to question the Protestant habit of individual reading of the Bible as a book of piety and so forth. No, the text was first of all spoken; later, as it was written down, it lost its creative power, and in order to recover this the text must be heard, it must be made relevant because it is spoken by a person who utters it for himself and for others. Relatively speaking, this is the experience of lovers of poetry: they know that a poetical text was composed to be spoken aloud and not read in silence. This is all the more true here! Neither is the revealed truth expressed or transmitted by good works, political action, involvement with labor unions, or in human commitment to others. I am not denying that those things might be useful! It is certainly true that faith must be expressed in actions; love for our neighbors must certainly be shown in concrete ways and not just in words; but this only comes *afterwards*, and never replaces the proclamation of the Word. Living together and serving others transmit absolutely nothing of the revealed truth. With these one comes back to righteousness by works!

Why this preeminence given to the Word?[8] It has no magical virtue or any greater suggestive power. The preeminence comes from the fact that God acts through his Word and only through his Word. It is by the Word that he created the universe. It is by the Word that he wakens man. It is by the Word that he inspires the prophets. It is by the Word that he declares, "This is my beloved Son." It is by the Word that he made Jesus alive again and raised him. The Word of man takes its importance from the radical quality of God's Word; only our word can possibly in turn become the Word of God. And the Word calls the heart to the righteousness of faith: one believes with the heart by receiving righteousness, but a word never remains without effect, without an echo. This received Word must lead to a testimony (how can they hear without someone preaching to them?). It is therefore not possible, the text asserts, to be awakened to faith in the Lord without immediately becoming a preacher, a speaker for God. "From now on, your mouth must speak also" (v. 10): it must declare the word that someone else spoke to you! It is only as such confessors arise that "the others" will hear and believe. The others? All of them! For Jesus is indeed the Lord and Savior of all ("I will draw all men unto me"). The Jews as well as the Greeks, but—the Jews first!

8. See the outstanding book by Gabriel Vahanian, *Anonymous God*.

Yet the exclusive importance Paul gives to the Word marks a difference between Jews and Christians. The Jews refer essentially to what is written. It is the letter, every letter of the writing, that holds and transmits truth. For Christians, it is the Word, and this was even truer in the first generation of Christians when the Gospels had not yet been written and there was no "New Testament." Everything was transmitted orally then, and preaching was essential—for Paul too—and was based on what was to become the "Old Testament."

Finally, we come to the third remark on these verses: "How can they preach unless they are sent?" By whom are they sent? I believe that Paul does not mean the church or the political authorities. The preachers are sent by God. He is the one who sends those who must carry the Word (because he is the one who puts his Word within them). Thus— and this is the decisive argument—God is always at the origin of salvation, not only in a vertical sense by addressing his Word to men, but also in a horizontal sense, that is, by sending messengers, the bearers. They will accomplish a human task, and a human word is addressed to others human beings. Yet it is a human word sent by God—which will be decisive—because the birth of faith depends on its being heard. Thus, according to these verses, the apostolate is the first task of the church. This is not a church that sends apostles, but rather a church *made up* of bearers of the Word!

In verse 18, we are faced with a surprising statement! Did the Jews not hear? Quite the contrary, exclaims Paul: they heard perfectly well! Of course, they knew that the Word of God was announced in Jesus Christ! We believe that only a small portion of Jews were able to hear Jesus, and that an even smaller portion was able to discern the Messiah in him. This is what the Gospels show us. And we are apt to follow a novel such as *L'Ombre du Galiléen*, by Gerd Thiessen, which shows with great clarity that most Jews and even those who later acknowledged him were only able to find traces of Jesus. They discerned a shadow, and from this shadow they were able to get to the person. Thus, the great majority of the Jewish people (and even more if we take into consideration all the Jewish colonies throughout the empire) has in no way been able to hear this Word, and consequently was unable to believe! That much is obvious! Yet Paul has the audacity to say that they *all* heard!

One could say that, by that date (AD 57), Paul was convinced that the gospel had been preached in all the Jewish communities of the known world, the Roman world. The fact that he wrote in Rome would prove that point. Yet, he would have known that in many of these communities the Jews had rejected the message concerning Jesus. It is true that there are very few Jewish names among the known believers. Paul would then have extrapolated that the Jews, having heard the gospel, and having been placed in a situation where they might choose, had everywhere rejected the revelation concerning the Christ Jesus. They heard, they did not want to accept. Under these circumstances, they are set aside from God's project. These are only a historian's hypotheses, however. What Paul says in his statement is not founded on this; he is not saying this based on some information, he is saying it based on Israel's Holy Scripture. First, by quoting Isaiah: "Lord, who has believed our message?" (53:1). Certainly, some will claim that this is *Isaiah's message*. But what Paul means is that when one announces a gospel to Israel ("How beautiful on the mountains are the feet of those who bring good news, who proclaim peace . . .") Israel does not receive it! This is not a new fact.

The most surprising use of these texts by Paul is the quotation from Psalm 19:4: "Their voice goes out into all the earth, their words to the end of the world." He uses this phrase and applies it to the bearers of the gospel, but . . . the text says something completely different, its purpose being to describe the splendor of creation: "The heavens declare the glory of God; the skies proclaim the work of his hands. The sun rises at one end of the heavens . . ." and "There is no speech or language where their voice is not heard." Then comes the phrase that Paul took out of context (this is not at all about the evangelists but about the splendor of creation, which declares the glory of God)! Paul says that the perfection of the world is a *Word!* "The word of Christ . . ." Have they *not heard?* The Jews should have been able to understand the fullness of the Word of God in the universe from the Torah. And this fullness is not complete until the love of God has been made incarnate. So this very gospel is announced by the song of creation! The Jews, who knew the Scriptures well, should have understood the gospel as it was thus proclaimed, given that their Scriptures say that the skies testify to it. . . . If this is the situation, are they then rejected and left outside of salvation? We shall return to this point.

Earlier Paul asked the question, how could one convince them? Moses had predicted that his people would become disobedient, but this is no reason for God to abandon it given that he chose this people and loves it! Paul refers to two other texts by Isaiah. On the one hand, since Israel does not want to acknowledge *this* righteousness of God, he will make it known to foreign peoples, to those who were not chosen to be God's people, "to those who did not seek me, to a nation that did not call on my name" (Isa 65: 1). And, Paul says, when the Jews see what is happening with the pagans after becoming recipients of grace, then Moses' prophecy will be fulfilled: "I will make you *jealous by those who are not* a nation."

"Through jealousy" Israel will then come to see the truth of this revelation that fulfills the revelation of which it had been a bearer for so long.

Israel, so proud of being the only people to have received the revelation, will be jealous as it sees the pagans now receiving and accepting a deeper knowledge of the God who reveals himself! This does not, however, in any way imply that God has turned away from his people. Quite the contrary: God's heart remains constantly open; he is always calling *his* people: All day long I stretched out my hand towards a rebellious and stubborn people . . ." (this concerns the call of God's Wisdom, according to Prov 1:24). God is still extending his hand toward Israel. It is seen in those deeply moving texts contained in Scripture in which God declares his suffering in the face of man's indifference, and Israel's indifference in particular ("My people, what have I done to you?"). This again evokes the Father of the parable erroneously called "the Prodigal Son" (we should call it the parable of "the Patience and Love of the Father"!), a father who ceaselessly waits for his son without ever despairing of him. These verses are a testimony to the error of the lofty declarations on the damnation of Israel!

In concluding my meditation on chapter 10, I would like to make two additional points. One concerns the people and the church.[9] In spite of everything, Israel remains *the people of God*. The church *is not* the people of God. Nowhere in the New Testament is there a formula for a "new people of God." On the contrary, as we have seen in these preceding verses, it is stated that Israel remains a nation and that its jealousy will be aroused by that which is not even a nation.

The theology of the people does not belong to the past; it is not obsolete. It determines the understanding that the Jewish people has of itself still today. "In all rabbinic literature, Israel and the Jewish people

9 See Franz Mussner, p. 10–26.

are considered theologically identical."[10] Even in the texts announcing that Christians are a people in God's sight, there is no question of Israel's being replaced by another people. The church, as we shall see in the next chapter, merely participates in the root (Israel). The people is now made up of Jews and pagans, but this does not change anything as far as All Israel is concerned—it is the Father's nation and a people, true and unique. Israel always remains God's people, *beside the church*! Maybe Mussner is right in saying that the church is God's people in a spiritual sense, whereas Israel is so in a total, spiritual, and national sense: it remains God's distinct property, God's "inheritance." It is a *people*, and also *God's* people. It is one of the causes of the inner tensions that exist within the Jewish people, tensions within which the Jewish people live and must live with respect to other peoples and also with respect to the church! In particular, for a Jewish person the hope of the restitution of the Land is a result of his unshakable faith in the God of the fathers! This is why the church and Israel are exactly complementary, as we shall see when we follow Paul in chapter 11.

Finally, my last remark will be concerning Barth's commentary on this chapter. Barth had the audacity to apply all of these texts to . . . the church! This is why he entitled this part of his commentary "The Guilt of the Church." It would be too easy to rid ourselves of this terrible proof by applying it to others, and for us Christian Pharisees to designate the "guilty party"! No, he says, this is meant for the church with and through the Jewish people. The church is inseparable from the Jewish people and has already committed one bad deed with respect to Israel: it has *appropriated* the revelation by excluding the Jews. The church has taken for itself the covenant (which it has declared "Old") and has taken the Hebrew Bible (also declared the "Old Testament"). It has in fact dispossessed this people of the revelation given to it, which neither Jesus nor, as we said earlier, Paul ever denied! The church appropriated the revelation (exactly that for which Israel was rebuked!), took it as its own, claimed that only it could interpret it and complete it, and gave itself the virtue of infallibility (Israel never went so far!).

Secondly, we find the same resemblance and same accusation in Paul: the church transformed the gospel of Jesus Christ into a moral law. It turned righteousness gained through Jesus into a system of morality!

10 This should put an end to the terrible inconsistency of many Christians who declare themselves to be anti-Zionist while loving "the Jews"! This is a lie and hypocrisy.

It changed the law of freedom into a series of commandments. By distinguishing between commandments and "precepts," major and minor sins, it created a catalog of virtues, ordinal and cardinal and a catalog of sins. Here again, the church went further than the Jewish people in its error. And, finally, it believed and taught that righteousness could be acquired through works, and Barth asserts this not as an attack on Catholics but that it applies to all Christians!

Thirdly, the church, no matter which denomination, is faced with pagans. But it did not know how to evangelize them because it did not bring the gospel, but presented instead either a doctrine or a law. So it made the same error as Israel! Finally, if today we deplore the decline of churches and the loss of Christian faith, the church itself is guilty for its own plight. This guilt consists, first of all, in refusing to acknowledge the fact! It refuses to acknowledge that its present plight comes from the failure to accomplish the task it has been given. Let us as Christians radically face our situation: to attempt to deny or escape the plight of the church would be to try to escape from God himself.

4

The Grafted Olive Tree

"AGAIN I ASK: HAS GOD REJECTED HIS PEOPLE?" IT IS OBVIOUS THAT this question asked by Paul was blasphemous to the Jews of his time, for until the third century B.C. Jews had lived in fear of being rejected. They had feared that this sovereign God would "turn away his face." This had been their greatest fear. That God would turn away was more to be feared than his anger ("Why do you hide your face?" Ps 44:24). Their experience is that their God is sovereign, so that what he wants always comes to pass and is also unquestionable. Psalm 74 is deeply moving: "Why does your anger smolder against the sheep of your pasture? Why *have you rejected us forever?*" This terrible possibility exists! And they remind God of the promises he made: "But you have rejected, you have spurned, you have been angry with your anointed one . . ." (Ps 89: 8). Among the prophets of the exile, too, we constantly encounter the same question: God has abandoned us. Jerusalem is deserted, the temple has been destroyed . . . and the prophets do their best to raise the courage of this people and proclaim that, in spite of historical circumstances, God is not indicating that he has abandoned the chosen people or cancelled the covenant. Without giving way to despair, these prophets of courage and of hope do keep the *possibility* of a final rejection in the background . . . Yet, from the third century on, an obvious change of opinion and of theology takes place! The Jews become very certain that their election is definitive, that the sovereign God would never reject them. Many texts testify to this: the time of uncertainty is over; Israel goes forth with its

God. This is due both to historical events and to a new understanding of the Torah.[1] As Maillot says, "God's election is *captured* by Israel!" We find ourselves back with the problem of appropriation. It is perfectly correct that Israel now receives a better understanding of revelation. Although God may reject the one he has chosen and loved, he does not reject "forever." When he turns away, he never loses the memory of his covenant. The experience of this period is that, yes, God may reject but it will only be temporary. He can be trusted. One can rest assured. God does not reject forever, but let us not forget on what the permanence of this covenant rests. What God has promised he will always keep, and the covenant that he has declared, he will also maintain throughout the vicissitudes of history. *Everything* rests on God himself. If the other party is unfaithful, *God* remains faithful. The covenant is thus maintained, but it rests only on the faithfulness, love, forgiveness, and patience of *God*. We cannot take any credit for it. The only thing man can do, as he travels through this temporary "rejection," is to acknowledge his God, in spite of everything, as the faithful God and pray always to him as "my God."[2]

The change here is that Israel has become much surer of itself! It is so sure that God will not abandon it that it turns the belief into a kind of property. This goes without saying. Yet Israel forgets that, here also, it is *by grace* and faithfulness to himself that God does not reject "forever"! In other words, just as Israel had appropriated the revelation (which it was supposed to bring to all) and the covenant (which it was supposed to announce to all as the gospel), now it is, in a way, appropriating the faithfulness of God and its own election! It becomes far too sure of itself. This is why the question that Paul asks is scandalous and blasphemous for the Jews of his time. For the point of view of the historical understanding of their history they should, at the very least, have asked themselves some questions about the scandalous and harmful periods of the Hasmoneans and the Herodians as well as their submission to the Greeks, to the Seleucids, and to the Romans, etc.

Now Paul is not only raising this question but also providing a stunning argument to testify that God has not rejected Israel! The proof

---

1   Baron, *Histoire du peuple juif*; and Saulnier, *Histoire d'Israël*.

2.   The decisive example of this confidence and this trust in God's faithfulness is given by Jesus on the cross when he utters the terrible, "My God, my God, why have You forsaken me?" But in this cry, we can also see his faith, for he does not reject God, and still calls him "his": "*My* God." This God who is for *Me*, in spite of everything!

is Paul himself! Has God rejected his whole people? Certainly not, since I am here! He is a full-blooded Israelite, of the tribe of Benjamin (which was, let us not forget, the only native tribe that remained attached to the house of David at the time of the break between Israel and Judah). And this is a tribe that in history and before God represents "All-Israel." Benjamin is called the Beloved of the Lord in the benedictions attributed to Moses in Deuteronomy 33: "Let Reuben live, may Judah find its covenant with the Lord, may Levi be faithful, Dan and Gad will be ferocious warriors, Zebulon will be rich, etc., but of Benjamin it is said: 'Let the beloved of the Lord rest secure in him for he shields him all day long; and the one the Lord loves rests between his shoulders.'" In fact, all throughout history, Benjamin has played a leading role in God's plan. This importance recurs in Jeremiah, who was also a son of Benjamin. It was about this tribe that the message was first proclaimed: "I establish you today over the nations and over kingdoms . . ." through the voice of the prophet of Benjamin!

Yet, Paul could have given other examples than himself to testify to the permanence of God's covenant! He could have said that the principal witnesses of Jesus, on whose word the entire gospel rests, were Jews who had followed Jesus. He could have reminded his listeners that in Jerusalem there was a Judeo-Christian church almost completely made up of Jews! Yet, he does not mention these facts and uses himself as the only example. Did he do it out of pride? Perhaps he did, yet he also had a great sense of responsibility. All of Israel was now summarized in this fragile witness! Paul has a considerable additional argument for choosing himself as a witness: he was a persecutor of Christians, an ardent zealot for the destruction of this heresy; and here he is now a convert. These two phrases testify that All Israel is in the same position. God has not rejected his people when even a persecutor is reclaimed by God to become a witness. Paul is thus a sort of living pledge of this all-powerful grace. For if God had finally decided to reject his people, he would have started by rejecting the "elite" of the people; he would have rejected what was most representative of all, and Paul belonged to this elite!

Moreover, God "foreknew" this people. This connotation is essential as Paul showed in chapter 8: "And we know that in all things God works for the good of those who love him, who have been called according to his purpose. For those God *foreknew* he also predestined to be conformed to the likeness of his son. . . . And those he predestined he also called, those he called he also justified, and those he justified he also glorified." When we consider the precision of Paul's thought and vocabulary, we must admit that it is not by chance that he uses the phrase: "His people, whom he foreknew." This phrase necessarily entails all the rest: predestined, called, justified, glorified.

Here, I will go out on a limb: "Predestined to be conformed to the likeness of his son." Christians will spontaneously think, "The Son Jesus being who he *was*, Christians are called to *become* conformed to the image of Jesus." Many texts imply this for instance, the texts saying that the servants will be treated like the Lord. Is it not possible however to read these texts in a way that is "backwards in time"? "This people was predestined to be conformed to the image of his Son . . . ," that is, throughout history; the people was what Jesus was going to be during his history. The Jewish people is the prophetic image of the Son of Man, the Son of God! Let us not be scandalized—rather, let us consider. After establishing the starting point, Paul continues by demonstrating that God actually did not condemn anyone nor reject anyone. There is however, what Luther called the right hand of God and the left hand of God. I believe that it is not correct to translate the right hand of God as grace and salvation and the left hand as righteousness and damnation. It seems to me that it means God works in different ways and that there are works that he accomplishes with his right hand (the church) and works (also positive ones) accomplished by the left hand, particularly in Israel. In the same way, Barth named two chapters of his commentary "The God of Jacob" and "The God of Esau." Even as the latter is "hated" by God, he is certainly not thrown into hell, not damned, nor outside of God's love! For if there are indeed two covenants today, there is only one Savior *for all*.

In verses 2 to 5 we come to the comparison with Elijah. The story is well known. Elijah flees into the desert after his triumphant victory over the prophets of Baal (1 Kgs 18) and after having had all of them killed. The whole people had been convinced by the miracle, but now Elijah is fleeing. He proclaims two things: I am not any better than my fathers (I believe Elijah is stricken by remorse for having had the four hundred prophets of Baal put to death!), and secondly, after God has passed by, he asks him to take his life because "I am the only one left." The whole nation was guilty of betrayal. By referring to this episode, Paul seems to identity more or less with Elijah as an intermediary between God and men. But there is a considerable difference between them. Elijah was condemning all of Israel: they have all abandoned your revelation—the Torah—they have killed your prophets, they have overturned your altars . . . so the whole people must be rejected. On the contrary, Paul pleads for Israel; and that is why he insists on the end of Elijah's story. God answers him: "Yet *I* have reserved seven thousand in Israel, all whose knees have not bowed down to Baal." "You do not know them," says God, "but I do. And when you accuse them you do not know what you are doing!" Seven thousand: this number calls for two remarks. In 1 King 20:15, we are told that King Ahab decided to review all of Israel's army and therefore assembled all the men, of whom there were seven thousand! What irony: I reserve seven thousand in Israel, but the whole army is exactly seven thousand! In other words: all of these men have actually remained faithful, even if you do not know it. This is not surprising for, at the time of the conflict, we are told that the people cried out, "The Lord is our God!"

We must also remember the elementary symbolism of the number seven thousand: it is the number of perfection times one thousand and, of course, one thousand is (like all multiples of ten) an indication that the number is huge. The two indications converge so the symbolism is even more complete and limitless than the narrative. It is also possible, however, to think that this number of seven thousand indicates a limited number of the people of Israel under Ahab, and then the preceding remarks plus this fact would mean that God has reserved within the people of Israel a *remnant* and that this remnant has sanctified the whole people. This is the interpretation that Paul chooses, and he shows it in the latter part of his argument: in the same way, in the present time, there is a remnant according to the election of grace.

Paul will come back time and again throughout all his letters to the central statement: if it is by grace, then it is not by works; if it were by works, it would not be by grace! Israel can thus accumulate works by being faithful to the Torah; it is of no use when it does not acknowledge Jesus as the remnant of the remnant in whom all the salvation of Israel lies. Once again, what Israel wanted to acquire *at any price* (the assurance of its salvation) was not obtained in this way! Certain individuals in Israel are thus pushed away: Israel, in its entirety, did not find assurance of salvation. The election obtained salvation and those who do not receive this election with humility are therefore pushed aside or "hardened" (or *drowsy*). Here Paul, who so often quotes the Torah loosely, hardens the text of Deuteronomy. The text says, "God has not given you a mind that understands, or eyes that see or ears that hear" [. . . this refers to the saving miracles that God accomplished *in* and *for* Israel]. Paul changes this into a positive action on the part of God: "God gave them eyes that could not see and ears that could not hear." We are again faced with the idea that this is not about ill will on Israel's part; this is not a spirit of rejection; God did it (and therefore . . . Israel is not responsible!). Paul however, adds the phrase "to this very day" (v. 8). to the text of Deuteronomy. This indeed corresponds to the hope that Paul continues to announce: "to this very day" means that anything is possible tomorrow. Once more, we have the hope of Israel: everything is possible tomorrow because God remains the God of Abraham. He is faithful, and tomorrow he might awaken all of Israel and give it eyes to see! Paul continues this slightly improper application of Scripture to Israel. He takes Ps 69:22–23, where David speaks of his enemies, to repeat that their table (which in reality is the altar of the temple), loaded with sacrifices and offerings (which are another aspect of works), becomes a snare for them. In addition to ethical and religious works, sacrifices and offerings, which are a sign of obedience and generosity, also lead the people of grace astray. They inevitably lead them to think that these offerings give them assurance of a salvation, which is not free.

We always come back to the great reversal that we have already spoken of: When one places works and offerings in the foreground, one does so in order to be saved. On the contrary, when one knows that one is saved by *grace alone*, one accomplishes these works and presents these offerings *because* one is assured of salvation. They are an act of gratefulness and thankfulness! Thus Israel, by its very election, is placed (as it was and will be) before a decisive choice. What Israel wants more than anything else that is, to be the people of witness and the people of truth, it must cease to seek at all costs through its own strength, its own will, its own scruples and, its own intelligence, which are all its own initiative.

I might add as a postscript to the meditation of these verses 1 to 10 that Paul puts himself into the drama of Israel in a most subjective way. In no way does he want to be separated from his people: "I am here"! And that should remind us of one essential truth about Israel: One cannot speak *objectively* of Israel. One cannot commit oneself either for or against. Israel is indeed a people set apart, and its presence necessarily calls us to reassess ourselves. This is why, as soon as Israel is present, passions surge for or against. The very life of this people presents decisive questions: the question of election, the question of God's freedom, and the question of the adventure of God's presence.

Of course, those who hate and persecute this people do not know that in doing so it is God himself whom they hate and persecute in his faithfulness, his patience, and his presence. This is still true today as Israel is temporarily set aside from God's work because of its rejection of Jesus. Yet God has not taken anything away from Israel! Thus, in addition to the tragedy of persecutions, there has been the added tragedy of the error of theologies that objectivize the history of Israel and these chapters by Paul. To draw a dogmatic theology from this, no matter how orthodox and biblical it may be, is precisely what we cannot do! Election and predestination are not *loci theologici*, they are not philosophical themes, they are not "problems," they are not neutral stones useful in building up a theological construct; rather, they are instances of having "one's back up against the wall," they are a call that requires a decision because it is the decisive business of any human life! The presence of Israel, whether it is the remnant that acknowledged and loved Jesus as the Messiah or the other part that remains waiting out of faithfulness, inevitably causes trouble—either joy or hatred.

VERSES 11–15

We are now entering the heart of the mystery of Israel: the mystery of the "fall." "They stumbled." Of course they did—because God gave them eyes that *they might not see!* What else could have happened! But Paul uses a rather surprising term: when one slips, or stumbles etc., one does not necessarily fall! Theirs was only a misstep, but they stumbled on the rock. The rock on which this people actually rested! Paul asks a strange question too: why did they make a misstep, and why did they stumble against a reef . . . ? If this happened, we might ask with Paul: did God want to lose them? Far from it, Paul exclaims again! One might get the impression that this text is unclear. On the one hand, Paul says, "Was it in order to make them fall? No"; and on the other hand, "Because of their fall, salvation became available. . . ." So, on the one hand, he seems to say: they slipped, and God did not want to make them fall. On the other hand, he talks about their "fall"! So they must have fallen! Yes they did, but everything rests on this: for what purpose? Was it *in order to* make them fall? Was God's purpose simply to make them fall so he could condemn them? This is not at all God's objective. He certainly never seeks to condemn his people; rather, the fall makes the salvation of all possible!

That is the objective. The *purpose* is not to make the people fall *and* thus to be rejected! The purpose is to save all men by making them fall! He does not say that they did not fall we have seen the snares. This is simply the means of God's mercy. Because the Jews did not fulfill the mission with which they had been entrusted (namely to carry the good news of the covenant *to the world*), they left an empty space! So God chooses another way of reaching the whole world, and God is waiting for Israel to follow that same path and be saved along with all others. The fall of Israel made possible the coming of the ultimate remnant: Jesus Christ. And in Jesus Christ the universality of salvation is being proclaimed. This fall starts a wonderful new adventure between God and man! Should we then say that the rejection of Jesus by a majority in Israel is a *felix culpa* (as has been said about Adam's disobedience)? Certainly not! Never can a fault, a fall, an attempt by man to take over, be called *felix*. This fall is horrendous, as is any sin against God. It is horrendous but not tragic. That is, it entailed countless adversities, countless defeats, and the hatred of the nations—but it is not tragic in that it is not a destiny, an inevitability without future or hope. Now, the wall that separated pagans and Jews is fallen. Pagans were outside the covenants (yet not outside Noah's covenant), outside the promise (given only to Abraham and his descendants); they were without hope and really atheists, in that, lacking the revelation of the Unique One, "they invented for themselves gods which are not true gods." Now these pagans have been reconciled to God. God has reconciled himself to all men through the blood of Christ, even if they do not know it. And the gospel consists in proclaiming to all: "Now you have been reconciled; the covenant is also for you and you have been called to life."

So the "fall" of the Jews makes the salvation of pagans possible. Following this path, Paul inverts the pattern of the promises of the first covenant—the Jews are God's people who are to carry the promise to all, and all will be saved through this proclamation. The faith of the pagans is now a testimony to the gospel, and the Jews are to receive from the pagans this new covenant, this new promise of salvation. Obviously, this could not (cannot) be received and heard by the Jews. Paul is accused of having profaned the Law, but he is convinced that God has not at all abandoned the Jews, quite the contrary—he crowns the work of his grace by *also* saving them freely, which would imply their conversion.

This good news can only be announced to the Jews if, on the one hand, pagans show that grace is given to them, and on the other hand, if one attests that the grace given to the Jews is greater than the one given to pagans! Indeed, there was a fall, there was a rejection, but a rejection that, since the coming of Jesus, can no longer be final: it is necessarily partial and temporal. Paul shows that he understands his ministry under the eschatological aspect of the conversion of the Jews.[3] God willed the fall of Israel so as to make it possible for salvation to be preached to pagans and he expects that the acceptance of this salvation will cause a "jealousy" in Israel that will lead the whole people to turn again to their God, whom they will recognize in Jesus Christ. This "jealousy" can only come from the fact that they will see in pagans signs, expressions, and manifestations of the grace of God, which will suddenly convince them of the excellency of the revelation in Jesus Christ. This is the work of grace among these pagans; in the end, it is even more extraordinary than the grace they have experienced throughout their 1200 years of history! They will become jealous of the good that God accomplishes through the pagans. . . . This must consternate Christians! The Jews are still rejecting Jesus Christ because when they see what Christians are, they are not moved to jealousy.

The total responsibility for the rejection of Jesus by the Jews is *exclusively* caused by what Christians and Christian churches are. If Christians had evidenced before the Jews a higher virtue than that which can come from the observance of the Law,[4] a holiness, a purity of behavior (customs) *before which one could only bow*, a purity in the worship of the Lord, without mixing in pagan rites, childish beliefs, and confusions (which I would call idolatrous); if they had evidenced a complete love of neighbor, and if they had lived according to the royal law of liberty acquired in Christ; if Christian societies had been models of personal, social, or political justice for all to see—then without any doubt Paul's prophecy, which is God's plan, would have been fulfilled.

3. This excludes, on the one hand, seeking the conversion of a particular Jew, and on the other hand, the controversy in trying to convince. We will see later the kind of relationship Jews and Christians can have.

4. I have often given as an example the gift of tithes: To tithe one's income is the application of the Law. If grace is infinitely superior to the Law, then Christians should give infinitely more than a tithe! And if they don't, they should *at least* apply the Law!

Convinced by this kind of life, the Jews would have recognized in Jesus the Messiah who changes men's hearts and from this transformation of the heart transforms the world.

Instead of this, however what have we Christians shown?[5] Incoherent and often despicable lifestyles, societies of conquest, of power and avarice, societies evidencing hate among Christians and a general triumph of injustice. And particularly towards this Jewish people, Christian societies have abounded in persecutions and injustices. They have lived in a constant hatred of the Jew, which, humanly speaking, is incomprehensible and which is only motivated by the fact that this people of faithfulness remains an unbearable witness to Christian infidelity.

Far from "moving" the Jews "with jealousy" (which would mean that they would attempt to do better than the Christians and acknowledge that this "better" comes from Jesus), the example of our lives and our societies have been a constant counter-witness that could only push them far from Jesus! The Jews really had no reason to convert and to come to *this* Messiah! When the acknowledgment will happen at the end of time, it will be because, on the one hand, the working of the Holy Spirit will be so strong that the church will again in truth become the church of Christ, and because each of our lives will be changed (in the twinkling of an eye, we will be transformed), and at the same time the Jewish people will recognize its Messiah.

In the meantime, the delay in bringing Jews and Jesus the Messiah together is caused by Christians and our churches. In the meantime. . . . So the temporary setting aside of the Jewish people enabled the preaching of the gospel to the world and brings pagans to recognize in the God of Abraham, Isaac, and Jacob, the only true God, the Unique One. "Through their fall, salvation was opened up for pagans, the reduction of their role became riches for the pagans."

Israel had indeed been shown the path of the gospel, but it moved away; and this moving away caused the gospel to be preached to all pagans. So Paul does not ask the question, "What will happen when Israel finds again the path of the gospel?" No, he goes even further: "What will happen when it finds itself at the *very heart* of the gospel?" Their "reintegration" means that once the Good News of Christ the Redeemer and Lord has reached the whole world, the Jewish people will again take the place that it had occupied at the beginning of election history—a

5. On the causes of this mutation see Ellul, *The Subversion of Christianity.*

place at the very heart of the revelation! For this is indeed the meaning of this reintegration![6]

Their distance brought God to reconciliation with all humanity past, present, and future. What will their own reconciliation then bring? What a miracle it will be when Israel ceases to be "a disobedient and obstinate people" (vv. 10, 21)! Paul says it will be life coming from the dead! (v. 15) The accomplishment of God's redeeming work is total "vivification." This word "vivification" (which Maillot translates as "life surging out of death") is not quite identical with resurrection. According to certain commentators, it is a rabbinic term expressing the ultimate realization of God's love, the indisputable triumph of the Living over the Realm of Death. For us, the Father made Christ come back from the dead and thus manifested his glory. Yet this glory will have to break out into the whole universe, and this is what we confess when we say that Jesus is "the first born of the dead" and that his resurrection is the final defeat of death. The conversion of Israel, as it receives and acknowledges its Messiah, will bring about universal resurrection. At that resurrection, the redemption of the whole world by God's gift of his Son will be manifest rather than his judgment. I think we need to stress that the end and the aim of the resurrection is not judgment and the separation of the "good" from the "evil," with the dispatching of the evil to hell. The end of the resurrection is the "heavenly Jerusalem," the triumph of love and the annihilation of the powers of death and of death itself, and those who should have been condemned are pardoned.[7]

This reconciliation by the setting aside of Israel and this rising of life out of death as Israel is reintegrated reminds us exactly of what Paul says in Romans 5:10: "For if, when we were God's enemies, we were rec-

---

6. This is also the meaning of the text in Revelation (7:4–10) where we see the totality of the people of Israel assembled in one place in front of the Unique, and behind them, the huge crowd that could not be counted with people belonging to every people, tribe, and language on earth (the church).

7. I know that this thesis, which I have explained many times, scandalizes. I cannot here take up all the texts about damnation. I have already shown that they were either parables serving as *warnings* and which cannot be used *to establish a dogma*, or statements showing the evil that exists in all men (and that evil is condemned to disappear) and not the person. We know that *committing a theft* does not make a person *a thief*. Furthermore, if salvation is by grace, it is of course for those who would have deserved a condemnation. One pardons a condemned person, not an innocent person! I came to save sinners not the righteous! This is obvious!

onciled to him through the death of his Son, how much more, having been reconciled, shall we be saved through his life (his resurrection)."

This passing from death into life is not only about the final fate of Israel, which is already assured of life by its "reintegration"—it is the salvation and life of all humanity. Reading Romans 5:10 and 11:25 shows once more that our three chapters are not in any way a parenthesis or a later addition! The humbling of the Servant, the death of Christ, and the setting aside of Israel have already reconciled the world. So much more will its rising bring salvation! The rising was accomplished in the resurrection of Christ, which was only vaguely seen in the case of Israel, seen vaguely as the Epistle to the Hebrews tells us about the cloud of witnesses carried by faith—Abel, Noah, Abraham, Isaac, and Jacob. "All these people were still living by faith when they died. They did not receive the things promised; they only saw and welcomed them from a distance" (Heb 11:13).

> As the risen one, Christ gives us access, in the secret of faith, to his final victory. Israel, still immerged in a history that is not yet over, continues to carry the sins of the world and waits for its uplifting, which will also be that of humanity. (Michel Remaud)

So the people of Israel remains a unique and singular people. It is the bearer of a promise of a better world, and related to this, Wischer emphasizes, God implanted into the Jewish soul the desire to change the miserable state of humanity into a happy and just condition. This is linked to the promise of the "re-establishment of all things" in the righteousness and truth of God. But this promise created a will. This explains the frequent participation of Jews in revolutionary movements, with the intention of establishing the kingdom of God on earth right away. Often the position of Jews reminds us of those of the millenarists, especially when a Jew ceases to be a faithful believer. The social justice of certain prophets takes the place of the expectation of the kingdom that God will establish. This fact, this "particularity," explains why the Jews have a hard time believing that Jesus is the Messiah; that the poor Crucified One is the glorious Redeemer. The usual argument is: "We do not see that Christ has changed the world." It has been prophesied that the coming of the Messiah would cause a mutation of the universe and of human society in particular. Nothing has changed. So then one expects a material and visible change. Yet this is much less about changing material consequences than about changing the human heart! "The mouth speaks out of the abundance of the heart"; a tree that has rotten roots cannot be made to bear good fruit: the important thing is to change the heart, the root, etc. This is the only possible beginning of a new creation. But . . . this faith in the change of the heart can only be acquired by a Christian witness.

Hence, we will say with Paul that God has started his work through the Jews, and he will also complete it through the Jews. When they acknowledge their Messiah, then we will see the kingdom and the triumph of life and the restoration of the universe! So we may say that the unbelief of the Jews (and their search for human means to replace the sovereign act of God) is delaying this. And so it is "their fault"? No, for they can only convert if the church and Christians present the kingdom of heaven already here on earth, if they can clearly see that faith in Christ . . . fulfills the complete change in man. We have already said however, that the picture presented to the Jews by Christians can only keep them away from Christ and not convert them! Consequently, the heavy responsibility for the delay in the fulfillment of God's project can be imputed to Christians and only to them—for they are keeping the Jews from coming to faith.

VERSES 16–24

In these impressive and remarkable verses, Paul returns to the privilege (never rescinded) that was given to the Jewish people! And he will explain that Christianity is a branch of the Jewish people.

When he talks about the first fruit he is probably alluding to some rite: when one baked bread, one used to take part of the dough, the first fruit, to make a cake and give as an offering to the Lord (Num 15:20–21 and Lev 23:10–17). The first fruit is not, for once, Jesus Christ but Abraham and Isaac, as the rest of the text shows: the *first part* is given to God so that the rest might be "received" by God, and then eaten by people. Abraham is indeed the first man reserved by God, "devoted" to God, and who offers his son Isaac as the first fruit! If the first fruit is holy (because it is God's part), the branches are too. Therefore, the whole people of Israel is sanctified.

Some branches were cut off, no doubt, by God himself. Many prophets tell us so! So does Jeremiah: the Jewish people is first of all an admirable people. "The Lord called you a thriving olive tree with fruit beautiful in form, [but can you stay in my house, where crimes are committed?], but with the roar of a mighty storm he will set it on fire, *and its branches will be broken.*" Some space is created on this trunk by cutting off branches, which brings us the great image of the grafting: the cultivated olive tree and the wild olive tree. The cultivated olive tree is the one that gives good fruit, that is, olives that produce oil.

A certain number of authors (for example Lietzmann) have made fun of Paul, who really did not know anything about agriculture because grafting is always done the other way around—on a wild tree, you graft a little branch from a cultivated tree, from the tree that bears good fruit. For the olive tree, it is the same thing: you graft from the cultivated olive tree to the wild olive tree. Certain scrupulous authors have even in their travels sought to find out whether there were areas in Greece, for example, or in Asia Minor where this "counter-grafting" was practiced. . . . Of course, they did not find any. To understand the meaning, however, we simply need to read the whole text to find that Paul resorts to an astonishing inversion revealed at the end of the paragraph. In verse 24, it is stated that we, the pagans, belong by nature (*kata physin*) to the wild olive tree. In the same way, the Jews belong *kata physin* to the cultivated olive tree. But *we have been grafted contrary to nature* (*para physin*) onto the cultivated olive tree, for the text says "contrary to" and not, as many translations say, "contrary *to your* nature." The grafting is accomplished "contrary to nature"; it does not go against the nature of the wild olive tree! This is a grafting contrary to nature, that is, a grafting that goes against the laws of botany and arboriculture! Vischer does not ignore the fact that this parable is "monstrous," but this is the very reason that the parable is full of meaning! This act is not that of a technician, but of God; and what God accomplishes does not conform to the nature of things, but it is an act of God's grace and freedom designed to humble the pride of Christians.

First, the cultivated olive tree was bearing good fruit, not because it was naturally good, but because it had been chosen by the grace of God; from then on it could bear good fruit. It did not, therefore, represent nature and its laws in history, but rather the grace and freedom of God! So the action of God as he grafts the pagans onto the root of Israel is not an action according to nature—it is against nature! And Paul is not making a mistake at all!

In this comparison, the grafting is not the only astonishing thing, however! There is also the "affair" of the root. You do not bear the root;

rather the root bears you. This is not very clear! Let us not forget that in the Hebrew Bible we encounter a whole theology of the root. The root is not only the part of the tree that is in the ground and from which it draws nourishment, it is also a kind of force that causes the production of leaves on each branch, and therefore the root is not only the root as we understand it but also the stalk or the trunk.

We have already mentioned (building on all the scholars of Hebrew studies that I have read) that Jews have a global way of thinking. Franz Mussner argues that the word *yad* means "hand" but can also mean "arm," *regel* can mean "foot" or "leg" . . . and very importantly, *rabbim* means literally "much, many" but also "all," and corresponds in fact to *our* "all." We need to reread the gospels in that light when the text is translated "many will be saved . . ."

Therefore, the root does not literally bear the grafted pagans, but the trunk does. This implies that the trunk had to remain as such! The root would be the patriarchs, but the trunk is Israel, the Israel of Paul's time but also of our time! Israel remains the fruit-bearing olive tree (*elaia, Kallie-laios*). Paganism is the wild olive tree. God does not ennoble this wild tree by grafting in it branches from the cultivated olive tree—it is the other way around! We must say that we have become disciples of Jesus and believers in this unique God "against nature." This, of course, implies that our theology must totally reject the idea of a good nature and of a (religious) super-nature that is beyond and completes the first. This is decisive if we seek to understand what God's love and grace are!

Thus, this parable teaches us that we Christians, we the church, are only *grafted branches*, "added pieces" (as Maillot says and whose analysis we have followed to a great extent in the preceding text). We are a bad species by nature; we do not bear fruit to the glory of God in our works; we have been implanted into the holy people—which remains such in spite of everything. Thus, our fruit and our oil do not come from us but actually from the marrow (rather than the fat!) of the first and cultivated olive tree. Here again, as Maillot remarks, Paul makes a certain identification between Jesus and Israel. (According to Frédéric Godet, "There is always something of the Christ himself in the people of Christ.") This reminds us of Jesus' words on the vine and the branches. The Jew remains the original Jew, but we "only" hold on to the trunk by faith! Henceforth, we constantly need to remember that if God was so severe in his dealings with his people and cut some branches off, how much more severe will he be to us if we make the same mistakes they made! "Do not be arrogant, but be afraid. For if God did not spare the natural branches, he will not spare you either" (v. 20–21). This completely justifies Barth's reading, which applies this text to the church.

If the error of the Jews was, as we have tried to show, pride in being the chosen people and appropriation of election, then we need to ask ourselves: what is the status of the church and of Christians?

We learn from this text that we are all a church *per se*, surviving in spite of everything and everyone; and when we consider the huge deviations of *all* churches, the displays, we must honestly ask ourselves the question: do we still exist before God? When we witness, in so many churches, a rejection and hatred of the Jewish people and Israel, we must honestly ask the question: are we still grafted on the true trunk? "Do not look down on the Jew, rather fear!"

When I see Christians being passionate for the Arabs and Islam but relentlessly rejecting and accusing Israel, is there even a fragment of Christian truth left? Have we maintained even the slightest idea of our situation as a body and people grafted onto the "old trunk of Isaiah"? We are nothing more than grafts, and we receive the nourishment that will express itself in our work, our worship, and our theology from that very trunk. This statement will scandalize. Because of that we need to return to the beginning: to the Jews *belong* the adoption (to us also, adopted subsequently), the covenants (ours derives from theirs), the Law (for our ethics comes from the Law), worship, the promises, and the patriarchs (9:4–5). All this is our common heritage and our Savior was born of them. And the Lord is *their* Lord! All of this is still true today.

Behind Paul's metaphor, we see a theology: the sole people of God is made up of Israel *and* the church. Israel and the church are not juxtaposed as two heights independent of each other. No, the church, coming out of pagans, is grafted onto the trunk of Israel. Both are linked to each other in the history of salvation. Israel has not been replaced by the church, and God has not planted another natural olive tree next to the first natural olive tree; quite the contrary, there is only one olive tree! And the branches that were for a time cut off will be grafted back again at the end (v. 24) and this time it will be "according to nature"! This implies that in the "in between" these branches are kept without withering or burning (Mussner). On the other hand, if the church were to claim to live separate from Israel—which it has unfortunately done so often—it would cut itself off from its root and would only wilt. This is why Barth is right to tell us that *there is no real ecumenism without Israel,* so that "in the end" everything will be in order, that is, saved. As we have said, Paul's way of relating everything to the end, in an eschatological way, excludes current judgments, this or that exclusion, this or that rejection or refusal, for such current judgments tend to freeze God's salvation plan. We must think of everything in the light of this end.

5

Mystery and Renewal

VERSES 25–36

THE KEY VERSE IS OBVIOUSLY VERSE 32.[1] WE ARE TOO MUCH IN THE habit of ceaselessly thinking about our fault, our sin, and, vice versa, our personal salvation. This is not only because of our Protestant individualism! This is equally true in Catholicism. Here, the question of disobedience and salvation takes on a universal dimension: "All men." For all of us, each one of us belong to this all. Yet, we are somewhat hurt by this affirmation that God has "bound" all men into disobedience. Is that to say that God, because of some form of sadism, would have *made men sin*, would have led men into some sort of inevitable sinful fate? No, man is perfectly capable of sinning by himself! There is no need for God to nudge him into it. But we must understand that sin is not such or such an error that we could enumerate or check off, it is not instances of disobedience, transgressions, or neglected duties, etc. Sin is "only" refusing to live according to the double teaching we find in the Torah and reiterated by Jesus: "You shall love the Lord your God with all your heart, with all your soul, with all your strength, and with all your mind, and you shall love your neighbor as yourself."

All possible faults belong to this violation! I said, "the refusal to live according to . . ." This refusal is very rarely explicit. Very few will dare to say that they refuse to love God; they would rather say that God does not

---

1. "For God has bound all men over to disobedience so that he may have mercy on them all."

exist. And even fewer, in these days of freedom and fraternity,[2] will dare to say that they hate their neighbor. This would not be approved of. One would much rather not say that in order to support the poor Palestinians one would need to hate Israelis, or that in order to love the poor black people of South Africa (whom one has never met) one would need to hate the whites, etc. Anyhow, with a heart overflowing with ideology, one "loves" people . . . But the question of disobedience is not a matter of feelings: it is a matter of *a way of life*, free of any justifying statement. For once more we need to remember that Paul is Jewish, his "thought patterns" are Jewish; and for a Jew, love is not at all a matter of feelings (and this goes for faith also!), an inner matter, but rather it is a practical matter, it is *a way of life*. Who then could claim to be living within a *total* and exclusive love of God and within a total and exclusive love of neighbor? Yet this absolute demand—and its very content—is realized with perfection for us in the life of Jesus, totally giving himself to others, totally obedient to his Father and forgetting himself in all things so that he may identify with the one who suffers and despairs.

This absolute demand, which was only realized once, shows clearly that there is no righteous person, not even one. Thus, God did not manufacture a prison of disobedience into which he would lock men up; rather, men entrap themselves by living outside of love *and* by justifying the fact that they do so. For the prison is closed when man provides his own justifications. Rather than owning that he is not righteous, he is willing to admit that he makes mistakes, but always ready to find various reasons and excuses for them. This is the very thing that prevents forgiveness and justification; this is the reason why man is bound in his disobedience.

I remember the terrible word of Hébert Roux to a lady of high society whose son was becoming a horrible . . . let us say "hoodlum" (yet quite distinguished). They were Protestants, and as Roux was telling her about the serious actions of her son, the lady replied, "But I assure you, pastor, my son certainly does many stupid things, but all things considered, he is good!" He answered, "No, Madam, on the contrary I often

2. We are all familiar with the overabundances of freedom proclamations. The car will free us, the genetic engineering of abortion will free us. Since decolonization, African peoples are free people. Communist peoples are free since they got rid of capitalists. Hitler had already perfectly formulated this ideology in his sign *Arbeit macht Frei*, which was posted at the entrance to concentration camps.

see your son do perfectly laudably things; but all things considered, he is bad!".

Now, God will use this disobedience to show the universality of his love! "But where sin increased, grace increased all the more" (or overflowed)! Thus the key words in this verse are "in order to." Just as we saw earlier (in verse 11), what was most important was God's design: to show mercy to all. The purpose of God's work is that all may know his love, his grace, his forgiveness, one way or another, and that they might thus recognize who they are and turn to this mercy. So disobedience is but one moment in the history of each one (although this "moment" can of course last a lifetime!) and the objective of this disobedience, its "theology," we might say, is to understand this love.

No doubt, if God wants to save all men he can do so, but I will never cease repeating that the God of Abraham and of Jesus is not a magician. He will not save men through some kind of objective mechanism outside of man, because salvation is about realizing, about living of, in, and by this love. Certainly, this love of God becomes "sensitive to the heart," as Pascal says, but since it is the fullness of love, it is not only sensitive to the heart, but engages the whole person—just as the whole "person" of God invested himself in Jesus. This is what converts man when God *gives himself* in order to fulfill his mercy.[3] "Having loved his own who were in the world, he now showed them *the full extent* of his love" (John 13:1): he gave them the supreme proof of his love. Certainly, God *can* save all men; and the gospel consists in discovering, proclaiming, and acclaiming that God *wants* to save all men. When we pray, "Thy will be done," let us remember that we are not submitting to some kind of fate that we accept. No, it is instead a declaration of the fact that we love this will because it consists in wanting what God can do, namely, save all men. Thus, the whole world is under condemnation (Rom 3:19, 23), but God gives the gift that can redeem any condemnation (without any wonderful work accomplished by man), and the sentence that judges man and condemns him is the very sentence that saves him and places him back inside God's love (Rom 2:1). We must be saturated with this

3. God does indeed do this. Here is the essential difference between the biblical God and Allah, who is so often called "the Merciful" in the Koran. The mercy of Allah is the mercy of the despot, of the sovereign dictator, who from on high lets his mercy come down as the president pardons a person sentenced to death. The mercy of the biblical God is the mercy of the God who stoops all the way down to man and gives mercy because he takes on himself the punishment intended for man.

foolish logic—foolish for our human understanding—if we want to understand the mystery of Israel.

Verse 25

Here Paul is addressing a mystery. It is undoubtedly true that this word has been much abused in Christian theology, and too often we have called "mystery" the incomprehensible constructions of theologians! Here the mystery is about the relationship between Israel and the pagan world. As Vischer[4] showed very clearly, a mystery is always related to the end of time; we are talking about a mystery when there is the revelation of a secret from God concerning the end or the goal—it is not the incomprehensibility that makes something a mystery!

$$\text{Telos} \left\{ \begin{array}{c} \text{end, final} \\[1em] \text{end, objective, goal} \end{array} \right\} \text{of all things}$$

Other examples of this are found in 1 Cor 15:51; Eph 1:3–9, etc. Thus, the birth *and all of Israel's history* are a mystery. And this raises the "Jewish question." The absolute disgrace of anti-Semitism is fundamental; it is purely demonic (and with this anti-Semitism I target those who attack Jews in particular, as well as those who attack Israel today). It is demonic because it is hatred of God's design, not only hatred of the people that God chose. It is a hypocritical hatred because one claims that it is founded on "reasonable" arguments. There is no need to repeat them here for we have heard them a hundred times.

It is no longer a question of making philosophies of race, or of history, or of the political or economic actions of the Jews: this is about God's whole design, established at the beginning and in the end, on the Jewish people! This is *the only "Jewish question"*! Paul reveals the mystery that is in Israel so that precisely we, the pagans, would not consider ourselves wiser by inventing gnoses and philosophies. As Maillot clearly said, Paul reveals this mystery not in order that we might have a better knowledge of things, but that we may change our attitude, our behavior (that you may not consider yourselves wise!). If there is a "fall" of a certain part

4. Vischer, "Le Mystè[insert grave accent on e]re d'Israël," 1965.

of Israel, it is so that the totality of pagans may "come in" (the kingdom, by faith!). Then will the end come. The enigma of the existence of the Jewish people, even for the unbeliever of good faith, is in direct relationship with the end of history. Its solution consists in universal redemption. This means that the refusal (the hardening) of part of the Jewish people will continue until all pagans believe in Jesus Christ, that is, until Christ has, in *Truth*, been preached throughout the whole world. Instead we have the sad misunderstanding so often encountered when, rather than going out to the world to preach salvation, joy, freedom, love, truth, one has preached morality, dogmatics, constraint, and austerity, all the things that can push away pagans (and rightly so). And all the while, the Jews remain as a perpetual question and as a legitimate refusal to accept what is not a proclamation of the true Messiah that Jesus was. When the totality of pagans have heard a real gospel, and when all the pagans have entered the kingdom, then, says Paul in a surprising declaration, then "All-Israel" shall be saved.

Verse 26

The first and crucial question is: what is meant by this "All-Israel," *Kol Israel*? Israel designates the Jewish people endowed with its "honorary title," the Jews as God's people. "Israel is a sacral concept designating the totality of those who are chosen by YHWH and who are united in His worship."[5] But there is a double aspect, or rather two aspects that do not perfectly overlap. On the one hand, there are all the descendants of Israel (belonging to the people), and on the other hand, Paul says there are "those who are Israel" in relation to election and not posterity (Rom 9:6). We need to remember the rule of part for the whole (*pars pro toto*): those who are elected as the true Israel bear in themselves the All-Israel (people). This is clear when one contrasts the texts that are about the Israel that believed in Jesus and those that are about the "hardened" Israel. But which is the case here? Paul talks about All-Israel although earlier he said "not all." Thus, All-Israel is composed of those who now have accepted Jesus as the Messiah, united to all the others. This All-Israel is the addition and the gathering. This gives us the meaning of the beginning of the verse. "And so" does not mean "as it was announced in the text in Isaiah," but rather, "when all have joined into a common wor-

---

5. Gerhard Von Rad, *Old Testament Theology*.

ship, when the branches that had been temporarily cut off are grafted back."

Finally, there remains one problem for this All-Israel! Certain exegetes think that in this sentence Paul means the Jews of his time and that he is not asking about the Jews who died in their rejection of Christ, nor future generations of Jews. A detailed study by Mussner on the "diachronic" basis and the use of tenses in these three chapters shows that in chapter 9 Paul is talking about a prophetic proclamation, in chapter 10 (in the present) he is recounting the rather negative experience of the "Christian mission," and in chapter 11 the topic is the eschatological end. Starting from his eschatological understanding, Paul talks about All-Israel from the beginning to the end of time.

How then will Israel be saved? Either because at the end of time Israel will convert—and in the final course of history come to faith in Jesus Christ—or because salvation will happen in a special, unique way. First of all, we should note that nowhere in our text is there any mention of a massive conversion of the Jewish people, but rather of its salvation. I believe Mussner is right to distinguish between the meaning in our verse of the phrase *and so* (All-Israel will be saved) from the word *as* (it is written). The word *as* means "in accordance with" the way it is announced in Scripture, but also "because" it is announced. The Liberator comes from Zion, which definitely remains the messianic center of God's kingdom. This is certainly an eschatological event: the decision to save comes neither from the Christians nor from the act of conversion of the Jews; rather it is the initiative of God, who is merciful to all! Christ's Parousia will save Israel without any previous conversion of the Jews to the gospel, by a special means, also drawn by *sola gratia*. The text quoted from Scripture is a contraction of Isaiah 59:20–21 and Jeremiah 31:33–34. The one who *will come* from Israel will be the Christ in glory, the Liberator, who is the *Goël*, the one who redeems the debts of others and frees them from their captivity. This means that in reality the Jews are in a different relationship to Jesus Christ than we converted pagans are!

Yet, the same work is accomplished for Israel and for the pagans (an internal covenant and the blotting out of sins). Once more, the announcement of Christ coming from Zion will deliver each one from sin. As Maillot wrote, "The Jewish Christ is the reading grid for all of salvation history, and here it is brought into play by the covenant of forgiveness. The Christ is in the background of all other citations." This has two equally extraordinary dimensions. The first is that pagans are now part of All-Israel. One might say that in the Prophets *Kol Israel* was the reunion of the kingdoms of Israel and Judah. Now this *Kol Israel* is expanded to include us, for that is the indisputable meaning. "Until the full number of the Gentiles has come in, *and so* All-Israel will be saved"! In other words, we might even say that *we are the ones* entering Israel, as opposed to Israel entering the church! The second mystery is the answer to the question, *why* is All-Israel saved? This answer comes progressively as we read the passage:

- because God has not rejected the people he chose long ago and his word does not fail (9:6);

- because God is powerful enough to graft the hardened part of Israel back onto his cultivated olive tree, to which it has belonged to by nature (11:23–24);

- because God's gifts and his call are irrevocable (11:29);

- because the Jews are loved by God on account of their fathers (11:28);

- because, finally, as we saw earlier, God bound *all* men into disobedience with the purpose of showing mercy to *all*. In this universal as well as ultimate grace, let us remember that it is not man who wants and strives, but God alone who *gives mercy* (9:16). This universal salvation of All-Israel will manifest the final victory of God's free grace, which not only surpasses any intelligence, but also takes away any obstacles and infinitely exceeds our ill will.

Thus, God used Israel's refusals as a means to convert the pagans and he will use the conversion of pagans to make certain the return of Israel. But this must be understood as a serious warning for us Christians. As I have said before, "We are fed by the bread that the children of the house let fall, and we are taking advantage of grace . . . at the (temporary) expense of the Jews." Our rejection was temporary and so is theirs (v. 30), and we must never forget, first, that the Jews are not outside of God's love; second, we must never forget all that we owe them!

Verses 28–30

These extraordinary verses represent the last word on the condition and the situation of the Jewish people for two thousand years! The proclamation of the gospel has not removed election! The election of Israel is not, however, the whole gospel. And so the Jews became enemies (and one usually adds "of God" . . . but these words are not in the text and I do not believe that is the meaning; they became "enemies" of Jesus on the one hand, but on the other hand they are treated as enemies by all other people!). They became enemies as far as the gospel is concerned, so that this gospel might be proclaimed to all. Thus, they became the enemies of all, *because of you*, you who have been able to hear the gospel because of their refusal. Nevertheless, they remain God's beloved because of their patriarchs and because God never cancels his promise. It is not their virtue and faithfulness that make them the people of God, but the love of God for these fathers and his faithfulness to his word.

Now these gifts and this call are also given to us. *Now*. These three instances of the word *now* have been very wisely emphasized. *Now* (v. 30) you have received mercy, *now* (v. 30) they are unfaithful, and *now* (v. 31) they receive mercy. Salvation, the righteousness of God, and his mercy are for Now. *Hic et Nunc*. It is the Today of God. Let us note the strange construction of verse 31: they are unfaithful now and already now (not in the new creation) they are shown mercy. Christians must never forget that it is thanks to the Jews that God loves them. They are also called to love these Jews and to carry them in their hearts and help them. Therefore, Israel must always be at the center of Christian theology so that we might effectively take into account this "All." It is certain that, without Israel, the church will never have anything but a lopsided theology and that God's family, from whatever angle one might consider it, is a "grieving family" (Franz Lovsky).

However, this admirable revelation of God's lessons and design, which are clear to anyone reading the Scripture seriously, as Paul does, must not cause us to forget what came before in chapters 9 and 10, any more than, as Maillot says, the glory of Easter should makes us forget the cross of Good Friday: the two are inseparable. It is from the vantage point of Easter that we must see and understand Good Friday, and chapter 11 gives chapter 9 all its truth.

This glory that has been promised and assured to Israel must not make us forget the horrible adventure of the present time: both the Shoah committed by the Nazis and the one prepared by Muslims. It is true that, as Lovsky has often repeated, the Shoah must lead us to rethink all of Christian theology. We can no longer think of, pray to, and worship the God of Israel and of Jesus as we did a century ago . . . The murder of the Jewish people is also Christ crucified again. On the other hand, I do not at all agree with Maillot when he says that Paul probably caught a glimpse of the coming of a "third force," neither Jewish nor Christian, but similar to Islam or communism. "To some extent," he says, "these movements show in their own way, 'a zeal for God' but a zeal without intelligence . . . " This appears to me to be fundamentally wrong in light of the three chapters that we have read.

First of all, Paul already knew this "third force": it is the great pagan crowd who surrounded him! It is obvious that Paul is including the cult of Mithra and various remnants of Greek and Latin traditional cults under the term *pagan*. The religions that came later did not show any novelty. Whether it is Islam, communism, the idolatry of money, Nazism, or Maoism, none of these presented anything new from a spiritual or theological point of view. That Islam would claim to be the point of culmination, of perfection, and of completion of Judaism and Christianity is nothing new (many deviations from Christianity—Gnosticism, etc.—have made the same claim). We must note that it is a huge step backwards from a spiritual, moral, and human point of view. Islam is a Judeo-Christian heresy, just as Montanism was. It is neither more nor less. As for exhibiting "zeal for God," we must not be taken in by the alleged possibility of meeting monotheisms. As much as Jewish "monotheism" agrees with the "Trinitarian monotheism" of Christianity, the solipsist monotheism of Islam has nothing in common with Christianity because Allah has nothing in common with the God of the Bible.[6] He is in every way the opposite. Furthermore, many other "monotheisms" were known within paganism; for in contrast to the common error, almost all "polytheistic" systems recognized one unique God, superior to the universe of gods, but one who could neither be named nor known. Muslims are pagans like all the others. Everything Paul said of the pagans applies also to them. As to subsequent political systems (communist, Nazi, Maoist), in no way did they claim to be serving God, naming God, or founding a religion, but, in fact, it is exactly what they did! In all of these cases, a religion was produced by the ideology made explicit

6. Ellul, *Allah et le Dieu biblique.*

in these political systems. Of course, they had no intentions of serving God! These were obviously simply paganism, the kinds of paganism of which our times are fond (and which are used to replace Christianity, which has become a little worn!).

The essential point here is that one cannot possibly compare Islam or modern forms of paganism to the chosen people, nor can one apply to these what Paul says of the Jewish people. On the other hand, we must take up the battle that the prophets waged against false gods, *on a spiritual level*. We cannot expect to find anything positive in these religions, and globally they belong to the world of the pagans. For these, let us remember that Paul only sees one possibility—their conversion to Jesus Christ. Today, there is no "third force" in history. There is only a fresh upsurge of paganism in other forms and, we might add, next to secular religions,[7] the genuine religion of science, which is also a form of paganism.

Anyhow, God's design has not changed. The only characters are the chosen people on the one hand, and on the other, Christians who are to live by faith according to the Spirit as well as the great crowd of pagans, who are called to become Christians because they belong to this set of people bound into unbelief.

Now the immense revelation of the immense design of God concludes with admirable thanksgiving (verse 33–36)! "Oh, the depth of the riches of the wisdom and knowledge of God! How unsearchable his judgments and his paths beyond tracing out!" Here again, let us not be mistaken. Paul is not saying, "You do not understand anything," but rather he is saying, "I have explained it all to you!" When he expresses his adoration by means of this admiration, he wants to say precisely that all the things he has explained so far are only a tiny part of God's immense design; they are only that small part that God choses to reveal to us and to let us understand, a small part infinitely exceeded by all the greatness of the glory of God himself. Paul is no doubt speaking about himself when he asks, "Who has known the mind of the Lord?" Paul is the first to bow down in adoration and to acknowledge that he does not know it! Who can have been God's advisor? Who can have given him anything . . . that would not first have been given by God? Thus, the limited understanding we might have of one small aspect of God's

7. On modern religions, see Ellul, *New Demons*.

design should not make us proud; quite the contrary, it should lead us to worship and fear[8] the Lord.[9]

At the same time, Paul informs us that what we have just read and tried to understand in these three chapters is in no way the construct of a gifted theologian, nor is it an example of subtle jugglery with words: "it is a revelation of God's design . . . " It is the revelation, not concerning the Jewish people, its "destiny," or the future of pagans, rather it is the revelation of the richness of God abounding in love. It is the revelation of the wisdom of God, the only wisdom able to lead man, without coercion, toward life and salvation. It is the revelation of the science of God who knows, ahead of time, every conceivable action of this creation and every possible event that might occur in every instant of human history! But we cannot grasp this richness, this wisdom, this science. We are incapable of understanding, *hic et nunc*, the work and the stage of his project, his way of acting and the paths he follows so that we may end up without coercion where he is waiting for us (let us remember Jonah's adventure!). Nobody knows the thoughts of the Lord, although it has sometimes been the illusion of mystics to have known them; but the truly great mystics were very well aware of the fact that they knew nothing of the Lord's thoughts: "How well I know that flowing spring in black of night . . . She calls on all mankind to start to drink her water, though in dark, for black is night . . . " (Saint John of the Cross, *Mystical Poems*). The prophets had already warned us: "For my ways are not your ways, and my thoughts are not your thoughts" (Isa 4:8).[10]

Finally, we reach the adoration of verse 36: "For from him and through him, and to him are all things. To him be the glory forever. Amen." To him *alone* be the glory. But this doxology should draw our attention to . . . the Trinity! For in Colossians 1:16, Paul uses the same formula to designate Jesus Christ. "For by him all things were created,

8. Fear in the biblical sense does not mean fright. See Ellul, *A Reason for Being*.

9. This is somewhat similar to the present situation of scientists: the more they advance in their knowledge, the more they discover unimaginable domains that are vaster and more elusive, and the more they are led towards humility through knowledge. This is happening after a period of pride when we were convinced that the universe as well as possible combinations were limited so that we would eventually know everything through science!

10. Let us once again note the stupidity of those who, in such conditions, claim to be judging God to be unjust, cruel, despotic, etc. They do not have even a shadow of a clue of what they are talking about.

things in heaven and on earth, visible and invisible . . . All things were created *for him* and *by him*. He is before all things, and *in him* all things hold together." Finally, in the First Epistle to the Corinthians (1 Cor 8:6) there is a form of sharing: "There is *but one* God, the Father *from whom* all things came and *for whom* we live; and there is but one Lord, Jesus Christ, *through whom* all things came and through whom we live . . . " This echoes a phrase of Jesus: "The father and I are *one*," and strongly affirms that all of God's work is done by the Father and the Son, through the Spirit. Nevertheless this glorious and magnificent end, which is our horizon, and which is the total reconciliation of Jews and Christians, must not make us forget the beginning of the Epistle to the Romans, or chapter 9; and we can say that, in its insane behavior, the world is in fact sinning against its own end, its hope and its future.

This is the tragedy revealed by the world's rejection and persecution of the Jewish people.

12:1–2

Here begins the part that is usually called the "ethical," "paraenetic," or simply "moral" part of this epistle. Why do I think that it needs to be attached to this explanation of the Christian theology concerning the Jewish people? I think so because of the simple little word "therefore": "Therefore, I urge you . . . " As we said in the beginning, many exegetes believe they can skip chapters 9, 10, and 11 and attach chapter 12 directly to the eight earlier chapters which concern the theology of salvation by grace. But this seemed to us to be a serious mistake, in as much as the true meaning of the last chapters concerning the "behavior" of Christians is not at all a moral code in the traditional sense of the word . . . The "therefore" is not connected to the first eight chapters—on the contrary, it is precisely connected to these three preceding chapters. It is not at all a friendly little teaching on good behavior for the time of Paul. The Jews have been set aside so that the gospel might be proclaimed to all, but they will convert and along with the pagans, they will constitute All-Israel, with its Messiah, when they come to be "moved by jealousy" as they see God's work among the pagans and as they see the works that the Holy Spirit can accomplish among the pagans.

Yet, we have made this simple observation: the example that the Christians have been giving for the last two thousand years is certainly not going to move the Jews! This is simply because the lives of Christians are not exemplary. So Paul addresses these Christians and says: What do we need to *be* (much more than *do*) so that the Jews might recognize a work of God in our communities? What should we manifest as an action of God's grace to cause the Jews to ask such a question? If the Jews are to be moved with jealousy, this is the life testimony that we must live! Since God guided the history of Israel and the history of the pagans for their salvation, in spite of their rebellion, and since God did it without coercing anyone and while respecting "man, the rebel," and "man, centered on himself," since God has remained for all the one who liberates and gives mercy to Jews and pagans—now that you know all this, and especially in this tragic separation of Israel and the church, tell us, Christians, what is your conduct, what is your way of life going to be? That is the problem. And it must be posed in terms of the Jewish people since Paul has already given much ethical advice with respect to the behavior that is expected in a pagan environment (chapters 2, 3, 6, and 8).

The "therefore" is relative to our life before and with the Jews! This includes All-Israel as well as each one of those who will be reading this letter. "I urge you in view of God's mercy" (or by "the immense pity of God" in Maillot's translation). This indeed can only be an exhortation. Paul has shown that the Law is obsolete as a duty, an obligation, or a demand. With a "Christian morality" we are not going to fall back under the Law and the framing of life within a finished set of principles that we merely have to apply. Paul does not command anything, he exhorts: since you have been liberated by the Liberator, this is how you have been called to live in liberty!

How then are we to manifest our liberation from both the obligations of this world and from the fear of God? This is an exhortation in the name of the great compassion, the great mercy! We cannot do without this mercy since we have been saved by grace and grafted onto the true tree! Whoever is "in Christ" knows better than anyone else how far he may have gone in sinning; whoever believes in the resurrection can only count on mercy since Jesus—who became a dead body incapable of anything—was raised by the love of God. We are in this situation. The greater our faith grows, the more we need this mercy. But I believe that when we translate the Greek word *oiktirmos* by the English word "compassion," we are adding another dimension. Compassion means to suffer with.

This is indeed true as far as Israel is concerned: God suffers with Israel; he suffered with his Son, and he suffers with us in our inability to truly live according to his grace! If we are led to live the way Paul will show us, it is because of God's compassion! Once again, God does not coerce but manifests his compassion to us; and if we feel it, how can we refrain from entering upon the path God opens before us! The example that we have just been given of God's compassion for his people Israel must prompt us to understand to what depth this compassion goes, also for us!

"I urge you to offer your bodies . . ." This seems to me to be very important: it is not a question of offering our souls! Neither here nor later in the text is this about our inner life—even when Paul speaks of love, he is not concerned with feelings. The Christian life is not a transcending life, a life superior to everyday life, or worse, a life that we would only lead on one day (on Sunday!) and that we could forget during the rest of the week! Offer your bodies: Your spirit already belongs to God. Your soul has just been converted . . . so what is left to drag you into passions and off the path? The body.

Thus, the Christian life is first of all a life sensitive to the physical expression of the faith, to its translation into action! And this will *open up* a whole new ethic and restore the unity of being—this is why translations that say "offer your being" or "offer all of yourself" are correct. There is no separation between the spiritual and the material; each depends on the other. Henceforth, daily life is involved. Ernst Käsemann (quoted in Maillot) groups all of the following text under the rubric, "the righteousness of God in everyday Christianity." How is this grace that Paul spoke about in chapters 1–8 and this relation to the Trunk of Israel in chapters 9–11 to be lived out in everyday life? Real worship of God does not take place in heroic exaltation or inner spiritual contemplation, but rather in everyday life. Offer your bodies! Should we deliberately seek martyrdom and cause death? No, certainly not: offer your bodies as a *living* sacrifice. We need to acknowledge that our whole existence is the object of divine claim. Since the cross, there is no more need for any other (mortal) sacrifices, as the Epistle to the Hebrews clearly shows. God's joy is this living sacrifice: a man, a woman accepts God's claim, which will now order life, because this man, this woman wants to! It is to place oneself freely at God's service. This could easily make us think of monastic vocations—yet, without challenging the value of some of these vocations, I do not believe that they are what the text is about. What made me think of them is the kind of death rite that certain monasteries celebrate over the person who gives vows. I know that it signifies death *to the world*, but we shall see that this is precisely not the meaning of Paul's text. This is the sacrifice of someone who remains perfectly alive, and who yet is going to be "holy," that is, separate from the world, but not because of a monastic "fence." "They are *in the world*, but *not of the world*," said Jesus. "See, I am sending you as sheep among wolves." We shall soon see how this holy sacrifice will be made explicit.

The important thing here is that in this verse we find an echo of what came before! This is not a development that is unrelated to what has just been said! First of all, concerning the injunction to "offer your whole bodies . . . ," we need to remind ourselves that, in the Torah, the most beautiful sacrifices were those that involved burning *all* that was offered. Secondly, the mission of "the originality of worship in the Old Testament" was to "bring the Israelites back into everyday life" (Maillot), not to take them away from life: quite the contrary, sacrifices as well as worship were rooted in a very concrete life and offered this life to God. Paul is therefore only continuing to express . . . a Jewish way of thinking. But now, we offer ourselves, so that the offering and the person who offers are identical. And from now on this is the sacrifice that will please God. This is the sacrifice that can convince the Jews of what the action of the Holy Spirit is.

In verse 2 Paul explains in what ways this sacrifice will be holy: do not conform (to the present century, to this world, to your times). The world—our society, our times, our means of communication, our knowledge—gives a certain shape to everything that it can lay hands on and influence. This shape is rather easy to see, to recognize. What are the key ideas of *our* society (but also of *all* societies historically known)? Covetousness and the spirit of power.

In truth, our society expresses and is indeed founded on this will to power (which one might also call the "will to persistence" in a being) and this covetousness (is it not commonly known that "whoever does not progress and expand himself, fails and will tend to disappear?"). If we adopt the form of the world, we will enter into this game of the will to power and claim that covetousness is a motive for all our actions. There is no need to repeat Genesis 3 here! It is always the same story politically, economically, and spiritually. And the end of our conformity is always death. Let us consider two examples from our own times. The will to power, pushed to the utmost by Adolf Hitler, resulted in the death of thirty million people—and in his own. Covetousness, in our "live at any cost," "consume at any cost" society leads us to the major risk that makes us put the very life of our planet at stake (pollution, waste that cannot be broken down, ozone, accumulation of CO_2, radioactivity, etc.). Our present epoch (*aiôn, eon*) features, to a worse degree, the same characteristics as all of history and gives the same shape to everything. The use of this word shows that this time is still "present"! This is not pleasing to God.

He does not require a mortal sacrifice, but rather a living sacrifice. "I set before you life and prosperity, death and destruction." That is the choice that the "form" given by the world removes. Thus, the first act of a pardoned person will be to refuse this form, to refuse to "enter into the struggle for life" or into happiness through consumption, etc. Do not follow fashions. "Judge all things and hold fast to what is good." Judge all things; this is precisely what the Torah wanted man to learn and understand! This refusal means, to the pleasure or displeasure of many Christian intellectuals, a break between the world on the one hand, and Christians and the church on the other. This rejection of "the form of the world" pleases God as worship because it leads man toward life, and the preservation of life (which is certainly not to be despised or considered unimportant!) and not toward destruction, which is always the triumph of nothingness, and which God refuses. Be transformed: instead of the shape given by the world, receive another shape! The correct translation "trans-formed" implies with "trans" the passage to something beyond. It does not only mean "to change," it means that beyond the form that the world can give there is another form that is "further off" (in a metaphorical sense). In other words, you need to get beyond the struggles of the world, its passions, and its ideologies. Do not let yourselves be imprisoned in the shapes of the world, that is, in its passions, in what it believes, what it struggles for, and what it takes a stand for. All the things that "inform" modern man (always "modern" again and again, in each successive century!), you no doubt need to know them, to discern them, but you also need to go beyond them. It goes without saying that you cannot go beyond them in a new form if you do not know them! This is what I find so disappointing with many Christian intellectuals who want to be "present to the world" (which is good), but who enter the form that the world is imposing on them because they do not know anything about it and because they are not transformed!

I am thinking of all the Christians who, in good faith, were travelling companions of Stalinist communism as long as it was fashionable, and those who entered enthusiastically into scientist rationalism at the end of the nineteenth century, which was also the result of a fashion, and those who are now fascinated by Islam and ready to make any concession without realizing that this is exactly what Paul is warning us against. After getting to know the forms of the world, we need to get beyond them so that our lives may gain another meaning. Because of this change of direction, this new life takes on a different form! We have exactly the same idea, a little further on in the text, in this very Epistle to the Romans: "Overcome evil with good" (12:21). Paul is not talking about a conflict between two equal forces, evil and good, but of going beyond evil. Evil is well known to you, now leave it behind! For good is not the simple opposite of evil, it is what takes us beyond! As we said earlier, this of course implies that we remain in the world! We need to start from this good and from this new form and go on to accomplish some action in the world; this action is not to be participation in what the world does, but rather the taking of a "critical" stance (not simply refusing or negating!). The essential part of this stance will be *within* the very works of the world, a *testimony* against the form of the present times and *for* the form of the world to come! It will become an action within this world and glorify God in it.

How is this kind of life possible? Curiously, Paul does not talk about piety or morality: he tells us that this world will be produced by the renewal of our minds, our intelligence. Among so many side roads, faith and this vision of a world oriented by divine love, with the addition of hope, change the mind of the Christian, change his conception of the world and of its future. Let us remember that a Christian is not a nihilist: a change in the understanding does not trigger a desire to destroy this evil world, but rather to change its form. We should see this in conjunction with what we said previously, following Vischer, about the frequent resort of Jews to revolutionary movements. Rather curiously, this is a change of direction for the intelligence! It is in our intelligence (and not in the "soul," or in some vague "spiritual" place) that this change occurs. It is so, first of all, because one must criticize the form of the world, and this is done with existential intelligence. Second, if we are to act to change the form of the world, one cannot act without thinking! Therefore, thought is the human starting point for faith. Let us make one important reservation: this is not "pure" thought, "rational reason," or self-meditative thought; as always in the Bible, it is existential thought, that is, it is linked to our life, it expresses our life—for out of the abundance of the heart the mouth speaks. The first indication of a change in the intelligence is the commandment, "You shall love the Lord your God, with all your heart, with all your soul, with all your *mind*, and with all your strength." We must worship with our whole mind, and think as we worship the Lord

So we see that Christian faith does not require a *sacrificium intellectus*, but only a *sacrificium intellectus mundi!* This reversal, this renewal, which is also repentance, means that in our thought knowledge will intervene and become the engine of our will! It is the knowledge of grace and our worship of the way God leads the world. The way God leads the relationship between Jews and Christians, as seen in detail in these chapters, is a perfect example of this. This reversal is the will to become an instrument of God's strategy in the world as we acquire this knowledge!

Therefore, all that will follow in chapters 12–15 is not a moral code or a condition for acquiring salvation, but an explanation of how to become an instrument in the hands of God so that the world might be transformed as well, how we in particular can be that instrument for the expression of God's faithfulness towards his people! Our mind, which is the seat and the means of trans-formation of our being, enables us to discern, *hic et nunc*, in our concrete daily life, what the will of God is (not so that we might submit to it, but so that we might *do* it!), what our behavior should be. To discern by discerning the spirits, of course! Therefore, several translations are possible: "What the will of God is, what is good, pleasant and perfect," or "That the will is good, pleasant, and perfect," or the translation of Maillot, which I prefer: "What the will of God is, what is good, *what pleases him, what is well done*." Look for what pleases God, just as in the world we seek to please those we love! To know how to give God joy, what a task! And this is only possible in the freedom of love and not in the strict application of a certain morality! Also, "what is well done," that is, "what is properly brought to its end," which actually was the first meaning of "perfect" (*per-fectum*) before the word took on its present meaning! What one has to do must be done well.

Therefore, the renewal of the mind indicates that a Christian life must include research and discernment. It should not be thoughtless spontaneity just because we have "faith," nor should it be the conviction that in all things the Holy Spirit is causing our actions. Certainly, the Holy Spirit enlightens our intelligence, but we should also use it to discern what is good, what pleases God, and what will be done well! We certainly do not lose ourselves, quite the contrary. Just like the Jewish people, the Liberator gives us the free use of our minds, which we should not despise!

Does this mean that faith and the Christian life are only something for intellectuals? Not at all! Indeed, quite the contrary! For an intellectual is full of a clutter of philosophies, ideas, knowledge, etc. that must be gotten rid of before the Word can be heard or must be turned over to the inspiration of the Holy Spirit. But any person has an adequate mind for what Paul urges! But the mind must be renewed. Thus we see that this Christian life, for which Paul will start giving directions, has a departure point: grace, election, the covenant (which still belong to the people of Israel!) and an objective: the joy of God. Between the two, it is up to us to draw our route, which we will freely choose according to the gifts God has given us! We need to decide on which points, and according to which principles, we must be nonconformists and be transformed! This is our living sacrifice, and this chosen path will be our worship. Here again there are many traditions: One usually says *a reasonable act of worship*, which Barth retains, but we could also say *a logical act of worship*. This would be a more literal translation, and why not—if we consider the preceding "therefore"! This is God's strategy within his covenant, within his election, and within the way he leads the chosen people and the pagans, so that logically you have to offer yourselves as a living sacrifice; that is, you will enter into God's design! This design is to bring the pagans to perfection and to convince the Jews of the love of Jesus the Messiah! This is indeed the only act of worship we might offer, and it is an act of worship that follows from the logic of the preceding text! Maillot prefers: *an act of worship in keeping with the Word*! This really means the same thing. In any case, it can neither be a "rational" act of worship (in keeping with our reason, produced by reason[11]) nor a

---

11. We have seen this too often in the "worship services" of the last twenty years, where the personal fancy of the pastor or even of the priest is replacing the slow creation of the act of worship by the communion of saints.

"spiritual" act of worship! Maillot also believes that "logical" would be in accordance with the *logos* and that would be a cutting polemic remark to the many impenetrable religions that were then multiplying and said to have declared themselves to be "in accordance with the *logos*"—esoteric, mysterious cults.

Paul maintains that, according to Jewish worship, it is an exoteric worship, practiced by all, all the time and in broad daylight, since it is the work of each person's life! And the act of worship is "reasonable" because it is placed within the action of God revealed in the preceding chapters. It is thus, as Barth says, "in keeping with its object." We can easily see the difference between our "acts of worship" on the one hand—liturgy, hymns, sacrifices, prayers, vows, explanations—and on the other hand, the only act of worship in keeping with its object: the living sacrifice of our existence in God.

Epilogue

WITH THIS INDISPENSABLE OPENING TO THE CHRISTIAN LIFE, WE ARE able to see the unity of God's work for the salvation of all, and can also see the role that we Christians, we the church, are called to play. We can also see that Israel has not completed its role. Too often, because of our delight in the *New* Testament and the "*new* covenant," we have the feeling that Israel no longer counts in God's plan! What a dreadful mistake! Does Israel still have a salvific function *after the Christ*? Does Israel have a special rank in the history of salvation? Admittedly, when I was in Israel, I heard Israelis say that they had had enough of being the "chosen" people and that this had only brought persecutions upon them! If Israel refused its election, then God's grand plan would be compromised. But since the Shoah, the great majority of Jews seem, on the contrary, to have become much more aware of its *positive* specificity and of its *decisive* role in the history of salvation.

It seems to me that there are now fewer Jews who want to "assimilate." I knew some before the war who would tell me, "But we are French, first. To be Jewish is only a religion, it means obeying the commandments . . . " The Shoah proved to them in a horrifying way that Israel is first of all a people (not a *race*, of course!), the people chosen and loved by God (this will inevitably entail the hatred of the world—for Christians too), and there is nothing Israel can do about it. Its worship, all the rites of Leviticus and Deuteronomy, as well as the whole Torah, are there to constantly remind the people that they belong only to God. Why did God maintain his people as such after Jesus Christ? Why are the Jews still Jewish after all the persecutions and dispersions? There is no need to look for political or sociological reasons . . . Here we have only a "theological" aim if I may say so, and I will simply summarize the admirable text provided by Mussner to this huge question.

1. The Jew is God's permanent witness present in the world and, as such, he is "a proof of God"! One can only explain the permanence of the Jewish people if one acknowledges that God himself supports his people as their defender. This has been said in various ways. Augustine declared that God protected the Jews in order that the church might understand the power of his mercy: "and therefore he has not slain them. That is, he has not let the knowledge that they are Jews be lost in them, although they have been conquered by the Romans, lest they should forget the God of law and their testimony should be of no avail . . . " (*City of God*, XVIII, 46). Furthermore, as far as Augustine is concerned, the Jews are witnesses to the permanent value of Scripture because when they are dispersed among all peoples they testify to the authenticity of the prophecies—which, he says, have obviously been spoken in reference to Christ. Thus, they prove that these prophecies are not the invention of the church. Assuredly, Barth joins Augustine when he says that "the Jew is the only visible and tangible evidence of God."

2. "The Jew is the permanent witness to the *concrete* character of Salvation History." Of course, "science" claims that Salvation History is an "idealistic superstructure," an ideology. The existence of the Jew (much more so than the existence of the church) questions this scientist ideology. Ever since the discipline of history was developed, it has been given its own logic: Hegel or Marx. But now the Jew gets in the way of this beautiful philosophy; the Jew does not enter into the dialectic of history. This is why Hegel talks about the "somber enigma of Israel" and Marx is anti-Semitic! The Jew does not enter into the "normal" paradigms of universal history; he is the only one that is different and he is so because he is the only permanent witness to the concrete character of Salvation History. It is not taking place in someone's brain or in the sky but actually within history itself, which cannot be conceived as simply profane. It is at this point that anti-Semitism is born.[1] The Jew attests to the *incarnate* character of Salvation History.

3. The Jew is the witness of the "hidden God" whose ways are unsearchable. This has always been proclaimed by the Prophets: "Israel, your God is a hidden God" (Isa 45:15). God does not show his game, and it is

1. I know that this statement will trigger most violent reactions. For me, the existence of the State of Israel is more than a profane fact. It is a sign of the action of God in history, a sign announced in the prophecies on the restoration of Israel.

in mystery and sometimes much later on that one finds a trace of this hidden God! The Shoah poses in a tragic fashion this hidden character: no Jew and no Christian can say why God allowed this! I believe that our meditation on the three chapters of the Epistle to the Romans has proven that one can clarify the action of God in, by, and for Israel to its limit! The Shoah drives us up against the wall: either God does not exist, or he is the hidden God whose mysterious ways nobody can know and whose witness *must be* and actually *is* the Jew upon whom God has always put his hand!

4. The Jew will not let the messianic idea disappear from the world! As Christians, we too often have the feeling that "the messianic question" has been solved! Jesus was the Messiah and he fulfilled the prophecies, etc. In the end, it does not preoccupy us too much anymore! For the Jews, however, Jesus is not the Messiah: they are waiting for the Messiah (consciously or unconsciously), and therefore we are also forced to wait for the glorious Messiah, who for us is the Messiah returning in glory. Therefore, I believe we need to be reconciled to the fact that the coming of Jesus (which caused such a change, sometimes a negative change for Israel) opens the messianic era. This will be the era of expectation of the coming from a Jewish perspective. From a Christian perspective, it will be the era of expectation of the return of this Messiah who will bring all things back into the kingdom of God. Precisely because it is a question of life and death for Israel, however, it is much more vigilant and exigent than Christians. We are often too satisfied with the coming of Jesus and the church! This messianic era is an era of expectation, during which Israel and the church each have their testimony to bring—a testimony of faithfulness to the foregone revelation (Remember . . .), a testimony of hope in the certainty of the kingdom to come, and a testimony of vigilance and faith in a God who never goes back on his promises. Both of them together bear witness to the total truth of God: Christians proclaim "already," the Jews "not yet." But the pair "already–not yet" characterizes faith in the God of Abraham and of Jesus, as Kierkegaard and Barth have shown. In any case, even though we may note the divergences in the understanding of the person of the Messiah, one cannot get away from the fact that the idea of the Messiah was born in Israel.[2]

---

2. Many Jewish writers, quoted by Mussner, attest that when the Messiah comes, if this Messiah is the Jewish Jesus, there will be no refusal or scandal.

5. The Jew keeps his eyes fixed on a better world: Marx and Ernst Bloch are witnesses to this will to bring about a better world. Their mistake, which is often denounced in the history recounted in the Hebrew Bible, is to want to bring about, through one's own effort, that which can only come from a decisive act of God. Remember Abraham, who attempted to realize the promise, but Ishmael was not the son wanted by God. Among Christians too there have been millennium movements that claimed to establish the kingdom of God on earth through human efforts . . . The Prophets do announce that God alone will establish this new earth and all of them, like Paul, see this in an eschatological end. Yet, for the Prophets, this reality must be earthly. One of the major errors of Christianity has been to transport this to heaven or worse, to some "Paradise." Whereas, Revelation brings us back to a *new heaven* and a *new earth* where righteousness will dwell, and to the coming of a new *city* for humans: the new Jerusalem![3] These are indeed earthly realities that need to be brought to salvation and perfection, as we saw in Romans 11:12–15. Thus, next to the often-fluctuating faith of Christians, the *persistent existence* of the Jew refers us by itself to an eschatological future.

6. Friedrich Wilhelm Marquardt writes: "Israel is, in the history of the world, the one who attests to the 'not yet' of God's will." We have already mentioned this "already–not yet." Marquardt's[4] explanation is quite impressive: "Through its 'No,' Israel represents the eschatological reservation of God himself (that is, maintains God's absolute freedom, according to Barth). It is opposed to the Christian pathos of time, of truth, and of final judgments. It exists as the decomposing ferment of wrong perceptions." Here we are getting to what we have caught a glimpse of in our three chapters of the Epistle to the Romans: the Jewish refusal is not "outside of God's design"! The current presence of salvation in Jesus Christ *has begun*, but God wants all men to be saved. The end of time has indeed come, in the sense that *nothing new* for the salvation of the world, creation, and men can ever occur. However, the end of time is not fulfilled, the final time has not arrived. It will only start when All Israel is saved (Rom 11:26). This is what we need to call "the eschatological reserve of God himself." Henceforth, in the course of history, the

3. Ellul, *The Meaning of the City.*

4. Marquardt, *Feinde um Unsretwillen: Das judische Nein und die christliche Theologie.*

Jewish people is a people of the temporary, who possess nothing that is completed, closed, or self-contained. Whether Israel wants it or not, it is the corner thrust into the hardened heart of the world, and there it will remain until this heart is changed into a heart of flesh.

7. Through Judaism, the history of the world has become a holy history, that is, the place where all the action of a holy God takes place. There is a universal conception of history in which God acts incessantly (but he does not impose conditions!). God is indeed the God of all creation. Throughout its history and throughout its fidelities and infidelities, willingly or unwillingly, the people of Israel repeats this truth ceaselessly. It is something that Paul echoes here in his doctrine of Christ, the New Adam, and in his doctrine of the church, the body of Christ made up of all men.

8. In spite of the christological "shrinking" of the historical church, Israel did not cease (even after Christ) to be "the servant of God," atoning—with the Christ and through horrible suffering—for the sins of the world. For Christians who are too strict, too "fundamentalist," this will seem to be scandalous. But let me repeat again: Jesus cannot be separated from his people, and the Jewish people cannot be separated from Jesus. The Shoah reminds us of this in such a harsh way that many Christians prefer not to think about it! Thus, even after Christ, Israel has a universal salvific function in the world.[5] In order to provide a complete testimony to the God of Abraham and Jesus, Israel and the church must be inseparable. Does that mean that I am taking anything away from the unique and universal work of Christ? Certainly not, not any more than Paul when he proclaims, "I fill up in my flesh what is still lacking in regard to Christ's afflictions." Everything is "in Christ." And his people first! Why do we never remember Simeon's song: ". . . your salvation, which you have prepared in the sight of all nations: a light for revelation to the Gentiles, and *the glory of your people Israel . . .* " (Luke 2:29–32)?

I would like to end by mentioning the admirable book *The Star of Redemption.*[6] According to Franz Rosenzweig, the Christian needs the assistance of the Jew! The Jew helps him not lose his identity, for Israel remains the tree on which the church is grafted. "But that Israel is more

5. Moltmann, *L'Eglise dans la force de L'Esprit.*
6. Rosenzweig, *The Star of Redemption,* 438.

than an idea, he knows it and sees it. For we are living. We are eternal, not as an idea may be eternal, but we are so, if we are so, in full reality. And so for the Christian we are that which really *cannot be doubted*." This, assuredly, is one of the reasons of anti-Semitism!

Appendix

The Suffering Servant[1]

THE BEAUTIFUL STUDY BY ARMAND ABÉCASSIS ON THE SERVANT IN Isaiah is exemplary. In the second essay, called *Metaphysics of Suffering*, he starts with the sociopolitical Servant (Isa 49), moves to the spiritual Servant (Isa 50), and finally to the suffering Servant (Isa 52). In the third part, he cannot avoid a meeting with Christian faith and theology. For Christians, the suffering Servant portrayed here is Jesus the Christ. Abécassis, however, argues that because Isaiah was writing almost six centuries before the birth of Christ it is obvious that he could not be thinking of Christ . . . for Isaiah could only reflect on the events occurring in his time (in my view, this seems to greatly reduce the scope of the prophecies!). Each suffering Jew is included here, and Isaiah's proclamation must be understood as moving from the idea that the righteous suffers because of a fault (committed by himself or by others), to the idea that suffering comes from God's decision to lay on the righteous the depravity of all. The righteous becomes the person who offers himself. The death of the servant carries the sins of all before YHWH. This, says Abécassis, is a veritable "lecture" on hope.

What Abécassis refuses to accept is not that Christians have given *one* possible interpretation of this text, but that they claim that this interpretation is the only one. Although the Jews have endured unthinkable suffering for the past two thousand years, the rabbis have not deified their people. Jewish thought parts company with Christian thought when the latter maintains that only a divine being could accomplish God's plan. Christians are "adding" to the text in Isaiah. How can Jesus be *servant*

1. Abécassis, *La Pensée juive.*

and God at the same time? Furthermore, Jewish thought abhors human sacrifice, especially the sacrifice of children. Moreover, Hebrew law excludes the possibility that a dead God could save humans. Christianity shifted animal sacrifice to the sacrifice of God himself . . . which is completely foreign to the Torah. Nevertheless, Abécassis shows—with great finesse—that suffering appears to be "an inevitable part" of the divine project (in the promise to Abraham), and his argument provides an extraordinary key for understanding Jewish suffering. The Hebrews, he insists, suffer in Egypt because they cannot enter the Promised Land. They are unable to do so because the Canaanites commit immense evil, yet God grants them time to repent and change their lives. The righteous (Hebrews) suffer to atone for the sins of the Canaanites. He then shows, very decisively and very clearly, that the meeting of three stories leads to the theology of the suffering Servant: first, the prayer of Abraham for Sodom and Gomorrah (if only he could have been allowed to go as far as *one single righteous person!*); secondly, the text by Hosea (11:8–89), according to which, God, very angry, nevertheless declares that his compassion is stirred and that he will not punish his people because he himself is "God, the holy one among you"; and finally, of course, the text in Isaiah. If the Servant is suffering for the sins of men, if the presence of the Servant can save the city, and if God himself declares he is in the middle of the city, then Christian theology, which is "simultaneously true and false," can be explained. This theology is true as far as the suffering of the righteous and the innocent is concerned, that is, for atoning suffering. "Someone needs to take on undeserved suffering and death so that life may continue and flourish." Abécassis writes a beautiful passage on the love of the suffering righteous. But according to him, the Christian interpretation is false in that it comes as an explanation, instead of simply being an interpretation of the biblical theme of the atoning suffering of the righteous. An idea foreign to the biblical text and to Jewish thought has been added "from the inside." This idea has been borrowed from other civilizations.

"What exactly is the meaning of the death of God as necessary for the atonement of evil and the liberation of humanity? Could man not be liberated from his guilt in some other way? Why would God have to sacrifice himself for human faults? And why does God need to become man?" Abécassis correctly criticizes the notion of "mystery," which has been used to excess. He obviously points to what is most incoherent and incomprehensible, namely, God becoming man. This is impossible. Would not the very act of removing imperfection from a being also remove existence? God would be liberating man through non-divine mediation. "The notion of creation as radical separation introduces nothingness between God and the creator. God cannot make himself man, nor can man make himself God."

"Judaism offers the Torah and the education of the Law to develop the responsibility of man and to dissolve his guilt . . . " and "Christianity, on the other hand, through its interpretation of Isaiah 53, offers the image of the suffering servant, a divine incarnation, who is sacrificed to clear man of his guilt . . . " I will not quote Abécassis any further, but I will retain his friendly and understanding words for Christians and their faith, because they obviously open up a dialogue. I do have some objections, though. Abécassis often mentions "the righteous," but *who* is absolutely righteous? Will it suffice to be put to death? Was Spartacus righteous? Who else but God is? There is none righteous, not one. Furthermore, the idea that believing in a "divine suffering servant" would come from a civilization foreign to Judaism . . . is quite strange! What religions then are we dealing with? I mentioned earlier that I agreed that the notion of "mystery" had been used excessively by theologians, but does that mean there should be no mystery at all? In that case, the God revealed to Abraham would have been a God who is totally clear, comprehensible, and knowable. One must acknowledge that the Torah and the Prophets are *also* replete with mystery! Furthermore, I was astonished by the assertion that *God cannot make himself* man. Could there be any limit to God's power? That is unthinkable; God can do everything.

Finally—this is only a brief statement of my main objections— Abécassis is wrong in stating that Jesus is sacrificed to take away man's *guilt*. No, this is a matter of sin and, above all else, a matter of a break with God. Only in Jesus does the final reconciliation take place, precisely because he is God and unites with man so that there may no longer be any break. The fundamental word is reconciliation. Having said that, I understand, hear, and accept all the objections. Assuredly, the key must be found in the exclusion carried out by Christian theologians and priests for centuries, as they took control over the suffering Servant and applied it only to the person of Jesus. One has tried to reduce the work of God to "either/or," whereas it should be expressed with "and." This study has shown to what extend the suffering Servant of Israel is at the same time both Israel and Jesus.

Abécassis' demonstration stops where worship of the Lord who is identified with his people can start for us, because there is a similarity between the historical destiny of Israel and that of Jesus "cut off from the land of the living."

> What was accomplished in Christ in a single moment of time—a sort of transhistorical event—goes on happening through time in Israel. The Jewish people continues under our very eyes to carry the weight of history and to live out the night phase of the mystery of the Servant. Israel continues to experience the silence of God . . . but Jesus overcame the trial of the silence of God. He retained his faith through trial and dereliction . . . In him is the promise of final redemption and of the glorification of the whole of Israel.

and

> We must acknowledge that the people of God, in its present situation, as well as through the centuries of history, in its suffering, hope, and prayers has held to the mission of Servant. This destiny is inseparable from that of the Gentiles. Israel bears the weight of the evil at work in the world, and its raising up will be that of humanity. Nor is this destiny separable from that of the paschal mystery of Christ, which sheds light on it and fulfills it. This conclusion—an intuition of faith—is no more communicable than faith in Christ itself, and it must be lived out largely in silence; but it forbids the Christian to reduce the suffering of Israel to a matter of the punishment of the Jews. By his resurrection, Christ gives us a pledge that Israel and the world will be raised up. By its endurance and by its hope, Israel reminds us of the historic and therefore unfinished character of redemption . . . Finally, because the suffering endured by the Jewish people is in large measure due to Christians, its presence at our side forbids us to be arrogant and to forget our own need for redemption."[2]

I insisted on including this long quotation as a counterpoint to Abécassis' discussion because it enables us to find our bearings in our dialogue and in our communion correctly.

---

2. Remaud, *Israel, Servant of God*, 25–31.

Bibliography[1]

BASIC WORKS

Fasching, Darell. *The Jewish People in Christian Preaching*. Lewiston, NY: Mellon, 1984.

Mora, Vincent. *Le Refus d'Israël*. Lectio divina 124. Paris: Cerf, 1986.

Mussner, Franz. *Tractate on the Jews: The Significance of Judaism for Christian Faith*. Translated by Leonard Swidler. Philadelphia: Fortress, 1984.

Rosenzweig, Franz. *The Star of Redemption*. Translated by Barbara E. Galli. Modern Jewish Philosophy and Religion: Translations and Critical Studies. Madison: University of Wisconsin Press, 2005.

ON ANTI-SEMITISM

Isaac, Jules. *Genèse de l'antisémitisme: Essai historique*. Paris: Calmann-Lévy, 1956.

Lovsky, Fadiey. *Antisémitisme mystère d'Israël*. Paris: A. Michel, 1955.

Poliakov, Léon. *The History of Anti-Semitism*. Translated by Richard Howard, Nathalie Gerardi, George Klin, and James Carroll. 4 vols. Philadelphia: University of Pennsylvania Press, 2003.

ON THE *EPISTLE TO THE ROMANS*

Barth, Karl. *The Epistle to the Romans*. Translated by Edwin C. Hoskyns. London: Oxford University Press, 1968.

Cambier, Jules. *L'Evangile de Dieu selon L'Epître aux Romains*. Studio Neotestamentica, studia 3. Paris: Desclée, 1967.

Cullman, Oscar. *Le Salut dans L'Histoire: L'existence chrétienne selon le Nouveau Testament*. Bibliothéque théologique. Paris: Delachaux, 1966.

Leenhardt, Franz J. *L'Epître Saint Paul aux Romains*. Commentaire du Nouveau Testament 6. Paris: Delachaux, 1957.

Maillot, Alphonse. *L'Épître aux Romains: Epître de l'œcuménisme et théologie de l'histoire*. Paris: Labor et Fides, 1984.

Viard, André. *Saint Paul, L'Epître aux Romains*. Sources bibliques. Paris: Gabalda, 1975.

Wilckens, Ulrich. *Der Brief an die Römer*. Vol. 2. EKK 6. Zurich: Neukirchener, 1989.

1. The 2012 edition has expanded the bibliographical information from Ellul's original, but there may remain some incomplete parts.

ON OUR THREE CHAPTERS:

Lovsky, Fadiey. *Antisémitisme mystère d'Israël.* Paris: Michel, 1955.

Lovsky, Fadiey. *La déchirure de l'Absence: Essai sur les rapports etre l'église du Christ et le peuple d'Israel.* Paris: Calmann-Levy, 1971.

Lovsky, Fadiey. *Le royaume divisé: Juifs et chrétiens.* Paris: Ed. Saint-Paul, 1987.

Remaud, Michel. *Israel, Servant of God.* Translated by Margaret Ginzburg and Nicole François. London: T. & T. Clark, 2003.

Simon, Marcel. 1948. *Verus Israel: A Study of the Relations between Christians and Jews in the Roman Empire (AD 135–425).* Translated by H. McKeating. Littman Library of Jewish Civilization. Portland, OR: Vallentine Mitchell, 1996.

Timothée number 10. for a reading of Romans 9 to 11.(BP 6, Groissiat, 01870 Martignat).*

Vischer, Wilhelm. "Etude biblique sur Rom. IX à XI." *Foi et Vie*, n.v. (1988) n.p.*

———. "Le Mystère d'Israël: Une exegèse des chapîtres 9, 10 et 11 de l 'Epître aux Romains." *Foi et Vie* 64/6 (1965) 427–87.

ADDITIONAL WORKS
(FOR CITATIONS LISTED IN THE 2012 EDITION)

Abécassis, Armand. *La Pensée juive.* Vol 3, *Espaces de l'oubli et mémoires du temps.* Le livre de poche, Biblio essais, 4100. Paris: Librairie générale française, 1989.

Baron, Shalom Wittmayer. *A Social and Religious History of the Jews.* 18 vols. 2nd ed. New York: Columbia University Press, 1952.

Ellul, Jacques. *Allah et le Dieu biblique. La France catholique.* February 1989.

———. *The Ethics of Freedom.* Translated by Geoffrey W. Bromiley. Grand Rapids: Eerdmans, 1976.

———. *The Humiliation of the Word.* Translated by Joyce Main Hanks. Grand Rapids: Eerdmans, 1985.

———. *The Meaning of the City.* Translated by Dennis Pardee. Eugene, OR: Wipf & Stock, 2011.

———. *The New Demons.* Translated by C. Edward Hopkin. New York: Seabury, 1975.

———. *The Reason for Being: A Meditation on Ecclesiastes.* Translated by Joyce M. Hanks. Grand Rapids: Eerdmans, 1990.

———. *Si tu es le Fils de Dieu: Souffrances et tentations de Jésus.* Paris: Centurion, 1991. English translation: Eugene, OR: Wipf & Stock, forthcoming.

———. *The Subversion of Christianity.* Translated by Geoffrey W. Bromiley. Grand Rapids: Eerdmans, 1986.

Grelot, Pierre. *Introduction à la Bible.* 2nd ed. Paris: Desclée, 1976.

Maillot, Alphonse. *L'Épître aux Romains: Epître de l'œcuménisme et théologie de l'histoire.* Paris: Labor et Fides, 1984.

Marquardt, Friedrich-Wilhelm. "Feinde um Unseretwillen: Das judische Nein und die chrisliche Theologie." *Treue zur Thora: Beiträge zur Mitte des christlich-jüdischen Gesprächs: Festschrift für Günther Harder zum 75,* edited by Peter von der Osten-Sacken, 174–93. Veröffentlichungen aus dem Institut Kirche und Judentum bei der Kirchlichen Hochschule Berlin 3. Berlin: Institut Kirche und Judentum, 1977.

Moltmann, Jürgen. *L'Eglise dans la force de l'Esprit: Une contribution à l'ecclésiologie messianique.* Cogitatio fidei 102. Paris: Cerf, 1980.

Rad, Gerhard von. *Old Testament Theology*. Translated by D. M. G. Stalker. 2 vols. New York: Harper, 1962–65.

Saulnier, Christiane. *Histoire d'Israël*. Vol. 3, *De la conquête d'Alexandre à la destruction du temple*. Paris: Cerf, 1985.

Thiessen, Gerd. *L'Ombre du Galiléen*. Paris: Cerf, 1988.

Vahanian, Gabriel. *Anonymous God: An Essay on Not Dreading Words*. Contemporary Religious Thought. Aurora, CO: Davies Group, 2002.

tionalism, reducing them to become only copies of the machine-like people who preceded them—and, unfortunately, may be teaching them?

Jesus' words, "Unless you become like little children, you cannot enter the reign of God," speak volumes in our present situation. To become childlike, not childish, should be the goal of all education. It is also the goal and condition of prayer. Stemming from the Latin word "educare," meaning to draw out or to lead out, education should be a drawing forth of the imagination of the individual as well as imposing past ideas and present facts on the memory and mind.

In the child is the possibility of playfulness flowing from an energized imagination. This yields enjoyment in life. In a sense, this may be what is meant religiously by justification by faith. In the child, "educated" to be an adult, the essence of life is work which yields production and consumption. Adult life becomes justification by works. In this adult world, play is produced for distraction. Its natural child-quality of spontaneity is suppressed. The work-oriented adult is even made to feel guilty about too much or too creative play. According to Alves, "Our society, dominated as it is by productivity, is the grave of the child and therefore the end of play, since the expansion of things produced and consumed depends on the repression of man's drive toward enjoyment.... Children's play ends with the universal resurrection of the dead. Adults' play ends with universal burial. Whereas the resurrection is the paradigm of the world of children, the world of adults creates the cross.... In play, each day begins with grace, not law.... The truth of play will become history when impotence becomes power and when that which is now power becomes impotence."[25] In Alves' mind, resurrection is not merely a doctrine to be affirmed by the intellect. It is also a symbol to be received by the imagination in order to create, here and now, life in abundance.

Obviously what Alves is talking about in education is revolution, turning things upside down. I am suggesting nothing less than a revolution in regard to teaching and celebrating Christian faith and the ritual celebrations of faith. The culture, which has tried to nourish and sustain itself primarily on the dark diet of rationalism from the Enlightenment in the eighteenth century and the Catholic neo-Thomist revival in the nineteenth century, has withered in the sunshine of real life. People cannot take the twentieth century experience very seriously and still find their faith grounded in the proof-texts of theology manuals or the questions and answers of a catechism. These products of the sell-out to reason must be supplemented by works that give imagination its due. Faith begins, according to Cardinal Newman, not in the notion or concept, but in the image or symbol. He wrote: "For an assent to be rationally adequate it must first be credible to the imagination."[26] To return imagination to the forefront of Christian teaching and celebrating must not be seen as a reduction of theology, liturgy, and religion to art. It is rather to see that, as well as scientific and inferential disciplines, these are also aesthetic ones. Revelation's primary expressive form is aesthetic. In fact, it is always through forms of imagination—myth, parable, image, symbol, ritual—that God's claim upon us is expressed in Scripture. And it is the imaginative, not just the rational, response in persons that can interpret and distinguish such forms.

In the renewal of the Catholic Church which was officially precipitated by Vatican II, many felt their faith shaken to the roots. Newman's words offer a suggestion about why this may have happened. "A believer who was unable to understand the creative role of the imagination in perception (but was unconsciously influenced by it) would regard a reform of his belief as effecting a destruction of his perception of the world. His world would have appeared to have disappeared."[27] Isn't that precisely what has happened to many Catholics since the Council? Imagination does not, if used in a healthy way, undermine faith; rather, it creates the conditions of possibility for a human act of belief.

One can readily discern the presence of the creative imagination in the teacher or preacher of faith. The learner/listener feels the imagination engaged in a search for truth that transcends objective observation. Truth here is communicated through personality, person to person, heart to heart. Any one of us instantly senses the difference between what Gerard Manley Hopkins terms "an equation in theology, and dull algebra of the schoolmen, or knowledge that leaves ... minds swinging, poised but on the quiver ... the ecstasy of interest."[28]

The difference lies in the understanding of, the employment of, and the engaging of the human imaginative system. This is the soul in us which is both before and after all other faculties, embracing the whole of existence and seeking intimacy with the whole through presence.

Imagination then, in this sense, is not a faculty but the crossroads, the linking point of all the faculties. It is the intuition with which one participates in experience. It is the intuition through which one drinks deeply of life. It is the seeing into reality which supersedes looking at reality. It gets behind appearance. It discloses the substance of things to be hoped for.

Hopkins made a useful distinction in this regard. He said that we *look at* a landscape but we *see* the inscape, i.e., intuit the inner meaning and reality of Being expressed externally through the landscape.[29] "To see is to engage the inscape, the convergence that lies behind the phenomena."[30] Without such seeing we remain outsiders to the human dimension of life. We do not participate with warmth and passion but observe with detachment. For, according to Owen Barfield, "final participation" in reality is an act of the imagination, getting beyond merely thinking about the thinker. He contends that the imagination is the person's capacity to make the material an image of the spiritual.[31] And it is this capacity which characterizes an artist.

This "final participation" may be another way of describing the summary of the mission of Jesus: "I have come so that you might have life more abundantly."

Life is what imagination is all about, nothing less. Oh yes, imagination can get us into trouble. It can separate us from reality just as surely as can pure and narrow rationalism. All images are not accurate. Some cluster in our structured imaginations in bizarre, distorting, and destructive patterns. Such imagination gone awry is called pure fantasy; it is an escape from the real. It

fails to live in the world of facts, truth and reality. Reason rightly restrains imagination from destructive fantasy. Imagination is
creative; fantasy is not.

However, true imagination and healthy imaging builds on
facts, truth and reality. Reality in a sense dissolves, diffuses and
is recreated through imagining as cognition. And, in so doing,
imagination "moves forward by a judicious selection and re-
shaping of the representations of the experience that make up
our meaning."[32]

Institutions have always feared the imagination. Imaginations can unleash people into disorder, and institutions place a
high priority on good order, enforced by reasonable laws which
limit. That is the nature of institutions, whether of state or
Church. They provide for the common good by legislating, by
commanding and forbidding acts, based upon the meaning and
purpose and goals of the institution. Law can stifle imagination
and creativity. But not necessarily. Good law accepts exceptions.

Such human law, of course, as St. Thomas Aquinas said, is
always *ut in pluribus*, i.e., for the most part. It can never cover all
cases. Allowances need to be made for exceptions to the law. In
asking "Whether He Who Is Under the Law May Act Beside the
Letter of the Law" the Angelic Doctor holds:

> Since then the lawgiver cannot have in view every sin-
> gle case, he shapes the law according to what happens
> most frequently, by directing his attention to the com-
> mon good. Wherefore if a case arises wherein the obser-
> vance of that law would be hurtful to the general
> welfare it should not be observed.[33]

With this understanding of law and its limits, it need not
hinder the imagination. It can support the virtue of epikeia by
which a person, in certain actions, may behave in a way opposed
to the letter of the law in order to achieve the purpose of the
law. In such case, "we should take account of the motive of the
lawgiver, rather than of his very words."[34] Unfortunately this

traditional moral principle itself has usually been taught in Catholic circles by way of exception.

The Church is not now nor can it ever be totally at home with the imagination. Creativity is always a threat to the institutional control and order. Yet the creative imagination is the only way to a continuing, vibrant life within the institutional Church. The tension between rational control and imaginative creativity is inevitable and healthy although sometimes at least temporarily hurtful.

In Christian history, many movements of the imagination were movements of mysticism. The fourteenth century mystics developed and became popular at the same time as the system of rational thought called Scholasticism and ecclesiastical life declined. Mysticism seems to have been the interior spiritual reaction which retained vitality in an otherwise largely externally oriented and decaying Church structure. Persons such as St. Catherine of Siena, St. Bridget of Sweden, Julian of Norwich, Blessed Giovanni Valle, Meister Eckhart, Blessed Henry Suso, John Tauler, and Blessed John Ruysbroeck made significant contributions to this spiritual renewal. Their thought and experience influenced such groups as The Friends of God and the Beguines. And it was born of the imagination in prayer.

Their new mysticism was less philosophical and more volitional, aimed at moving the will or the heart. Although imagination was not a common word to their writings, the shift from an emphasis on the intellect to an emphasis on the will is surely related to today's new piety which Urban T. Holmes says involves the retrieval of the imagination. "The fundamental issue in ministry today," he says, "is the recovery of a sense of enchantment and the ability to be enchanting."[35] Like the mystics who, while faithful to Catholic tradition, were a reaction to a decadent Scholasticism, we, too, are trying to recover from an overdependence on the purely rational, "the clear and distinct idea" of Descartes. "The power of ambiguity, a sensibility to life, and the relation between beauty and goodness came to be lost to the God at the end of a syllogism."[36]

Imagination involved risks for the fourteenth century mys-

tics and reformers just as it does for us today. There is no guarantee in the life of the imagination. Like life itself, of which it is
the soul, imagination is a risky business. As Whitehead has said,
"Imagination . . . is a dangerous gift, which has started many a
conflagration."[37] In Germany, in the fourteenth century, the
Flagellants and the Brethren of the Free Spirit fell into heresy,
as did the Fraticelli in Italy. Twenty-six sentences from Meister
Eckhart's writings were condemned posthumously by Pope
John XXII, fifteen as heretical and eleven as rash and close to
heresy.

Part of the institution's problem with these mystics was
that their language was aesthetic and contained deep feeling. As
such it lacked the precision and exactitude of the technical language of Scholasticism. Therefore it may well have been not
fully comprehended by authority and was possibly, in good conscience, misinterpreted.

Much of this intuitive, volitional and feeling approach to
faith surfaced again in the late nineteenth century in the Roman
Catholic Church as theologians began to incorporate the find-
ings and the methods of history and the physical sciences into
their own investigations. Among these theologians were Alfred
Loisy, George Tyrell, Maurice Blondel and Baron Friedrich von
Hügel. These men were condemned in 1907 by Pius X, not by
name but under the label of "Modernism," "the synthesis of all
heresies."[38] And the near witch-hunt which ensued showed
both the ecclesiastical institution's fears of this approach and the
inadequacies of the new thought.

Although each one of these thinkers differed from the others considerably in both theological method and content, they
shared two things in common: their reaction against the over-
objectified and rationalistic character of the institutionally-
supported neo-Scholasticism and their concern to show the
authenticity of subjective religious experience. This was the beginning of the thrust toward what Bernard Lonergan would later call "The Return to the Subject."

Pius X summarized the Modernists' errors under three
headings: *immanentism* (religion is not dogma but an inner expe-

rience of transcendence by an individual), *agnosticism* (Scripture and dogma must be interpreted subjectively and religious truth is a subjective experience), and *evolutionism* (the Church is a result of an historical process and must continue to evolve in order to adapt itself to changing times).

But times do change in the life of the Church. The Second Vatican Council opened doors closed during the Modernist controversy. To those of us who live in the twilight years of that Council, these condemned positions, or at least their basic orientations, seem like at least partial truths to be assumed rather than errors to be refuted. Indeed, when Pope John XXIII delivered the opening address at the Council in October 1962, he used words which, fifty years earlier, would have classified him as a Modernist. He boldly affirmed:

In the present order of things, Divine Providence is leading us to a new order of human relations which, by men's own efforts and even beyond their expectations, are directed toward the fulfillment of God's superior and inscrutable designs. And everything, even human differences, leads to the greater good of the Church. The salient point of this Council is not, therefore, a discussion of one article or another of the fundamental doctrine of the Church.... For this a Council was not necessary. But ... the Christian, Catholic and apostolic spirit of the whole world expects a step forward toward a doctrinal penetration and a formation of consciences in faithful and perfect conformity to the authentic doctrine which, however, should be studied and expounded through the methods of research and through the literary forms of modern thought. The substance of the ancient doctrine of the deposit of the faith is one thing, and the way it is presented is another. And it is the latter which must be taken into great account with patience if necessary, everything being measured in the forms and proportions of a magisterium which is predominantly pastoral in character.[39]

This proximate-to-Modernist address is a far cry from the repressive condemnations by Pope Pius X in 1907. But the times had changed. The wheat and the chaff of the Modernists' positions had been sifted and the Church could, with clarity and confidence, begin to dialogue with the "new theology." This was a way of reflecting on revelation which took into account subjective religious experience. Yet many did fear Pope John's aggiornamento with its "open the window" agenda. A middle-aged pastor, a man by all accounts loyal to tradition, assured me shortly after my ordination in 1964: Pope John XXIII is the worst thing that has ever happened to the Church. He predicted dire consequences for the institution, many of which have been realized. But what neither the traditionalist pastor nor this young liberal Turk could foresee were the new sources of life surfacing even as some structures declined and failed to support life for many believers.

Just as the revival of mysticism in the fourteenth century helped to restore vigor and heart to ecclesiastical life, if not to Church structures, so today there has been a reawakening of an awareness of the Spirit in our lives as well as the power of the imagination for setting the Spirit free within us. Indeed, Pope John XXIII attributed his idea of calling an ecumenical council to a sudden and unexpected inspiration of the Spirit which was "like a flash of heavenly light, shedding sweetness in eyes and hearts."[40]

For those who still fear the inspirations of the imagination in religion as well as for those who take the risk to imagine the "what if," three criteria are available by which imagination can be disciplined by reason without losing its unique autonomy as the point at which all the faculties converge. First, the imagination's images must be appropriate to the reality represented imaginally. Second, there must be a pattern of consistent thought in the imagination's products. And, third, we must not confuse the image with the reality, the representation with the referent.

Urban T. Holmes suggests four "D's" to analyze the act of imagination and prevent it from leading to the demonic rather than the divine: description, discovery, development, and discipline. First, *description*. All the filters of consciousness need to be open to experience to let a full image of that experience form in our structured imaginations. Then reality is present in our consciousness through true images and their clustered relationships. Second, *discovery*. We discover images implicit within the description which are not our own pre-conceived constructs. We see holes in our world and hear the spaces between the sounds. Third, *development*. The images begin to be related, not to test for validity, but freely and playfully interrelating in patterns that shed new light, and new insight, into our experience. Fourth, *discipline*. This is where we analyze the product of our imagination in order to test its truth and validity and to clarify it for insertion into life and tradition. This final step away from pure intuition toward intelligence is the guardrail that keeps the imagination from plummeting headlong into the chasm of pure and destructive fantasy. As Holmes concludes, "The movement from imagination to thinking is always restrictive and limiting, as necessary as it must be. Only when we acknowledge the loss in that movement can we appreciate fully the power of the act of imagination."[41]

Although both reason and human institutions rightly try to curb imagination from the chasm of chaos and unreality, nevertheless the person who opens the windows of his soul to reality, the person who images, must personally move out of the order of our systems of thought and action to truly perceive the new. Revolutions are born because someone got far enough out of the center of things to see it all differently. And that reality, as Coleridge said so well, dissolves and diffuses and becomes recreated.

The place of imaging, according to Holmes, is at the edge of the abyss, where all of the impositions and limitations of reason and law are held in abeyance for a time. In the center of an organized society, much is taken for granted. There we live at the limited dimensional levels of feeling, common sense, and thinking, but all this works against that fuller way of knowing and living which is the imaginative mode, a way of cognition which both precedes and follows knowledge through discursive reason. In this mode, one becomes unchained for a time from the order of reason and law and risks experiencing on the edge of existence a fuller insight into life and love.

This is a great risk, of course. Moving from the center to the edge of our ordered existence creates the possibility of a point of no return to the center. Out there, near the precipice, we may fall headlong into nothingness, into a reality of total loss and chaos. We may never return to the center, enriched by passing over to another different and perhaps dangerous position or viewpoint.

For those Christians who fear this kind of "anti-structure," as Victor Turner terms it,[42] let them take heart from the example of Jesus whose whole life was a passing over, a paschal mystery. He often was alone to converse with God in the desert, the anti-structure. It was in the abyss of this desert experience after his baptism that he was tempted—and renewed. He was given a deeper insight into himself and his mission. It was in those many moments alone in quiet, out-of-the-way places that he came to terms with the cost of his mission. And it was at night, in a secluded garden, when he experienced the beginning of the abandonment of his personal, chosen support structure, that he accepted the lead toward the chaos of the cross: "Not my will, but thine be done." Crucified there on the edge of the abyss, stretched between heaven and earth, Jesus passed over to the center in the resurrection—but only because he had risked a pilgrimage into the wilderness.

I suggest it was Jesus' active imagination that, from a human point of view, opened him to the graces given in the anti-structure. There he saw in the dark the mystery beyond sight, the power and presence of God. The risk of chaos, the beckoning abyss was, for Jesus, the pre-condition of life in abundance. As one author has suggested:

> Is it not possible that for us this category "imagination" may not reveal the originality and mystery of Christ? . . . Imagination is a form of liberty. It is born in confrontation with reality and established order; it emerges from non-conformity in the face of completed and established situations; it is the capacity to see human beings as greater and richer than the cultural and concrete environment that surrounds them; it is having

the courage to think and say something new and to take hitherto untreaded paths that are full of meaning for human beings. We can say that imagination, understood in this manner, was one of the fundamental qualities of Jesus. Perhaps in the whole of human history there has not been a single person who had a richer imagination than Jesus.[43]

Let those who fear the loss of control implied in imagination's pilgrimage to the mystery at life's core be encouraged by these recollections of Jesus' own life's journey. Imagination is the fullest way to know God. And the place to imagine best is in the anti-structure. The anti-structure "confronts us with what is at the same time most frightening and potentially creative: the stuff of chaos. No one contemplates the possibility of a pilgrimage without the fear that they will never come back. Perhaps, however, the most deadly diabol is the rationalization we use for never going: the disapproval of the structures to which we have sold our soul."[44]

Imagination is the locus of holiness happening in the human. It leads us to the languages of liturgy. It is where Jesus' promise can most completely come true for us: "I have come that you may have life more abundantly."

Notes

1. Gilbert Durand, *Les Structures anthropologique de l'imaginaire. Introduction à l'archétypologie général* (Paris: Bordas 1969); *L'Imagination symbolique* (Paris: P.U.F., 1968).

2. Durand, *L'Imagination symbolique*, pp. 111–112, quoted from George S. Worgul, Jr., *From Magic to Metaphor* (New York: Paulist Press, 1980), p. 80.

3. Søren Kierkegaard, *Journals*, p. 243, and *Concluding Unscientific Postscript* (Princeton: Princeton University Press, 1941), p. 311.

4. Julian Hartt, *Theological Method and Imagination* (New York: Seabury Press, 1977), pp. 250 and 252.

5. William Lynch, *Images of Hope* (Baltimore: Helicon Press, 1965), p. 243.

6. *Ibid.*

7. *Ibid.*, p. 256.

8. Matthias Neuman, O.S.B., "The Role of Imagination in Fundamental Theology," unpublished essay, p. 14.

9. Robert D. Young, *Religious Imagination* (Philadelphia: Westminster Press, 1979), p. 35.

10. Neuman, *op. cit.*, p. 18.

11. *The Jerusalem Bible* (Garden City, N.Y.: Doubleday, 1966).

12. Theodore W. Jennings, Jr., *Introduction to Theology* (Philadelphia: Fortress Press, 1976), pp. 17–18.

13. John Shea, *Stories of Faith* (Chicago: Thomas More Press, 1980), p. 95.

14. Ernst Cassirer, *An Essay on Man* (New Haven: Yale University Press, 1955), p. 26.

15. Susanne Langer, *Philosophy in a New Key* (N.Y.: Mentor, 1962), p. 46.

16. Young, *op. cit.*, p. 25.

17. *Ibid.*, p. 27.

18. Owen Barfield, *Saving the Appearances: A Study in Idolatry* (N.Y.: Harcourt, Brace and World, 1965), p. 89.

19. Jennings, *op. cit.*, p. 13.

20. *The Washington Post*, March 22, 1979, Section A, p. 20.

21. *Ibid.*

22. *Ibid.*

23. Michael R. Real, *Mass-Mediated Culture* (Englewood Cliffs, N.J.: Prentice-Hall, 1977), Chapter 3, "Sports," pp. 90–117.

24. Ruben Alves, *Tomorrow's Child: Imagination, Creativity and the Rebirth of Culture* (N.Y.: Harper and Row, 1972), p. 72.

25. *Ibid.*, pp. 89, 91, 98, and 100.

26. John Coulson, "Belief and Imagination," *Downside Review*, Vol. 90, No. 298, January 1972, p. 14.

27. *Ibid.*, p. 11.

28. *Ibid.*, p. 6.

29. Cited in Urban T. Holmes, *Ministry and Imagination* (N.Y.: Seabury Press, 1976), p. 95.

30. *Ibid.*, p. 96.

31. Barfield, *op. cit.*, p. 137.

32. Holmes, *op cit.*, p. 102.

33. St. Thomas Aquinas, *Summa Theologica* I–II, Q. 96, Art 6.

34. *Ibid.*

35. Holmes, *op. cit.*, p. 8.

36. *Ibid.*, p. 2.

37. Quoted in *ibid.*, p. 103, from Alfred North Whitehead, *The Arms of Education*, p. 141.

38. Thomas P. Neill and Raymond H. Schmandt, *History of the Catholic Church* (Milwaukee: Bruce, 1957), p. 562.

39. *Council Daybook: Vatican II* (Washington, D.C.: National Catholic Welfare Conference, 1965), pp. 26–27.

40. *Ibid.*, p. 26.

41. Holmes, *op. cit.*, p. 109.

42. Victor Turner, *The Forest of Symbols: Aspects of Noembu Ritual* (Ithaca: Cornell University Press, 1967), pp. 93–101.

43. Leonard Boff, *Jesus Christ Liberator* (N.Y.: Orbis Books, 1978), pp. 90–91.

44. Holmes, *op. cit.*, p. 135.

Chapter III
The Languages of the Imagination

If it is true that imagination is the intersection where all the faculties function synthetically rather than analytically to disclose to us more than meets the eye and to give us ways of seeing in the dark, if it is true that faith is first and most fully encountered in the human imaginative system where our spirits are lured and grasped by God's Spirit, and if it is true that liturgy as faith-celebration is meant to address this imaginative system, then it is imperative that we who are Christian explore and understand various forms of imagination used in liturgy. These expressive forms could be called "languages of the imagination" because they communicate to the imagination as a knowing power. Parenthetically, doesn't it seem somewhat strange that those of us who profess faith in a God we cannot see yet and whose mission is to make the unseen God known and experienced by others are rather unacquainted with and somewhat ill-equipped to use those forms of expression which are the most effective ways to communicate that message and presence that can transform persons?

We who lead and minister in rituals are more comfortable with the languages of *explanation* than those of *exploration*. Our style is didactic. Perhaps that is the result of catechetical and theological training which was communicated through lecture methods, the content of which was highly rational and intellectual. We simply do unto others as we were done unto. We have been so accustomed to controlling religious truth with our reason and its language of questions and answers that we fear the ambiguity of the truth of mystery which is shared through less precise yet more revealing modes of communication, namely, modes of the imagination.

Again and again, in speaking with groups of priests, I am made aware of how well we all learned our seminary lessons. Precision and clarity have become our idol structures. Not only is this true for the purity of doctrine and the preservation of dogma where clarity must indeed reign, but it too often rules our preaching, our presiding, our praying, our way of dealing with people and, perhaps most tragically, our own way-of-being-in-the-world. With reason as king, rather than as *one* of life's guides, life itself is thwarted and constrained in its innate drive toward transcendence, toward life more abundantly. As Urban Holmes observes: "Both the dogmatist and the agnostic suffer from the same problem of placing their reason above that which is ultimately numinous. Wholeness is found in transcending these opposites to a new unity and mystery."[1]

Watch a person preach sometime and ask yourself if this person's very *being* proclaims the mystery and wonder of God or whether the language of the lips and perhaps the whole body symbolizes control and limitation in life. The latter is the spirit of reason working alone as a king. The former is the effect of a free and energized imagination. The mystery may be there but, for it to be communicated, we must be able to see it and hear it. If you are presiding at worship, watch the congregation's attention be seized when you tell a story and drift when you slip into dogmatic statements and tried and true explanations. What does that tell you?

We can save ourselves, our priesthood, and our people from such rational oppression by learning to understand and use, in addition to reason's tools and human sense, those symbolic forms of expression which address and engage the human imaginative system. We need to understand truth as Paul Ricoeur does when he says that in human knowing, the initial stage of symbol or image gives rise to the second stage, thought and analytical reflection. Then thought is informed by and returns to symbol as the fullest way of knowing meaning in the third stage of cognition. This return to symbol as cognition, which Ricoeur terms "transcendental deduction of symbols," is a kind of second naiveté. It has become a breakthrough in hermeneutics from the enchained experience of linguistic analysis and scientific positivism which were locked in the second stage of knowing, the rational stage. But there is much more to knowing reality than that kind of analytical knowing. We are radically symbol-making beings. An understanding "within the symbols," Ricoeur claims, "is necessary for the purpose of breaking with explicative and reductive thinking.... To understand ... is to display the multiple and inexhaustible intentions of each symbol...."[2] Let's explore the symbolic forms of knowing which are used in expressing religious faith.

There are five modes of expression for the religious imagination according to Theodore W. Jennings, Jr.: vision, symbol, myth, ritual, and apocalyptic.[3] Each of these uses images to communicate and disclose truth, a truth not contrary to but rather complementary to reason. This is truth which is inconceivable but not self-contradictory.

Vision is a private experience, coming from outside the person and revealing some dimensions of ultimate reality. It is a constellation or a congealing of images, words or dramas in the imagination which emerge either in dreams, trances, or ecstatic experiences. These patterns are judged to have revelatory significance by the one who has the experience. Some become accepted as disclosive of truth by a community to which they are communicated. Witness the many visions recorded in the sacred writings of the Judaeo-Christian tradition.

Symbol "is a fundamentally non-verbal representation of the conjunction of the sacred and the profane."[4] It is a kind of sign. St. Augustine called a sign "a thing which, besides the species it imposes on the senses, leads to a knowledge of something other than itself."[5] It is a present reality that points beyond itself to make known the other reality which is not immediately present and, in the very pointing, the "other" becomes present in the symbol.

Signs both reveal and conceal. One must pass through the

sign to arrive at the signified. Cyprian Vagaggini makes this point in lucid fashion: The sign is like a veil, though

> transparent; for the eyes that do not know how to pene- trate the veil, the sign is a screen. To penetrate the veil means to grasp the sign precisely in its value as signify- ing the thing. Hence for one who does not grasp the value the sign acts as a screen; for one who does grasp it, on the other hand, the sign acts as a bridge and infor- mant.[6]

Signs are called *real* if they arise from nature like smoke being a sign of fire. They are *conventional* if they result from a decision based on reason such as road signs.

Two kinds of signs interest us here: images and symbols.

Images reveal a reality other than themselves by being rec- ognizable likenesses of the other reality. Examples are pictures, statues, and models of buildings. To be successful, they must ac- curately represent that to which they point.

A symbol is a class of sign which is like the image in that it points to a reality it symbolizes. But symbols are richer and more intense signs because they make the other reality present without being identical to it.

To use an example: a photograph of a beautiful young woman would be an image of her to everyone. It would be an accurate likeness of her exterior appearance in some particular mood and context. To her fiancé, miles away on an extended business trip, the image becomes a symbol. By gazing at her like- ness lovingly, she becomes present to him in that sign without being the same as the sign. The photo has become a symbol— and he kisses it. It is a real presence through symbol, similar to eucharistic presence.

Symbols are synthetic agents of unity and convergence. In a symbol two things are present: the thing itself and that to which it points and makes present. Derived from a Greek word, *sum- ballo, sum-ballein*, which means literally "thrown together," a symbol brings together things not normally connected but usu-

ally separate into a unity that supersedes what either reality
alone is or means. What was many becomes one in a symbol.
What was separate is united in the imagination.

The most common and immediate symbol is our own body.
The body is our touch point with the rest of reality but it is not
all we are. "Your body does not exhaust your meaning," suggests George Worgul. "In short, your body is a symbol of all you
are. Your body points to you and makes you present, without
being identical to you. Your body, as a symbol, is an agent for
the unity of you as a person. In and through your body, the disparate elements of your unique reality converge to form a
whole."[7]

In religious terms, the symbol unites the sacred and the secular. Through matter, spirit is made present without being
identical to matter.

The third mode of religious imagination is *myth* or story.
While symbol is primarily non-verbal, myth is fundamentally
verbal. Myths are the linking together of symbols in the mode of
narration. The narrative of a myth tells a story which communicates core meaning about life itself. The central myth of Christianity is the story of Jesus' death and resurrection. It grounds
Christian existence by exposing its origins and exploring its destiny. All of the other narratives of Jesus in Scripture take their
meaning in relation to the primary myth of the paschal mystery.

To refer to Jesus' story as myth does not imply it is untrue.
As myth, however, the true historical experience, where retold,
in production or print, discloses more truth than a mere historical account. Myth in this context is not contrary to scientific
history. It is an interpretation of historical events which gives
those events their meaning for mankind. And, as such, it serves
as a guide to Christian human attitudes and behavior. Christians
live in the light of the Jesus myth. The myth deciphers reality
for those who live in that light. In one sense, to live in Christ
Jesus means to have as a primary image cluster the paschal mystery, the darkness made light, ascending and enclosed conjoined,
to use Gilbert Durand's terms. A Christian lives out of this
myth or root metaphor. All is seen in light of it. It holds the believer's life together.

Ritual is the fourth and most fundamental mode of religious imagination. It is a public dramatic action. By nature, it is social. It is "a group enactment of and participation in the presence of the sacred."[8] This is done through the linking of symbols and myths into a rhythmed, integral whole. All that was said about those two modes of religious imagination converges in ritual. Ritual is a constellation of symbols and myths that point to meaning beyond themselves and make that meaning present. This is a good description of the real presence in the Eucharist.

Ritual is related to culture both as cause to effect and as effect to cause. Ritual is effected, created, discovered by a culture in order to review and renew the group's values and meaning. In ritual we act out the meaning and values which are contained verbally in myth and non-verbally in symbol.

At the heart of every culture is what Worgul calls a "root metaphor" or what others call the central myth. The root metaphor arises from a primordial experience of reality. An example would be the experience of the struggle for and achievement of independence celebrated ritually every July 4. This "holy day" or holiday for our nation recalls and represents in ritual form the primordial, originating event which initially called us into being as an independent political entity. All of the parades, bands, fireworks and picnics not only recall that eighteenth century event. All this ritual also revives in the present the meaning and the feeling of that liberating event. Independence, as we know only too well, is not achieved once for all but is a continuing struggle, a permanent task. Ritual can enflesh the vision and energize renewed commitment to that liberation.

For Christians the root metaphor is the paschal mystery, the death and resurrection of Jesus. By our sacramental rituals which re-present that primordial, originating event of our community, that event becomes truly present again in symbol for the purpose of transforming our experience so that we might live in the likeness of the Man for Others. These repetitive patterns of behavior called rituals must, of course, be understood and shared in by the participants if they are to be living and powerful. Without intelligent and felt participation, they can become hollow, like meaningless recitations of recipes.

It is in ritual, then, that the social entity—family, club, state, Church—finds its keenest and most fundamental expression. Through these dramatic representations of their vision and values, they survive. Without vital ritual, cultures lack a center that will hold and disintegration is in process.

According to the cultural anthropologist, Victor Turner, the root metaphor celebrated in ritual has five effects upon any social group.[9]

First, it gives distinctive identity to the culture. It roots it as this rather than that self-understanding and self-expression.

Second, root metaphors set a culture's interpretive perimeters. All of life takes its meaning from this myth. It becomes the clue and the model for thinking, speaking, and acting for the group and its individual faithful members.

Third, the root metaphor enacted ritually gives a basis for corporate coherence and group binding. Such ritual brings the many into one by uniting them with their own charter event, thus reinforcing its meaning and value for all. It is experienced community that both triggers and is triggered by ritual activity.

Fourth, a social corrective is activated for a group through representing the root metaphor ritually. Communities and individuals need to be brought face to face with their raison d'être and be challenged to conform to its meaning and values in the present. The group untrue to itself will recognize this in ritual, whether that be a family meal when there is impending divorce or a parish Eucharist when there is division over policies and personalities.

Fifth, the effect of all this in the social group is to realize the existence of the group by evoking a presence which grounds that group. And all of this takes place, the connecting with the past in the present for the future, through expressive forms which allow us to see into the dark of the past and of the future.

Rituals bring groups and cultures into being and sustain them in existence. And yet these rituals were also created and discovered by the group. They are appropriate symbol structures which carry the largely incommunicable meaning of human existence. Rituals then are traditional. They are passed down. They are also dynamic. They evolve. Balancing the old and the new is the task of any community which attempts to renew and restore rituals that have become cluttered. Cluttered rituals tend to conceal what they are meant to reveal. For these very reasons, the community called Church began to renew its ritual life at Vatican II.

In one sense, every ritual action must be different since every community and every time is different. Yet, unless the fundamental ritual is recognizable as a representation of the charter event for all such communities in communion with one another through faith or, trust, in their root metaphor, ritual will fail. It will be faddish. Ritual must not become simply a period piece, an expression only of meanings, values and feelings of the day. Ritual must express the dignity, the mobility and the beauty of a meaning which is both present in all space and time yet transcends all.

Ritual, as both created by and creating a community, addresses the human imaginative system not simply to communicate information. Rather ritual activity energizes communion. Neither does ritual function to conceal and obfuscate the truth. It discloses, through dramatic action, the presence of Mystery in human existence. It leads to communal participation in the mystery of truth that is celebrated. It brings many into one, personally and experientially. It reconciles the opposing forces and experiences which move us toward disintegration and destruction whether as individuals or communities. For a nation, rituals overcome the dual opposition of liberty and law. For Christian religious communities, the polarities of life and death are united to the representation of the myth of the symbolic event of Jesus' dying in order to be raised to life.

The fifth and final form of religious imagination according to Jennings is called *apocalyptic*. It is verbal like myth, but cast in the form of a vision of an absolute future. It is usually anonymous or pseudonymous and generally more elaborate than vision. It is not of great importance for our concerns here since liturgy primarily involves these three forms of imagination: symbol, myth, and ritual.

These five modes of the religious imagination, in Jennings' view, function in four ways for individuals and communities:

representation, orientation, communication, and transformation.

First, representation. Access to the spiritual, which is present but invisible like the air, must be mediated by the material through re-presentation. In the Eucharist, for example, the relation of our existence to the sacred is presented through a kind of transfiguration, in which the ordinary—bread and wine—becomes luminous with the extraordinary. It is personal Presence as food.

Second, orientation. All of reality becomes oriented to the myth celebrated in ritual. Birth and death, war and peace, love and hate—all take their meaning and value cue from these forms of imagination.

Third, communication. The ritual forms and sustains community by communicating in symbol and myth the group's fundamental meaning and goals.

Fourth, transformation. These forms of imagination serve to transform the ways participants see themselves and, correspondingly, the ways in which they enter into relationships with others. This leads toward the goal of religious experience which is conversion. "It is clear that the mythos not only represents existence but places upon that existence a claim to interpret it in such a way as to alter everything."[10] For an example of such conversion, recall the incident related in a previous chapter in which a son-in-law found himself represented in the Prodigal Son story. He oriented himself in a new way toward his mother-in-law because the very meaning of his life as communicated in that story called for reconciliation in that relationship.

In summary then, to quote Jennings, "the religious imagination through the mythos serves to express and make effective the presence of the sacred in such a way as to represent, orient, communicate, and transform existence in the world."[11]

Summary

The languages of imagination which disclose and communicate religious truth and experience in liturgy are image, symbol, myth and ritual. Through these forms of expression the entirely inexhaustible and largely incommunicable Mystery of Christ is celebrated by the Church. Until those who exercise liturgical ministries know and can use the appropriate languages of Mystery and until the human imagination of our worshipers is addressed, engaged and energized in liturgy, our liturgical renewal and reform will remain something of a dead letter on the pages of sacramentaries, lectionaries and rituals. The *texts* of the rites will have been reformed but the communities' worship *life* will not have been renewed. Such renewal involves a new mindset for the ways of worship. It means having the mind of Christ whose whole life and death were symbols of more than meets the eye. He energized people's imaginations to see and hear in their lives, with eyes and ears attuned to a particular kind of perception, the kingdom of God which is in but not of this world.

Having such a renewed mind will lead liturgical ministers to the conclusion that liturgy, as an imaginative expression, is an art form. That realization is revolutionary—and as old as the hills.

Notes

1. Holmes, *op. cit.*, p. 151.
2. Paul Ricoeur, *The Symbolism of Evil* (Boston: Beacon Press, 1967), p. 353.
3. Theodore W. Jennings, Jr., *Introduction to Theology* (Philadelphia: Fortress Press, 1976), pp. 49–54.
4. *Ibid.*, p. 50.
5. Worgul, *op. cit.*, p. 39.
6. *Ibid.*, p. 40.
7. *Ibid.*, p. 42.
8. Jennings, *op. cit.*, p. 52.
9. Cited in Worgul, *op. cit.*, pp. 94–105.
10. Jennings, *op. cit.*, pp. 56–57.
11. *Ibid.*, p. 57.

Chapter IV
If Liturgy Is Art, Then What Is Art?

I
Liturgy: An Aesthetic Experience

The scene: a priest of middle age is simulating a eucharistic liturgy for a university drama professor in order to improve his celebrating style. The priest is at an "altar," facing the professor. He begins to recite the preface of the Eucharistic Prayer, only to discover that he is not on the right page of the Sacramentary. He begins the preface dialogue, "The Lord be with you," etc., while leafing through the book, eyes searching the pages for the proper place.

The drama professor interrupted: "Wait a minute, Father. What are you doing?"

"Well, I'm reading what's prescribed here in the book— 'The Lord be with you' . . . 'Lift up your hearts,' " replied the priest.

"But don't you realize," the dramatist said, "this is a dialogue? You should be looking at the people."

So the priest looked straight ahead and said with neither facial expression nor verbal inflection, "The Lord be with you," etc.

"Wait a minute, Father. What are you doing?" repeated the artist.

Now the priest became annoyed. With frustration evident in his voice, he replied, "I'm looking at the people just the way you told me to."

"But doesn't this mean anything to you? Could you put some feeling into your face and sounds?"

"Look," said the priest with restrained anger, "I'm not going to be an actor."

The dramatist shot back, "Well, Father, if you don't want to be an actor, take off the costume."

This incident rather vividly opens the whole can of worms regarding liturgy as a form of art. Ritual is, indeed, a species of dramatic activity. It is not "Hamlet" or "On Golden Pond," but the organization of ritual's energies is actually meant to be much more like those staged events than a static, communal reading experience.

The priest feared being a ham, putting on a show. He distrusted the advice to make the liturgy more subjective, more a projection of his personal feelings and interpretations. This is because he was taught to see liturgy as an objective text, governed by legal norms. It was without "personality." His priestly task: keep the rules and read the recipe. The objective nature of the universal ritual was said to bear its own meaning, its own truth. Nothing personal need be added.

Well, that word "added" is the key to the problem that surfaced between the priest and the dramatist. And it is the key to the experiential problems we face in parish liturgies today. We tend to see the arts as something "added" to the ritual as luxuries, as extras. They are nice but you can get along without them.

Really?

We think we can do without the arts because we conceive of liturgy as primarily textual. It is words, accompanied by some gestures. But this is not what ritual is. It is the reverse. Liturgy is, first of all, actions, not words. The action is specified by the words. And art is not some kind of decoration layered upon ritual action and ritual word. Art is the very core of the expressive forms that comprise liturgy.

Liturgy must no longer be conceived and celebrated as an experience which *uses* the arts, like frosting on a cake. Liturgy *is* an aesthetic expression and experience. Liturgy *is* art. However, a radical transformation of consciousness must take place before liturgical scholars and practitioners can approach the worship experience as an aesthetic experience. This conversion toward the aesthetic could be borne out by a reconsideration of Vatican II's description of liturgy as an expression and an experience of the Mystery of Christ and the nature of the Church from the *Constitution on the Sacred Liturgy*, n. 2.

Mass is meant to be an experience of the Mystery present in the gathered community. Mystery is the key. Mystery is what people miss at Mass. But what forms of expression best create the conditions of possibility for experiencing Mystery? The answer: aesthetic forms. Art discloses mystery in life. Liturgy discloses the Mystery of life.

"Expression" and "experience" are also key words in this exploration. It must be admitted, of course, that no forms of expression *create* the experience of Christ's Mystery. That is a gift of God, grace. It is his Presence in us through the Spirit. It is that Spirit-Presence heightened and intensified by the symbolic action of word and sacrament. Nevertheless, it is aesthetic forms of expression which more effectively and efficaciously *create the conditions of possibility* for experiencing Mystery both in the assembly and in individual worshipers.

The word "experience" may be somewhat problematic for Catholics as related to worship. We have not been accustomed to explicitly considering the *experience* of liturgy. How liturgy looks and feels has seemed peripheral to the substance, *ex opere operato*, of Christ's presence in the Mass. Yet, if liturgy is a form of art, then the *appearance* of things is indeed of the essence, not of the action of God, but of the action of the community through whose assembling for ritual God's action takes place. It is questions about just what the local liturgical *experience* is that can lead toward the transformation of liturgy from text into event, from ritual as recipe to ritual as rite. As any person in the pew knows, the way Mass is celebrated does indeed make a difference. "Good celebrations foster and nourish faith. Poor celebrations weaken and destroy faith."[1]

It is imperative that we consider the nature of aesthetic forms if we are to explore further the thesis that liturgy *is* art.

Just what kind of expressions are truly aesthetic? How are they created? What is an aesthetic experience? As the rest of this chapter is read, see it all in the light of the art of ritual. What is being said about art here is precisely what can be said about ritual. A specific reflection on these thoughts in relation to ritual follows in the next chapter.

II
Art and the Human

Before considering in detail the nature of aesthetic experience, it would be useful to roundly condemn the popular notion that art is a rarefied experience for the rich and the effete. This common misconception not only fails to appreciate the nature of art. It also misses the mark on what it means to be human. Life without aesthetic sensitivity is like body without soul. Life without a creative imagination is severely limited.

Every person is, in his or her roots, an artist. When the person's imagination is engaged in creating or in perceiving the creations of others, that person is most like the Creator. What specifies us as beings in the image and likeness of God is this capacity to create. It is in our imaginations that we best image the Creator. To create in his image is our human vocation.

Art, then, like ritual of which it is the genus, should not be relegated to some ineffable, remote corner of human experience. Art, like ritual, is at the core of what it means to be human. For art is a quality of *all* experience.

What does it mean to suggest that art is a quality of all experience? All of life involves interactions between living persons and the world around them. We are who we are because of our experience with and in our environment. We struggle to create ourselves and our worlds out of these changing dynamisms of tension and resolution produced by this interaction. Art is the expression of the quality of feeling, the *ideas* of feeling, which are present in this interaction. In this way, art heightens and intensifies ordinary experience. Its expressive forms probe the hidden depths of experience to disclose realities that eye cannot see nor ear hear. The one who lives life aesthetically sees more, knows more, and appreciates more. It is life more abundantly.

The artist extracts the various tensions and resolutions of our interaction with the environment and highlights them through symbolic forms. The one who lives aesthetically helps life make sense. This brings about a kind of balance, an equilibrium and simultaneity in our perception of our experiences. Present experience draws upon past memories as well as anticipations of the future. Past and future operate as directions in the present, intermingling simultaneously with the present. Tension is held in balance and experience is unified. A center clicks in and holds, at least for that aesthetic moment. As John Dewey remarks, "the past reinforces the present and . . . the future is a quickening of what now is."[2] Experience, then, "is the fulfillment of an organism in its struggles and achievements in a world of things." As such, it is art in germ. Life, "even in its rudimentary forms . . . contains the promise of that delightful perception which is esthetic perception."[3]

If art is not separated from life but is actually a quality of all human experience, what distinguishes ordinary experience from aesthetic experience? Dewey calls the latter "an" experience. Ordinary experience is continuous. It just keeps happening without much distinction between moments. *An* experience, on the other hand, is one complete in itself. It has a beginning and an end. There is a before and an after in *an* experience. Such a unified experience has purpose and brings satisfaction. It always carries with it an emotional quality flowing out of the deep interaction between the organism and its environment. Dewey terms this experience's aesthetic stamp. It is indeed this aesthetic, emotional quality which unifies *an* experience and moves and cements change in the one who shares in *an* experience.

Insofar as aesthetic experiences are controlled by the felt relations of tension and release, order and fulfillment, they become experiences dominantly aesthetic in their development. This is true for art and for ritual which is created and celebrated aesthetically. What Dewey says of a work of art can legitimately be said of worship: "Every work of art follows the plan of, and the pattern of, a complete experience, rendering it more intensely and concentratedly felt."[4]

Since life is an interaction between person and world, and since art resembles that living experience, it is essential for living and for art that humans remain in close contact with nature. We are of the earth. We are not mere minds entrapped in flesh. If we are to be whole beings, the body-spirit entity which we are must not lose its unity, its identity. Unfortunately, however, our Western overly rationalistic and voluntaristic education too frequently produces isolated minds looking out on separated worlds. Art, seen as a quality of all truly human experience, and liturgy, as an art form, can offer some salvation from this disjointedness. For both disclose that, in matter, there is spirit; in world, there is kingdom; in life, there is hope.

"Perhaps if we can redefine who and what we are we can find a more secure place for the arts," Dewey writes. "In a world dominated by the knowing will there isn't much of a place since the important instrument of thought is the verbal formulation of whatever the willful knowing has determined. But to redefine ourselves as human it is necessary to build on the fact that we are, at the same time, animals."[5] In union with all reality, we see ourselves as irrevocably and joyously enmeshed in matters of earth and flesh. We are residents of both worlds and, as such, we are "a vast interlocking web of structured energies."[6] With all that is, we are energies in tension. It is our art flowing from our symbol-making nature, which allows us to survive the rending caused by dual residency. It is the imagination that saves from madness and dissolution.

Once we experience ourselves and define ourselves as *part* of nature, then we can safely affirm that we are, at the same time, *apart* from nature. What makes us apart and unique in nature is our self-consciousness. We know ourselves as selves, distinct from others. This awareness transforms the self, indeed constitutes the self. It establishes conscious space between beings and brings about the possibility of true relationships between the self and the other. This self-consciousness leads to symbol-making for surviving and growing in and through these relationships. It is thus the condition for and foundation of the human and humanizing activity called art. Art, as such, is the symbolic ordering and relating of the tensions of reality according to the visions and values perceived by the imagination. It makes order out of chaos, draws meaning out of confusion. Art or forming, then, is the essential act of the human and we alone in creation can create our own forming. "Alone in the order of nature, we have the capacity to make something new in nature."[7]

We human animals merge and mesh, dissolve and diffuse the forms of nature in our imaginations. We link them in new ways—ways analogous to the creativity of God. Our creating is not, of course, from nothing. The material is given for our forming. We combine and interlock the gifts of nature in order to create something new. This is similar to the shifting and setting of the images in our structured imaginations. Images cluster, split apart and reform under pressure from our lived experience, our interaction with the environment.

Another description of the uniquely human activity called art is that it is metaphoric activity. It is "the linking of apparently different things by some profoundly felt connection between them. At this point metaphor is the basic act of thought."[8] In this metaphor-making and symbol-making, the mind imagining penetrates into the secret life of things to find the bonds between them. Thus, "art is not an ornament to an existing world; it is the primary means of forming that world."[9]

Our life in this world is not fundamentally a matter of words. It is first a mixture of sights and sounds, colors and textures, masses and volumes, lines and surfaces. It is basically earthy, tangible, solid, present. The human venture is to organize all these energies into a unified, significant experience, without ever losing touch with the reality given for our aesthetic forming. This is the art of living.

If art is understood in this way, it is neither an effete activity for special times, places and persons nor a relief from the real life of work. Art becomes a heightened form of all experience. It is a quality of knowing the inside and the underside of life which energizes all of life. "Art throws off the covers that hide the expressiveness of experienced things; it quickens us from the

slackness of routine and enables us to forget ourselves by finding ourselves in the delight of experiencing the world about us
in its varied qualities and forms. It intercepts every shade of expressiveness found in objects and orders them in a new experience of life."[10] That sounds like a paraphrase of Jesus'
statement: "I have come so that you may have life more abundantly." Could there be an intimate connection between aesthetic experience and religious experience?

III
Aesthetic and Religious Experience

Religious experience is not aesthetic experience. They are
not to be equated. Having said that, however, it can be shown
that the two have much in common. Although art is a human
process, seeking to understand and express the finite, and although religion's source is outside nature and seeks to express
the infinite, nevertheless the substance of what is expressed
might be same. Both use matter to reveal spirit. And, if the Spirit is active in the spirits of artists, then are not the interior experiences of the arts similar to those of believers?

Both aesthetic and religious experiences present heightened
and intensified experiences of reality. Both involve matter disclosing and making present spirit. Both share an epistemology, a
way of knowing, which is described respectively as "intuition"
and "faith." Both share a kind of immediate knowing, a knowing which is self-authenticating. The proof of the pudding is in
the eating, if you will. The experience itself validates the aesthetic and the religious vision. Both involve the disclosure of
spirit/Spirit. As M. R. Austin suggests, these similarities raise
the question of whether both art and religious experience may
not be at root the same thing but "known and experienced in
two contrary and mutually exclusive ways. . . ."[11]

The substance of both is "in but not of this world." It belongs to the world but is more than the world. As the painter,
Henri Matisse, notes from his own aesthetic experience, the artist "possesses an interior light which transforms objects to make

a new world of them."[12] Isn't this similar to a religious experience?

It seems, then, that the experience of art and the experience of belief are similar and that the languages used to express these experiences are also held in common. The revelations of these two different but similar experiences tend toward making "whole" the artist and the believer. As a matter of fact, "to make whole" is one of the meanings of the Greek New Testament word *sōzō* which means "to save."

Art, then, very appropriately can be used as a means to salvific knowledge and conversion. It can be useful in the process of making us whole. As such, it follows that it is an appropriate expressive form for experiences of worship. Artistically conceived and celebrated rituals can be a means of bringing about the transformation of vision and values which theologians call conversion. Through worship created, composed and choreographed aesthetically, an opportunity is provided for persons to experience some of the transforming freedom which is present when one truly encounters and participates in a work of art. The imagination is freed to see and feel new modes-of-being-in-the-world, "a new vision, a new order of reality, an ideal beauty."[13] But the creating of such an experience demands an understanding of the creative, artistic process.

IV
Creativity: The Experience

What is the aesthetic experience in life and in art? It begins with an encounter between the individual and the world of which he or she is a part, as has been stated previously. The self becomes consciously and intensely present to "the other," the object of aesthetic contemplation. There is an interpenetration of the self and the world of objects and events. This confrontation and communion creates tensions which the imagination seeks to resolve by some kind of reordering of the image clusters of the structured imagination. This aesthetic perception in the artist brings about a heightened experience of ordinary experience. It is, as was stated earlier, *an* experience. The person relates to reality not merely as a rational observer of nature's causes and effects. This involves the experience of participating in reality, from the inside, drinking deeply of the waters of experience. Such aesthetic awareness gives form and meaning to all that happens. Experience then takes on significance or import. And it becomes unified through the perception of its aesthetic qualities on the plane of meaning.

One *shares in* rather than merely *observes* experience through the operation of the imagination as a knowing power. As John Dewey claims, this is the synthetic and rather magical power of the imagination to fuse all the faculties together.

At this point, it would be interesting to consult Dewey's own description of imagination contained in his masterpiece, *Art as Experience*. This can be seen as a summary of the various insights into imagination offered in Chapter II. Imagination is

> a quality that animates and pervades all processes of making and observation. It is a *way* of seeing and feeling things as they compose an integral whole. It is the large and generous blending of interests at the point where the mind comes in contact with the world. When old and familiar things are made new in experience, there is imagination. When the new is created, the far and strange become the most natural inevitable things in the world. There is always some measure of adventure in the meeting of mind and universe, and this adventure is, in its measure, imagination.... An imaginative experience is what happens when varied materials of sense quality, emotion, meaning come together in a union that marks a new birth in the world.[14]

Drawing upon the evidence of history, Dewey recalls that it has always been through the imagination that matters of the spirit—whether in art or religion—have been expressed. An examination of ritual expression in the Middle Ages, for example, indicates that "the rites and ceremonies of the Church were acts enacted under conditions that gave them the maximum possible of emotional and imaginative appeal."[15]

Dewey also points out that theologies have laid hold on our imaginations through the centuries "because they have been attended with solemn processions, incense, embroidered robes, music, the radiance of colored lights, with stories that stir wonder and induce hypnotic admiration. Most religions have identified their sacraments with the highest reaches of art, and the most authoritative beliefs have been clothed in a garb of pomp and pageantry that gives immediate delight to eye and ear and that evokes massive emotions of suspense, wonder and awe."[16] What better way to make the current case for recasting our liturgical experiences in aesthetic forms of expression?

Dewey's insights into the functioning of the imagination and our probing of the relationship between imagination and worship lead back to the question of the nature of human creativity. What do we need to know about aesthetic forming in order to create, compose, and choreograph communal experiences of worship?

Creativity involves bringing something new into being out of the old and the familiar. In the aesthetic encounter, the artist sees through reality to the core which discloses itself to his or her imagination. This happens in a surrender to the encounter that is totally absorbing. Being so intensely caught up in the experience, a heightened form of consciousness is spawned. Reality dissolves, diffuses and is recreated.

It is important to note that this is not born of reason. It is not the working out of a purpose or a theme conceived in advance by the mind functioning discursively. Neither is it a conscious act of the will except insofar as the artist chooses to surrender the self to the encounter. One cannot will to see. One can choose to look. The seeing is a gift.

Such an intense encounter brings with it an experience of ecstasy in which intellect, will, emotions and body are unified in an insight into the perceived reality. This ecstasy is precisely what the word's Greek root means: *ex-stasis*, meaning "to stand out from." The usual split between subject and object, between artist and reality is overcome in the artistic insight. The artist merges in his or her imagination with the inner reality of the object of perception. This must not be understood as irrational, however. It is suprarational. It is that peak experience of artistic insight flowing out of a deep communion between artist and object.

This communion is always accompanied by feeling. According to Rollo May, "the person sees sharper and more accurately when his emotions are engaged. Indeed, we cannot really see an object unless we have some emotional involvement with it. It may well be that reason works best in the state of ecstasy."[17]

Seeing with feeling may be one of the most accurate descriptions of the aesthetic experience. And the artist's major function in life is to make conceivable and objective the subjective realm of human responsiveness, doing this by capturing and expressing the inner feel for reality in the art work's own aesthetic qualities. Art is, then, "the patterns and forms of human feelingfulness."[18] Or, to quote Susanne Langer, "art is the creation of forms symbolic of human feeling."[19] The created piece does not directly express emotion, however. It expresses *ideas* of human feeling, according to Langer. She says: "The making of this expressive form is the creative process that enlists a man's utmost technical skill in the service of his utmost conceptual power, imagination."[20]

Thus we see in the creative act the subjective pole—the conscious artist—and the objective pole—the world. Each acts upon the other through the imagination's perceiving with feeling. This powerful and alive encounter is the first stage of creativity.

In creating the ritual experience, the artist encounters two worlds: the world of the celebrating community and the world of the given texts and ritual actions. In the creative tension of this dialectic between the two worlds, the artist creates the expressive forms of worship for that existential community of faith.

V
Creativity: The Process

Having discussed the nature of art and the nature of creativity as a way of probing the meaning of creating liturgical expressions and experiences, it would now be useful to explore the process of aesthetic creation. Following the aesthetic encounter, what then happens in the process of *creating* the aesthetic expression of reality in the art work?

This exploration might well begin by drawing a distinction between communication and aesthetic creation. The latter is not, properly speaking, communication. In communication a clear signal (word, gesture, etc.) is given by one person to another in order to pass along information. The signal has a definition and can be translated. The signal is of interest only as a means to the communication of the idea to be conveyed. It is itself of secondary importance.

In aesthetic creation, the art work has import in itself. It is not a signal to share information. It is a symbol, bearing meaning in a less clear and untranslatable way. It is ambiguous enough in its expression to be open to several, equally valid interpretations. The art work is polysemous.

That which unites all the arts is the sharing in common of a medium of expression. For music, there is sound. For poetry, there are words. For drama and dance, there is act and there is gesture. For the plastic arts, there is matter to be formed: paint, stone, glass, etc. In working with the medium, the artist is not only creating his feelingful insight into reality. He is not only forming the aesthetic expression. The art work is, at the same time, forming the artist. The artist creates the art work, and the art work, in being created, creates the artist. This would be particularly obvious to one who creates a homily and finds personal transformation in the process. It can happen in one who creates ritual as well.

This reciprocal interaction between artist and medium imbues the material with the intensity and profundity of the artist's spirit, his imaginatively intuited insights into reality. This interaction differs from the more functional, utilitarian task of "making something." The latter is an activity for the sake of something else. Aesthetic forming is engaged in to explore and capture the medium's expressive potential. It exists for its own sake.

As Bennett Reimer notes about the artist's interaction with the medium:

> As an artist "works out" the expressive possibilities of his medium he is at once embodying his understanding about the nature of feeling and exploring new possibilities of feeling. The thing he creates contains his insights into subjectivity, capturing both what he brought as a person to the act of creation and what he discovered during that particular act of creation. The art work, then, can contain the artist's insights as they exist up to and including that particular work.[21]

In this expressive process, both the creator and the work created become transformed. Turbid emotions are clarified and, in the mirror of the created expressive form, our desires and emotions know themselves. In this aesthetic knowing, they are transfigured.

Such transformation involves a dialectic between present and past experiences for the artist. "What is expressed will be neither the past events that have exercised their shaping influence nor yet the literal existing occasion. It will be, in the degree of its spontaneity, an intimate union of the features of present existence with the values that past experience have incorporated in personality. Immediacy and individuality, the traits that mark concrete existence, come from the present occasion; meaning, substance, content, from what is embedded in the self from the past."[22]

Past and present interact and merge in the creating of the art form. As the artist translates his aesthetic insight into the medium of expression, some elements of what is being expressed are heightened, others recede in significance or are omitted. A selection of aspects of experience is made and then transformed in the aesthetic perception and expression. The whole is rearranged on the basis of the meaning perceived by the artist in the intense encounter with reality. In the silence of aesthetic encounter, the poet, for example, struggles "... with the meaninglessness and silence of the world until he can force it to mean; until he can make the silence answer and the Nonbeing be. It is a labor which undertakes to 'know' the world not by exegesis or demonstration or proofs but directly, as a man knows an apple in the mouth." So says Archibald MacLeish.[23]

Dewey's description of what happens as the artist creates is also illuminating for our purposes. He claims that the process begins with "an impulsion." This involves a turning outward and forward of the organism in relating to its environment. Resistance between organism and environment ensues. The old and the new, the past and the present, are brought into tension. A re-flection of the old and new takes place like an incubation. From this re-flection, expression flows forth, not as an emotional outburst but as a re-flective awareness of meaning and purpose. In an act of expression, Dewey says, "an activity that was 'natural' ... is transformed because it is undertaken as a means to a consciously entertained consequence."[24] Natural materials are employed, embodying meaning beyond but within themselves.

What happens as the artist works with the medium of expression could be called an organization of energies. The energies of the reality being expressed work on the energies of the artist's imagination and, together, they work to organize the material of the medium into a unified expression, *an* experience. This organizing of energies involves a sense of rhythm in space and time. Each of the parts of the work of art must ebb and flow into and out from one another. Each part or moment is rhythmed toward the next and from the last. Thus "perception will be serial in order to grasp the whole and each sequential act builds up and reinforces what went before."[25]

As Dewey points out:

> There can be no movement toward a consummating close unless there is a progressive massing of values, a

cumulative effect. This result cannot exist without conservation of the import of what has gone before. Moreover, to secure the needed continuity, the accumulated experience must be such as to create suspense and anticipation of resolution. Accumulation is at the same time preparation, as with each phase of the growth of a living embryo. Only that is carried on which is led up to; otherwise there is arrest and break. For this reason consummation is relative; instead of occurring once for all at a given point, it is recurrent. The final end is anticipated by rhythmic pauses, while that end is final only in an external way. Such characteristics as continuity, cumulation, conservation, tension and anticipation are thus formal conditions of esthetic form.[26]

The rhythm of the expressive form, with its tension and releases, reflects, "as a substratum in the depths of the subconscious, the basic pattern of the relation of the live creation to his environment."[27] The resistances of rhythm must be brought into a kind of unity. This can happen "only when the resistance creates a suspense that is resolved through cooperative interaction of the opposed energies."[28] It is precisely this resistance between old and new freshly organized which is experienced as aesthetic. It "defines the place of intelligence in the production of an object of fine art. A rigid predetermination of an end-product whether by artist or beholder leads to the turning out of a mechanical or academic product. The consummatory phase of experience . . . always presents something new. Admiration always includes an element of wonder."[29]

The force of such a work of art is in the interpenetration of qualities and relations flowing from the organization of energies and perceived with feeling and completeness of form. "We cannot grasp any idea, any organ of mediation," Dewey reminds us, "we cannot possess it in its full force, until we have felt it and sensed it, as much so as if it were an odor or a color. . . ."[30]

The artist's surrender to the encounter with his or her world is never a kind of passivity. Rather it is holding oneself alert and open to hear what being and silence may speak. "It is active listening, keyed to hear the answer, alert to see whatever can be glimpsed when the vision or the words do come. It is a waiting for the birthing process to begin to move in its own organic time. It is necessary that the artist have this sense of timing, that he or she respect these periods of receptivity as part of the mystery of creativity and creation."[31]

This points to the importance of psychic rest and relaxation for anyone engaged in aesthetic activity, including the aesthetic activity called the art of living. Aesthetic vision comes best when there can be uninterrupted engagement/encounter followed by free time for the imagination to draw connections and disclose meanings that surpass those of eye or discursive reason. Sleep and dreams are often times when this happens most effectively. Backing off from the ebb and flow of ordinary duties is essential for *an* experience, for aesthetic encounter. Backing off from the encounter is also essential for the creation of an art work. Out of fecund silence, art is born.

VI
The Art Work and Its Meaning

We have considered the process of creativity from the artist's encounter with the world through the artist's interaction with the medium in which he or she expresses his or her aesthetic perceptions of the world. Now we must explore the result of that creative process: the art work itself. We need to understand the way in which it contains the meaning expressed by the artist and the ways in which perceivers of the art work receive meaning for their own insights into reality.

First, it is useful to compare the meaning in an "expressive object," the art work, to the meaning in a "statement." The former is the product of the imagination; the latter is the product of discursive reason. The statement explains an experience; the expressive object explores it and discloses its inner nature as perceived by the artist and proposed to the imaginative perception of the participant-perceiver. The statement is a sign, pointing to a reality other than itself; the expressive object is a symbol which makes present aspects of the reality-experience which it re-presents. The statement gives the meaning of an experience; the expressive object yields the significance, the import. The statement directs to an experience whereas the expressive object constitutes *an* experience in itself. The statement is prosaic and scientific, whereas the expressive object is poetic and aesthetic. The statement makes known an intention, whereas the expressive object immediately realizes the intention. The statement indicates meaning; the expressive object contains its meaning.[32] Isn't this the way in which sacraments contain what they signify? Could not *in modo sacramenti* mean the same as *in modo artis?* Surely liturgy should never be experienced as a statement but rather as an expressive object. Sacramental expression is aesthetic in nature.

The expressive object is neither an exact replica of the reality encountered nor an object totally divorced from that reality. The form of expression called art "is not nature, but is nature transformed by entering into new relationships where it evokes a new emotional response."[33] It is imagination's interpretation of reality. It expresses what "is wrung from the producer by the pressure exercised by objective things upon the natural impulses and tendencies. . . ."[34] The primitive, raw material of experience becomes reworked in the expressive object, and the emotion called out by the original material is modified by the imagination as it finds expression in the new material.

The art work expresses an interaction between past and present for the sake of the future. "Art celebrates with peculiar intensity the moments in which the past reinforces the present and in which the future is a quickening of what now is."[35] In no way is it a literal representation of the past. Rather, it is "an intimate union of the features of present existence with the values that past experience has incorporated in personality."[36] In this way the work of art clarifies and concentrates meanings contained in scattered and weakened ways in the material of other experiences. It discloses unseen truths about the nature of all experience by presenting the world in a new experience which perceivers undergo. Sharing in that art work evokes, from both creator and perceiver, "a deeper sense of the nature of human life."[37]

As Dewey aptly points out: "Through art, meanings of objects that are otherwise dumb, inchoate, restricted, and resisted are clarified and concentrated, and not by thought working laboriously upon them, nor by escape into a world of mere sense, but by creation of a new experience. . . . But whatever path the work of art pursues, it, just because it is a full and intense experience, keeps alive the power to experience the common world in its fullness. It does so by reducing the raw materials of that experience to matter ordered to form."[38] And, in those forms, feelings are brought to cognition. Again, the work of art contains the insight into human subjective responsiveness or feelingfulness. It is there to be experienced with feeling.

Isn't that the description of a good worship experience? Aren't people hungering for a sense of the feeling of life in their liturgical experiences?

In what sense, then, can aesthetic, expressive objects be said to contain meaning and a sense of feelingfulness? This arises out of the aesthetic qualities of the work itself, out of the material embodying the meaning of human life, a meaning of spirit disclosed to the imagination and bodied forth in the expressive object.

The meaning of the art work surpasses the expressive potential of mere words which can be defined and translated. There is more truth to human life than the conventional symbols of words can bear. "If the only means available to humans to help them understand their nature were language . . . a major part of human reality would be forever closed off to comprehension."[39] The art symbol takes over where words leave off in order to express the ineffable, the incommunicable, the Mystery. This is true because what is most human in reality simply cannot be pointed to by signs but rather must be embodied in forms expressive of interiority, of Mystery.

Reimer helps us grasp the distinction between the power of conventional symbols to communicate truth and the power of expressive forms to bring about a kind of communion with the truth.

Conventional Symbols	Expressive Forms
non-art	art
information	insight
designative	embodied
consummated, closed	unconsummated, open
communication	expressiveness
intermediate	immediate
making	creating
discursive form	presentational form
meaning as knowledge	meaning as import and significance[40]

VII
The Perception of the Art Work

The human phenomenon called art has two fundamental moments. First, there is the encounter leading to expression in the artist. Second, there is the participation in that expressive object by a perceiver. What kind of encounter takes place between the art work and its perceiver? How does the art work have its effect upon its perceiver?

A person who shares in a work of art must become involved in a kind of dialectic similar to that which took place between the artist and his or her expressive form. Each works its creative power upon the other. Like the artist who surrendered his imagination to the intense encounter with the world in order to create the art work, so the perceiver must surrender to the expressive, aesthetic qualities of the art work.

In so doing the perceiver shares the artist's insights into subjective reality by coming to understand life more deeply through a kind of sympathetic participation in the art work. He or she gets inside the form and it, in turn, gets into the perceiver. The result: transformation of perceiver and art work. In fact, until aesthetically perceived, art is not a "work" but a "product."

In perception, which is an act of reconstructive doing and undergoing, persons see with emotion. It is an act of going out of energy in order to receive. In this perceiving, "a beholder must *create* his own experience. And his creation must include relations comparable to those which the original producer underwent."[41] This is a seeing of the world which far surpasses mere recognition and observation. The latter is too easy to arouse vivid consciousness such as is necessary for aesthetic encounters. In perceiving a work of art, the work is recreated every time it is aesthetically experienced. What was evoked in the expressive object "is substance so formed that it can enter into the experiences of others and enable them to have more intense and more fully rounded out experiences of their own."[42] Through the imagination's engagement with the work, meanings and insights into feeling are disclosed which may differ from and surpass those of the creating artist as he or she grasps more and more of the work's expressive subtleties. In this perceptive process of both sharing and discovering, the perceiver in a sense creates his or her own art work. And the art work, in turn, works its power on the perceiver, shaping his or her experience by the shape of its expressive content. "Doing and perceptions projected in imagination interact and mutually modify one another."[43]

Reimer summarizes this perception of the art work with great clarity. "Aesthetic perception is an active, outgoing, 'doing,' which intensely involves the person in the aesthetic qualities of the thing being regarded. The aesthetic quality of the thing, in turn, 'works on' the perceiver as he becomes aesthetically involved in it, as it does on the creator as he is shaping it. The 'doing' becomes an 'undergoing' as reaction takes place to what is perceived."[44]

The effect of such aesthetic participation or perception is that of transformation of both vision and values. Things merely observed take on new meanings when perceived. Connections which logic or senses would never make become disclosed to the imagination. A consciousness of an integral whole comes to be where before there was disunion and confusion. "The conception that objects have fixed and unalterable values is precisely the prejudice from which art emancipates us. The intrinsic qualities of things come out with startling vigor and freshness just because conventional associations are removed."[45]

For the person who lives life with aesthetic sensitivity, for the one who perceives rather than just recognizes and observes experience, the truth of one of John Dewey's observations is validated again and again: " 'Reason' at its height cannot attain complete grasp and a self-contained assurance. It must fall back upon imagination—upon the embodiment of ideas in an emotionally charged sense."[46] The same is true in grasping the Presence of the Mystery of Christ in worship.

Summary

Liturgy *is* art. This is the fundamental thesis of this book. In this chapter the inside of the creative process which produces art works has been examined in detail.

Four stages of the creative process can be garnered from this chapter in relation to the occurrent or performing arts: first, encounter; second, creation; third, performance; fourth, perception. These are the same stages involved in creating, composing and choreographing the art of ritual.

Notes

1. *Music in Catholic Worship*, n. 6.
2. John Dewey, *Art as Experience* (N.Y.: Minton, Balch and Co., 1934), p. 18.
3. *Ibid.*, p. 19.
4. *Ibid.*, p. 52.
5. John W. Dixon, Jr., *Art and the Theological Imagination* (N.Y.: Seabury Press, 1978), p. 4.
6. *Ibid.*, p. 5.
7. *Ibid.*, p. 137.
8. *Ibid.*, p. 12.
9. *Ibid.*
10. Dewey, *op. cit.*, p. 104.

11. M.R. Austin, *Aesthetic Experience and the Nature of Religious Perception* (New York: Seabury, 1980), p. 24.

12. Cited in *ibid.*, p. 28.

13. *Ibid.*, p. 29.

14. Dewey, *op. cit.*, p. 267.

15. *Ibid.*, p. 31.

16. *Ibid.*, p. 30.

17. Rollo May, *The Courage To Create* (N.Y.: W.W. Norton, 1975), p. 49.

18. Bennett Reimer, *A Philosophy of Music Education* (Englewood Cliffs, N.J.: Prentice-Hall, 1970), p. 8.

19. Susanne K. Langer, *Feeling and Form* (N.Y.: Charles Scribner's Sons, 1953), p. 40.

20. *Ibid.*

21. Reimer, *op. cit.*, p. 49.

22. Dewey, *op. cit.*, p. 21.

23. Archibald MacLeish, *Poetry and Experience* (Boston: Cambridge Riverside Press, 1961), pp. 8–9.

24. Dewey, *op. cit.*, p. 62.

25. *Ibid.*, p. 136.

26. *Ibid.*, pp. 137–138.

27. *Ibid.*, p. 150.

28. *Ibid.*, p. 161.

29. *Ibid.*, pp. 138–139.

30. *Ibid.*, p. 119.

31. May, *op. cit.*, p. 81.

32. Dewey, *op. cit.*, Chapter V, "The Experience Object."

33. *Ibid.*, p. 79.

34. *Ibid.*, pp. 64–65.

35. *Ibid.*, p. 18.

36. *Ibid.*, p. 71.

37. Reimer, *op. cit.*, p. 25.

38. Dewey, *op. cit.*, p. 133.

39. Reimer, *op. cit.*, p. 37.

40. *Ibid.*, p. 60.

41. Dewey, *op. cit.*, p. 54.

42. *Ibid.*, p. 109.

43. *Ibid.*, p. 52.

44. Reimer, *op. cit.*, pp. 80–81.

45. Dewey, *op. cit.*, p. 95.

46. *Ibid.*, p. 33.

Chapter V
Ritual: Created and Perceived

The relationship between *an* aesthetic experience and the formed expression of that experience has been explored. The argument has been made that liturgy, as an expression and an experience, is a form and a species of art. This argument is made, of course, only for worship as a human ritual. It is not meant to substitute the power of art for the power of God operative in worship. Faith is always a gift. However, the gift is garbed in human attire. That is the principle of the incarnation. If it is true that God deals with a person and with communities in human ways, it should surprise no one that the Spirit speaks to spirits through that highest of human activities, creativity. It is in the artist's reworking of raw materials into an art work that spirit becomes present in matter and reveals the more than meets the eye in life, a "more" Jesus called kingdom.

Now it remains to be demonstrated how the same processes of creativity which are activated in forming and perceiving an art work are the human processes that are energized to create and celebrate liturgy as an *expression* and an *experience* of the mystery of Christ. This chapter should be read against the background of the previous chapter. Frequent reference to the last chapter will be found helpful.

I
Worship: "An" Experience within Life

Like art, liturgy takes the ordinariness of life and expresses it in forms that heighten and intensify ordinary experience.

Only by being so related to real life can liturgy enlighten the insides and the undersides of people's joys and sorrows.

Two pitfalls must be avoided in relating life and worship. First, worship must not be a form of expression that creates an experience totally up on a cloud. Worship must not take us completely out of life. It is not a fantasy trip to utopia. Those who create worship as a completely or primarily other-worldly experience in a space without any feel of this earth would do well to remember that the kingdom which the Church exists to proclaim, serve, and make present is truly "in the world." The art of the incarnate God, Jesus, made this truth evident in the flesh. Worship must not deny the incarnation.

On the other hand, those who speak of God not as "out there" or "up there" but only "down here within us" tend to create expressions of worship which lead to experiences not much different from a town meeting or a rock concert. "Otherness" is absent in the craze for human community. God is, indeed, immanent for us. But God in himself is wholly Other, and his kingdom, while "in the world," is not "of this world." The experience of Isaiah in the presence of the Holy One, cited earlier, must not be excluded from our earthly expressions of praise and prayer.

To create and celebrate authentic worship then, and indeed to live as an orthodox Christian, calls for us to be something like a juggler. The juggler, to succeed, must keep all his pins in the air at once. To catch one and concentrate on it causes the others to fall. Catching primarily or exclusively the other-worldliness or the this-worldliness of worship creates heresy in practice. God is both transcendent and immanent. Jesus is both divine and human. The Church is the one Spirit in many spirits. Scripture is the Word of God in the words of persons. And worship must be expressed and experienced in a like paradoxical manner—never "either/or" but "both/and."

Liturgy, then, is a ritual expression which resembles life lived in the Spirit. It takes the ordinary and transforms it into the extraordinary so that the ordinary can be penetrated with more light than darkness. And this transformation takes place by the creation and perception of the aesthetic qualities of ritual activity.

Liturgy should have all of the characteristics of *an* experience in John Dewey's terms. Like every work of art, worship ". . . follows the plan of, and the pattern of, a complete experience, rendering it more intensely and concentratedly felt."[1]

Worship must be experienced as having a clear beginning and a definitive conclusion. This is why the secondary rites of entrance and dismissal in our liturgies need to be considered, created and celebrated so carefully. Unless there is this sense of opening and closure, it has not been *an* experience complete in itself, *an* experience different from, yet in some continuity with, ordinary experience.

The complete and unified liturgy has a clearly and aesthetically expressed purpose and carries with it a sense of satisfaction, like all art. We who celebrate ritual know well that sense of "good liturgy" when all has fallen together nicely. We know, as well, the frustration when a unified experience just doesn't happen. The center doesn't hold and the parts don't connect. "An" experience was not had.

The element that unifies "an" experience, according to Dewey, is the emotional quality contained in the expressive form, in the ritual. That infused quality must also be perceived by the imaginations of the participants. It is this felt relation of tension and resolution which makes worship "an" aesthetic experience as opposed to a disjunctive reading exercise. More on feeling later. Just remember always that feeling is not peripheral to either the liturgical expression or the liturgical experience. It is the mortar between the bricks of "an" experience of ritual.

To create and celebrate ritual as "an" experience requires that both creators and perceiver/participants live in close touch with all that is natural. The images and symbols that are rhythmed into ritual action are more to be discovered in our imagination's interaction with the environment than invented as novelties for a special occasion. There is something about good ritual that makes it more a classic than a period piece. It must flow out of a sense of symbolic relatedness to nature.

Bread and wine are more enduring than coke and pizza. If we did not fear it in liturgy, touching is naturally of universal significance. All of the natural images of growth and decline, life and death can be captured and ritualized in liturgy. This kind of natural-based symbol-making and ritual-creating enables people to survive the ordinary interactions between themselves and all that is "other."

The awareness of all that is "other" stems from the fact that we humans, alone on the earth, are self-conscious beings. We experience "otherness" out there and reach out to relate through our symbols. In ritual this means taking material common to the "others" and investing it with a meaning which can be shared.

Of course conventional symbols like words are part of this process in worship. But words which merely point to meanings which communicate information can never adequately bear the meaning of mystery which is present in liturgy. It is symbols which surpass communication by creating the conditions of possibility for communal experience of the Lord. Symbol, by its power to draw together, connects liturgy and life.

Liturgy, then, as a heightened and intensified expression of life, must be created through what could be called metaphoric activity. Liturgy's language actually is metaphor in that, out of one thing, connections are made to other things that exceed the reasoning powers. These are connections disclosed in the imagination's exploring the potential of earthly realities to bear spiritual presence. Out of the given, something new is made.

Take the example of a candle which, through imagination's power, becomes a metaphor of transcendent dimensions. In a homily a preacher holds before the community the symbol of an unlighted candle. He says: A candle is like a person. Let it be a symbol disclosing to your imagination, in a vivid way, what we are now as well as what we shall be that has not yet come to light.

This candle is like you and me. It has all it takes to be a candle—wax, wick, shape, color, odor. But it lacks something that alone will make it truly what it is. It needs a spark from outside itself, a gift of flame. Then it will give off light and warmth. Then it will be what it is meant to be. We are like that. We have all it takes to be human beings. Yet we need a gift, a spark of love from our God—a gift mediated usually through other persons and events. Then we glow. Then we become warm and give off light. Before that we are as incomplete as the unlighted candle.

But there is more to the symbol. When the candle receives the gift of flame, it not only gives off light and warmth. The flame also sears and burns and consumes the candle in the very process of becoming its true self. And so with us. The gift of flame that lights us with love and holiness, once received, if not quenched, will not only make us givers of light and warmth into the world. It will burn and consume us too. And, like the candle, perhaps we will be only truly ourselves when we are all gone up in smoke.

Used in a homily, such a simple symbol can turn listeners into participants in the mystery of their own lives. It gives them the space to walk around and find themselves. It can move them toward a commitment, a consummation in faith.

This engagement of the imagination in a worship experience ". . . throws off the covers that hide the expressiveness of experienced things."[2] Various shades of expressiveness are intersected by artist and perceiver alike. Both are alerted to see our relationships with other persons, other things, and events in renewed ways. Birth, life and death take on new, previously unseen dimensions.

We begin to lose ourselves in the interaction with the symbolic form and find ourselves living in a more deeply related, committed and alive way. Aesthetic experiences in worship can confirm the suspicion that the substance of art may be the same as the substance of religious experience. As the Lord said to the young man who was attracted to life's fullness by Jesus' imaginative words and deeds: "You are not far from the kingdom of God." So it can be for those who surrender to the encounters of life and liturgy with aesthetic sensitivity.

Worship as an aesthetic expression and experience transforms the vision and values of persons, and these, in turn, can change behavior. Human consciousness is converted to participate in, not just observe, reality. Here we are at the roots of true personal and communal conversion, an experience which, humanly speaking, is aesthetic. It is a transforming engendered by the imagination's envisioning of new modes-of-being-in-the-world. It is out of such imagination's knowing that "young men dream dreams and old men see visions"—and so do women!

II
Creating the Liturgical Expression

Worship, first of all, is something created by an artist or artists as an expressive form, an aesthetic object. It is better not to speak of this process as "planning" liturgy. This concept is spatial and static. It is better to speak of creating, composing and choreographing liturgy. These terms are more temporal and dynamic. This can create flow in ritual.

Secondly, the expressive form is activated in celebrations by communities for and with whom the aesthetic form was created. In this bringing alive of the ritual creation, the phase of creativity called perception takes place. These two aspects of creativity, namely, forming and perceiving, will be treated separately here, although they are, in reality, conjoined as distinct yet not separate moments in creative, aesthetic ritual activity. It is only in aesthetic perception that a product of art becomes a work of art. A particular liturgy, therefore, cannot be created as a work of art apart from a consideration of the community which celebrates. And such a liturgy only becomes an aesthetic experience when that community celebrates the created ritual.

First, then, some reflections on the process of creating the aesthetic, expressive form called liturgy. What does the artist go through to form the expression?

All creativity begins in the encounter between the artist and the world or worlds of which he or she is a part. For the artist of ritual action this means an intense engagement with two distinct but not separate worlds: the texts and the times. His task is to link these two worlds through symbol so that they may seem as one to the imaginations of the celebrating community for and with whom he or she is creating. To do this, the artist's own imagination must be intensely energized by the connections between these two worlds.

The texts are those of the universal Church's ritual. In the case of the celebration of the Eucharist, these texts are scriptural and ritual. They are given for revelation and celebration. It is essential that the artist take these given texts with the utmost seriousness. The task of creating ritual is not a free-wheeling, start-from-scratch experience. It begins with what is familiar, i.e., of the family of faith. The imagination-produced-novelty lies in creating the same familiar ritual action with such fresh energy that it discloses new meanings each time it is celebrated. The old breaks open the new. Like the wise householder of Matthew's Gospel, the artist of worship draws from his or her storehouse the old as well as the new.

This apparent limitation on the liturgical artist's creativity is actually necessary for true creative action. As Rollo May points out, "Creativity itself requires limits, for the creative act arises out of the struggle of human beings with and against that which limits them."[3] This includes ignorance, sickness and death. This is Dewey's notion as well, namely that the organism interacting with the environment produces an inevitable struggle. Creation is a resolving of these tensions, not by eliminating them, but by holding tensions in balance, in a kind of equilibrium and simultaneity. In this way all experience, including liturgical experience, is unified.

In order for the ritual creator to have an encounter with "the otherness" of the texts—in other words, for true self-consciousness to exist in the artist—there must be an awareness of limits. "The limits are as necessary as those provided by the banks of a river, without which the water would be dispersed on the earth and there would be no river—that is, the river is constituted by the tension between the flowing water and the banks. Art in the same way requires limits as a necessary factor in its birth."[4] Creativity in worship, then, is spawned out of the dialectic between spontaneity and limitations. "The controlled and transcended tension present in the work of art is the result of the artists' successful struggle with and against limits."[5]

Too frequently during the past few years liturgical creativity began without a sense of limitation by the givenness of the ritual. Experimentation seemed, at times, to mean: "Do your own thing." Novelty was the goal.

No such nonsense is meant when it is said that liturgy is art. The worship artist's imagination begins with a familiar form and then, as Matisse said, one listens in silence for the given to speak to the imagination.

It is form, then, that provides the essential boundaries for the creative act. This refers not primarily to the structure of the service, nor to the words on the pages of the ritual texts. Form is more the non-material, spiritual element present in the limits. Structure and texts are the mechanical form. This is external. It is norms and rules. If you are to create a sonnet, for example, you must have fourteen lines in a certain pattern.

The spiritual form is an inner and organic form. It is the passion in the poem. "When you write a poem, you discover that the very necessity of fitting your meaning into such and such a form requires you to search in your imagination for new meanings."[6] This form is never superseded in creating worship. It is contained in all the ritual action as a unifying force. Without form, spontaneity would vanish.

In creating liturgical forms of expression, then, the artist encounters, in an intense and contemplative way, the world of the ritual texts of word and sacrament. At the same time, the artist must be engaged in an on-going encounter with the times. The liturgist who drinks deeply only of texts will create rarefied expressions more appropriate to an academic exercise than to flesh and blood communities of believers. The liturgical creator needs to swim in the same stream of life as those for whom he or she creates ritual. This is not to say that the artist does not swim in other streams as well and inhabit other worlds as well. But, without living inside the world of his or her worshiping community, one of the creative limits is missing, namely, the times.

How can one create an authentic ritual for Good Friday and Easter if the pattern of the paschal mystery does not merge and mesh with his or her life as its unifying and interpreting form? How can an artist effectively compose a wedding ritual who has never known love or a burial rite without having known grief?

All ritual action, all aesthetic experience, is a heightening and intensifying of ordinary life to give it meaning, direction and hope. The artist preparing the aesthetic ritual must be thoroughly familiar with life as well as liturgy, with the times as well as the texts.

The link between texts and times is made in the imagination of the artist. "Imagination is the outreaching of the mind."[7] The perception to be expressed in ritual form is determined by this imaginative encounter between the two worlds. The artist knows the world, yet, in the creative encounter, the world comes to conform to our ways of knowing. What is seen by the artist is the product, then, both of subjectivity and external reality. Imagination infuses form with its own vitality and form keeps imagination from falling off the deep end. As May points out: "Artists are the ones who have the capacity to see original visions. They typically have powerful imaginations and, at the same time, a sufficiently developed sense of form to avoid being led into the catastrophic situation."[8] They can live on the edge and still return to tell about the near chaos experience.

In the aesthetic encounter with the two worlds of texts and times, an insight is born in the artist's imagination which links the two, even if only for a moment. The center holds and the artist experiences "this-is-the-way-things-are-meant-to-be." It is, if you will, a sharing in the very creative power of the Creator. Order comes out of chaos. Joy and ecstasy are felt as the artist perceives the self sharing in being as such. It is this aesthetic perception which needs an expressive form.

An example may help to bring all of this dialogue of texts and times together. A few years ago I was called upon by the musical director of the Peoria Symphony to create a eucharistic liturgy for the funeral of his wife. She was forty years old and had died after a long bout with a rare blood disease. The local community, however, had not been aware of her illness, or at least had not been aware of its seriousness. She had been a beautiful, bright private person who chose to keep her pain to herself. Her husband and two young daughters respected her wishes.

When she did die, it seemed to the community a sudden as well as a tragic loss. They were not prepared. The musical community of the city, loving and admiring its symphony conductor, floundered to express its grief and to comfort the forty-year-old widower and his family.

The wife had been a Roman Catholic and the daughters were raised in that faith. The husband, my friend, described himself as, at best, an agnostic, not a real atheist. In regard to God, he just doesn't know. "If there is a 'divine' for me," he says, "it is expressed and experienced in the performance of great music." The arts *are* the medium of the holy for him.

There was to be no wake or visitation. The family chose cremation. The only public event was an evening memorial Mass in our cathedral. I began to create the ritual by encountering the two worlds. My creative task: listen in silence to the potential rhythms of the given funeral ritual and listen actively to the community of family and friends of the deceased. In those few days, a kind of incubation period took place. It began with what Dewey calls "an impulsion."[9] My involvement with the experience and the ritual texts brought about a resistance which led to re-flection and produced *an* expression. The imagination reached out to link these worlds in ways that would bring light and meaning to the darkness of our grieving.

An aesthetically-oriented community would be, I assumed, especially receptive to liturgy as a form of art. But how to create and celebrate with them an experience which would be a "conversion of resistance and tensions, of excitations that are in themselves temptations to diversion, into an inclusive and fulfilling close"?[10] How to engage the community's imaginations to find and disclose the passion in the form, the living in the dying? How to rhythm the symbols of liturgy so that what the word "symbol" (*sym-ballein* in Greek) means could actually come to be, namely, "drawing together." The opposite, *dia-ballein,* the "pulling apart," is diabolic and is what happens where grief is not linked with thankful hope. Let me describe the resulting expressive form as well as the way it was perceived and shared.

The space for the ritual was arranged with the paschal candle centrally located where the coffin is usually placed. A large arrangement of flowers, a memorial from the woman's husband, stood in front of it. A prelude of Bach's organ music was played as individuals gathered to find some form to express what they felt. The family and I entered from a side door near the front of the cathedral during a choir's singing of the Introit and Kyrie from *Requiem* by Gabriel Fauré.

After my words of welcome and invitation to prayer, the large assembly, composed of both Christians and Jews, a good number of whom were not active in a faith community, stood to sing a chorale setting of a Judaeo-Christian psalm text, "O God, Our Help in Ages Past" (St. Anne), which was printed in the congregation's memorial Mass program. The warmth of this greeting and the gathering song began to transform these grieving individuals, helpless in the face of tragedy, into a spirited community of comfort and hope for the family and for one another. What was disparate and disordered took on a unified form as the assembly surrendered to the symbolic power of the created ritual.

The entrance rite had achieved its effect of gathering, opening and quieting the community for the hearing of the word of God. The Scriptures were selected to reflect the confusion felt in tragic and sudden deaths. Out of the scriptural text, my imagination linked up with the words of the situation, the words about the beauty of art disclosing the divine as expressed by the husband and experienced by many musicians. I spoke of the power of beauty to disclose a mystery in life that is more than meets the eye, a beauty which cannot always be easily labeled but which can be experienced by those who create it in the arts. This is a beauty which can defy even death. In my homily I created a verbal reflection on the aesthetic experience which was known and shared so deeply by that artistic community. With this expressive form, I engaged their own imaginations to experience Mystery, by whatever name they might call it.

It worked. The worlds came together. All felt this drawing together, this *sym-ballein*. There was a hushed silence that spoke volumes. Later some participants said: "We came confused and sad. But the ritual pulled us together and we began to feel hope and trust again." The ritual form had worked its aesthetic effect. This was the experience of the family as well. They felt more together after sensing the *sym-ballein*, the "drawing together" which took place among the people during those ritual moments. There had been an incarnation of Dewey's description of an imaginative experience. This is ". . . what happens when varied materials of sense quality, emotion, meaning come together in a union that marks a new birth in the world."[11]

The rest of the ritual flowed freely and rhythmically out of that liturgy of the word. It was not that all fully shared in or grasped the liturgy of the Eucharist. But the Holy had been evoked and was carried through the remainder of the ritual. It was borne also on the aesthetic experiences of a string quartet performing Mozart during the preparation of gifts, a brass quintet playing after Communion and the choir performing more sections of Fauré's *Requiem* during the Communion rite. In some senses it was a kind of "you had to be there" to fully appreciate the way the parts of the ritual were rhythmed together and to sense the aesthetic effect this had upon the assembly. If you had been there, you would have known it was right.

What happened is what Dewey suggests takes place in *an* experience, the aesthetic experience: "What is conceived is brought forth and is rendered perceptible as part of the common world."[12] The art work of ritual captured the aesthetic quality, the *ideas* of feeling. It contained them by expressing them in the medium of a liturgical celebration. And the result was not communication through signals. This would not have worked, for all present used different signals, labels, words to express what this event meant. There was, nevertheless, a communion in the event brought about through a transcending engagement of the imagination in the world of symbol.

In such experiences the expressive object called ritual creates for worshipers the conditions of possibility for exploring the meaning of human experience. It does so by making that meaning present as a symbolic, aesthetic expression which contains what it signifies for those who surrender to undergo the experience of the expressive object.

The creator of the liturgy must be an exegete and an interpreter of ordinary experience. Liturgists extract particular traits and dimensions of the object to be expressed. This selection is based upon the interest of the artist arising from his or her own integrated experience and from his or her perception of the interests and needs of the community for whom the work of art is being created. New possible modes-of-being-in-the-world are thereby disclosed as projects for the imagination. What may be inconceivable can be revealed as real and possible, like living coming through dying.

As the liturgist creates worship's expressive form, a past-present-future dynamic must be energized in the imagination. The artist's encounter with the worlds of the texts and the times are, first of all, in continuity with all of the person's previous encounters with liturgy and their disclosive power. It is also to be a present expression and experience of that past, central Christian event, the death and resurrection of Jesus. Every liturgy is a re-presentation of its originating event, the paschal mystery. This event is the root metaphor of Christianity. All life is lived and interpreted in the light of this faith-event. Even though it was a once-for-all event, in the expressive object of liturgy, that event becomes present again for those who surrender to the symbolic action of the ritual. It becomes not just the experience of Jesus and Christians of the past. It is rather presented for present perception so that the participants may make that experience of dying and rising their own. It can "... enable them to have more intense and more fully rounded out experiences of their own."[13] What is retained from the past and is expected in the future are joined in the imagination as directions for the present. Or, to cite Dewey again, liturgy, like art, "... celebrates with intensity the moments in which the past reinforces the present and in which the future is a quickening of what now is."[14]

It is the responsibility of the liturgical artist, then, to shape the ritual materials so that the worshipers' past and present experiences can be brought into an immediate, clear perception, giving insight with feeling into the deepest dimensions of both past and present with directions into the future. The personal elements and the material of the ritual are ". . . organically absorbed into the perception had here and now. They give it its body and its suggestiveness. They often come from sources too obscure to be identified in any consciously memorial way, and thus they create the aura and penumbra in which a work of art swims."[15]

In a ritual art work so created, the energies compressed from prior life experiences and perceptions into the present experience are impulsed forward with intensity into the future. Such compression is produced by selecting the potencies in things by which *an* experience has significance and value. Those potencies are then organized in their multiple resistances until an art work is produced which involves both rhythm and symmetry. Rhythm and symmetry cannot be separated in ritual. "When intervals that define rest and relative fulfillment are the traits that especially characterize perception, we are aware of symmetry. When we are concerned with movement, with comings and goings rather than arrivals, rhythm stands out."[16]

The rhythms and symmetry of ritual can do precisely that for the perceiver-participant, if the artists creating liturgy understand the aesthetic organization of energies. The artistic imagination reaches out beyond limits externally set by the material used ". . . so that the value of that material may be pressed out and become the matter of a new experience."[17]

The material of worship only becomes a medium when the artist uses it as an organ of expression. "Whenever any material finds a medium that expresses the value in experience—that is, its imaginative and emotional value—it becomes the substance of a work of art."[18]

These elements blend and fuse into a unity which physical things can only emulate. The penetrating quality which unites the individual parts into a rhythmed whole can only be emotionally intuited. "But without the intuited enveloping quality, parts are external to one another and mechanically related. Yet the organism which is the work of art is nothing different from its parts or members. It *is* parts as members. . . . The resulting sense of totality is commemorative, expectant, insinuating, premonitory."[19]

III
Perceiving Liturgy

The art work of worship is the matter of ordinary experience reworked and infused with spirit by the artist's imagination. The matter becomes ordered to form through the interpenetration of the material by the organization of energies called rhythm. But, for this expressive form to become more than a *product* but a true *work* of art, someone must perceive and participate in its rhythms. It must look and feel as the artist intended. And it must be able to yield meaning beyond the artist's intention. It must be understood and responded to with sympathy and engagement by the imaginations of perceivers. This is the second part of the creative process in worship: perception.

What is perceived as an opening hymn flowing into greeting and prayer should not be a simple recurrence, one thing after another. It should be experienced as one cumulative movement and experience in the entrance rite. What should be perceived are rhythmed relationships carried forward cumulatively to some consummation. This recurrence is both old and new, both a reminder and a novelty, never either/or. "Every closure is an awakening, and every awakening settles something. This state of affairs defines organization of energies."[20]

In liturgy, such organization of energies, such interaction of elements, move and stir, challenge and comfort, perceivers-participants. Different senses perceiving the liturgy function in relation to one another. The energies of one expressive form are communicated to other centers of expression and "new modes of motor responses are incited which in turn stir up new sensory activities."[21] Something is energized in the participants which opens them to the grace of the experience of faith.

All of these impressions must be integrated into a single perception, and the integrating, synthesizing agent is the perceiver's mind functioning as imagination. This is the organic push from within, turning a product of art into a work of art. Liturgy connects with life to give it light. What is experienced is the Mystery hidden but to be disclosed in the core of life.

Life experiences can become more intelligible through participation in liturgy as an aesthetic experience. However, this intelligibility is not that of reflection and science which renders things more intelligible by reduction to conceptual form. Rather, intelligibility is disclosed by presenting meaning "as the matter of a clarified, coherent, and intensified or 'impassioned' experience."[22]

The knowledge gained through involvement in liturgy as art is knowing transformed. It is "something more than knowledge because it is merged with non-intellectual elements to form *an* experience worthwhile as an experience."[23]

The word "mystical" sometimes is attached to such an awareness of the divine within the human, the extraordinary disclosed in the ordinary. This same word is often associated with the experience of a work of art. Both involve the seen revealing the unseen, the understood disclosing the incomprehensible. As Dewey says: "Every work of art must have about it something *not understood* to obtain its full effect."[24]

What is sensed, yet not completely understood, is that the aesthetic experience elicits and accentuates a perception of belonging to a reality larger than the self, an all-inclusive whole which is the universe in which we live. This helps to explain the religious, awesome feeling that often accompanies intense aesthetic perception. "We are, as it were, introduced into a world beyond this world which is nevertheless the deeper reality of the world in which we live in our ordinary experiences. We are carried out beyond ourselves to find ourselves."[25]

Those words of John Dewey echo the vision of Jesus: to be in the world but not of the world; and, to find oneself, one must be willing to lose oneself. In Christian worship, as in any work of art, expressive forms operate "to deepen and to raise to great clarity that sense of an enveloping undefined whole that accompanies every normal experience. This whole is then felt as an expansion of ourselves."[26]

One of the possible dangers of creating and perceiving liturgy as an art form is that it could become simply a beautiful "in-house" experience of warm fuzzies, something to transform visions without confronting values, something to bathe in aesthetically without being cleansed. Values and behavior could thus become isolated from and untouched by the beauty of worship. Such purely inward-looking experiences are to be eschewed with as much vigor as are the recitals of ritual recipes from which we are beginning to emerge.

If the aesthetic power of ritual does its deed on artist and perceiver alike, not only has a work of art been formed but both creator and participants have been reformed and recreated in the perceiving as well. Nothing, nothing at all, can remain totally the same, including our relationships with others in justice as well as in love.

Liturgy perceived as an art form can energize believers to be instruments for bringing God's kingdom of justice and peace into the world. In rhythmed ritual, the stirrings of dissatisfaction with the present social order and its systemic sin as well as intimations of a better future can be found. Here, new and more just images-of-being-in-the-world cluster in imaginations and are disclosed as possibilities. These changes in the climate of the imagination become precursors of changes in social existence, changes that affect more than just the details of life but touch the substance as well.

The imagination is thus in service of justice. It is the imagination which Dewey claims to be "the chief instrument of the good." "A man to be greatly good must imagine intensely and comprehensively," he says. "The first intimations of wide and large redirections of desire and purpose are of necessity imaginative. Art is a mode of prediction not found in charts and statistics, and it insinuates possibilities of human relations not to be found in rule and precept, admonition and administration." "Art has been the means of keeping alive the sense of purposes that outrun evidence and of meanings that transcend indurated habit."[27]

Thus liturgy as art has the potential both for creating more celebrative Christian communities and for stimulating a vision and a motive for establishing that kingdom of truth and life, of holiness and grace, that kingdom of justice, love and peace which is in but not of this world.

Summary

The efficacy of liturgical celebrations, from the point of view of both the creator and the perceiver of such expressive forms, depends to a great extent upon the degree in which the human imaginative system can be engaged. The philosophy of John Dewey has been called upon to undergird this basic thesis. Dewey recalls that the Church has, at its best, connected art with human experience, weaving a fabric of real life with its aesthetic rituals. Because of this, he contends, "religious teachings were the more readily conveyed and their effect was the more lasting. By the art in them, they were changed from doctrines into living experiences."[28] The Church must learn to do this again with our new ritual texts which came forth after Vatican II.

If human persons are to experience the Mystery of Christ present in the Church, as Vatican II claims liturgy is meant to do for worshiping communities, then this is more likely to occur if rituals are understood, created and celebrated as art forms, as aesthetic expressions. The consciousness of more than meets the eye in life, the awareness of mystery, is the work not of that function of the mind which we call discursive reason but rather of the mind operating as imagination. In this way our immediate experience is concentrated and enlarged. "The formal matter of aesthetic experience directly *expresses* . . . the meanings that are imaginatively evoked."[29]

Notes

1. John Dewey, *Art as Experience* (N.Y.: Minton, Balch & Co., 1934), p. 52.

2. *Ibid.*, p. 104.

3. Rollo May, *The Courage To Create* (N.Y.: W.W. Norton, 1975), p. 113.

4. *Ibid.*, p. 115.
5. *Ibid.*, p. 117.
6. *Ibid.*, p. 119.
7. *Ibid.*, p. 120.
8. *Ibid.*, p. 122.
9. Dewey, *op. cit.*, p. 62.
10. *Ibid.*, p. 56.
11. *Ibid.*, p. 267.
12. *Ibid.*, p. 56.
13. *Ibid.*, p. 109.
14. *Ibid.*, p. 18.
15. *Ibid.*, p. 123.
16. *Ibid.*, p. 179.
17. *Ibid.*, p. 189.
18. *Ibid.*, p. 229.
19. *Ibid.*, pp. 192–193.
20. *Ibid.*, p. 169.
21. *Ibid.*, p. 175.
22. *Ibid.*, p. 290.
23. *Ibid.*
24. *Ibid.*, p. 194.
25. *Ibid.*, p. 195.
26. *Ibid.*
27. *Ibid.*, pp. 348–349.
28. *Ibid.*, p. 399.
29. *Ibid.*, p. 273.

Chapter VI
Parables of Ritual

"The kingdom of heaven is like . . ."—so Jesus said many times. Through parables, the unseen became somewhat seen. The same is true of ritual. By comparing four of the arts with ritual, parabolic insight may be born into the creation and celebration of ritual. Ritual, as an art form, resembles four forms of the occurrent or performing arts. By comparing ritual analogically with the creative core of each of these art forms, we can learn something about the inner dynamism of liturgical creation and celebration.

Liturgy is like poetry in that, by infusing words with passion and import, they are transformed into forms of feeling. Liturgy is like drama in that ritual action is a species of dramatic performance, the acting out of story. Liturgy is like dance in that it involves choreographed movement and gesture in space. Liturgy is like music in that it reflects, in its ritual rhythms, the tensions and resolutions in sound which is the matter ordered to form by composers and performers of music.

The thought of the renowned philosopher of art, Susanne K. Langer, contained in her book, *Feeling and Form*,[1] will be used to explore the relationships between the ways each of these arts is conceived and articulated and the ways in which worship comes to be. These insights into the creative core of specific arts will give ritual artists some semblance of what their creative experience could be.

The occurrent arts, as Langer prefers to call them, bespeak their creator's imaginative grasp of the emotive life. Each takes a medium—story, sound, movement, words—and reworks it until it contains the new insights into the life of human feeling which the creator has perceived. What was unknown becomes known. This is the vital import or significance of these aesthetic forms. It is not so much a direct expression of the creating artist's own emotion as it is an abstract, symbolic form containing what the artist knows about the truth of the emotive life. In the forms' inner dynamisms, the very pattern of human life is expressed, felt and directly known through these forms of "sentience."[2]

Ritual resembles these occurrent arts in that, as symbolic action, it is a form of drama, existing to make known something previously unknown or only partly known, namely the Mystery of God present in human experience. It, like the occurrent arts, contains what it symbolizes and symbolizes what it contains. If aesthetically conceived, created and celebrated, ritual can effectively engage the imagination to know the truth about life lived in the Spirit and to know it with passion, with feeling.

Ritual, as an articulate but non-discursive symbol, is an activity entirely controlled by the artistic imagination, as has been previously explained. Word and sacrament, without this fuller, aesthetic and human expression, lack some of their power to change visions, values and behavior. For that reason, ritual should always be understood aesthetically as what Langer calls "significant form," "a symbol of sentience."[3]

If we are to understand ritual as Langer understands art, it would be useful to know her three principles of creativity. First, the material form to be used in the artistic expression must be abstracted from its natural, real context. If matter is to be shaped into expressive forms that disclose more than meets the eye, then the imaginations of both ritual artist and the celebrating assembly must float far enough out of the ordinary and deep enough down into the real to experience the new insight into feeling. This involves investing natural forms such as storytelling, gift-giving, and meal-sharing with new significance. The immediate effect should be to make the surface of life more visible in the way in which good decoration does for a surface plane.

Perhaps this principle of aesthetic abstraction, of creating a transparent form of otherness, is another way of describing the liturgy as "the summit and source of the whole Christian life" as has been done in Roman Catholic statements on worship. This phrase draws upon the image of a mountain as an analogy. As a mountain-moment, liturgy can allow us to see life from a higher vantage point. In peak moments, we can see the valley differently and return to the ordinary with our vision transformed. This happens in art perceived and in thoroughly participated ritual.

The second of Langer's principles for creating art is that the material used must be made plastic so that it can be manipulated to express more than itself, more than mere practical significance. In ritual art, for example, the materials of word, gesture and music must become more than themselves when they are subsumed into the commanding form of the ritual. This should happen much in the same way that the words of a poem become swallowed up in the music of a song. Words are digested into the music and become musical elements. In that same way, the arts which are used in ritual lose themselves in becoming part of the fiber of the ritual entity.

Langer's third creative principle: these elements which are taken up into the art form need to be so rhythmed, their energies need to be so organized, that they become transparent. Ritual, like every art, creates a primary virtual object or an illusion. It no longer has its original meaning and no practical significance as such. Participants are then enabled to give attention not to the "things" used but to the disclosive power of the created appearance, the semblance.

Such artistic forming of the elements of worship takes bread, wine, oil, gesture, word, sound and assembly and gives them a new embodiment. These isolated things are set free from their normal condition and reordered into a new constellation of elements called ritual. They are no longer "things" but appearance or semblance. This new semblance or illusion is what is immediately given for perception. For those with eyes to see and ears to hear, for those of faith, it reaches beyond itself, charged with a new reality. It is the very sensuous character of the ritual which serves this vital significance. Through such aesthetic forms, the Gospel becomes disclosed to the imagination with feeling. Anyone sensitive to those articulated forms can perceive this embodiment of spirit in reordered matter. For this to become possible in assemblies of believers, an on-going liberation of the senses is required. We must cease to live primarily in our heads during worship and come to live in our whole beings, our body-spirit person which perceives through and is unified by the imagination.

Seeing with the imagination as believers participate in ritual can give their experience the character of otherness, semblance, illusion, autonomy, self-sufficiency and transparency.[4] The symbolic forms become like a glass, allowing us to see beyond appearances to new and deeper presence and significance. At the same time these forms serve as mirrors, reflecting our inner life reacting in faith and feeling to our environment. Again, all of this might not seem so strange when we realize the way we speak of eucharistic presence as Christ truly present and disclosed under the symbolic *appearances* of bread and wine. The presence of our God in sacramental form surely resembles the way in which truth is present and disclosed in aesthetic form.

Now it remains to explore the ways in which the four occurrent arts of poetry, drama, dance and music resemble ritual in their creative cores. In each case we shall see that the artist's insight into the reality to be expressed guides the creation of the art work. The same is true in creating ritual.

Liturgy Resembles Poetry

Liturgy, although primarily action, obviously uses many words. These are, at their best, poetic more than prosaic expressions. Nothing stops the flow of ritual so effectively as the throw-away prose language of explanation.

For example: "Good morning. Our opening song today reflects the theme of God. This is the message of both our Old and New Testament readings today. Would everyone now please turn to page 712 and sing verses 1, 3 and 5. On verse 2, Bessie, our organist, will accompany the choir, and on verse 4, the tenor section will sing alone. Now will you all please stand and greet our celebrant, Father Ponderus B. Portley, by singing 'You Are Our God.' " Do you get it?

If ritual is to flow and not get dammed up, prose, explanation and narration must be minimized, if not eliminated. You cannot engage the imagination with reason's expressive forms. You stifle imagination's engagement. Ritual language is that of the imagination more than discursive reason. Ritual's special mode of verbal expression is the language of poesis.

What can we learn about ritual language from an examination of the creation of poetic words? As has been stated, every art creates an illusion, a virtual image. Something from life is abstracted from its ordinary setting, filtered through the creative imagination, and it becomes something new. It becomes an expressive or aesthetic object, an entity containing insight into the truth of human feelingfulness.

The poet's abstraction is words. Out of these materials he makes the poetic elements. In his imagination he experiences life and, out of that encounter, unique insight is born. With words he or she creates the *appearance* of an actual present experience with life. This semblance, this knowing with feeling, is the virtual image of life. It is not life itself reproduced or mirrored. By abstracting from actual experience, virtual experience is simplified. It allows the listener/reader to more fully perceive experience rather than the jumble of things which actually happen in a person's ordinary experience. The very first words in poetic expression must shift the perceiver from the realm of the discursive and conversational to that of the imaginative and the poetic. As Langer notes, "nothing can be built up unless the very first words of the poem effect the break with the reader's actual environment."[5]

The words of our ritual texts are attempts at this kind of language. A subjective situation is created; common sense is omitted. What disrupts this is the interspersed prose remarks of the ministers. Immediately one can feel the switching back and forth from literal meaning to artistic import, from explanation to exploration. In the poetic, the words are more carefully chosen and more tersely stated.

All greetings and introductions should flow out of the rhythm and the symbolic imagery which preceded them. Those same ministerial interjections should lead into the images which follow in the ritual. In this way a response similar to that which comes from reading poetry is achieved in the participant's perception in ritual, namely an integrated response to a strongly articulated virtual experience. Through the power of poetic words, every element in, let us say, an entrance rite springs from a common organizing impulse and is held together by this overarching form.

One such example might be unifying the gathering of the Advent Sundays around the words and melody of "O Come, O Come Emmanuel." All that is said and done would take its energy from this expressive form. In this way the virtual event of gathering is created and sustained. Langer's words about poetry describe as well what happens when we create the words of assembling. "In poetic events, the element of brute fact is illusory; the stamp of language makes the whole thing, it creates the 'fact.' "[6] Gathering is such a virtual event. The "facts" exist only to create an appearance with emotional import.

An entrance rite, expressed poetically, bears the same kind of fruition as a good poem. It goes from seed to full flowering. There is an experience of completeness similar to the life process itself. It feels like real life but is a created illusion of the organic. Imaginations have been engaged and opened. People are readied to receive and respond to the word by being led into the ritual realm, a world all its own—in but not of this world. They are like quivering arrows, waiting for the impulse to move forward to a target.

This is the virtual life created by the poetic expression and experience. Yet this is in no way an escape from reality. Ritual must always be related to life, "but a world created as an artistic image is given us to look at, not to live in, and in this respect it is radically unlike the neurotics' 'private world.' "[7]

Ritual resembles poetry, then, in that both create virtual events which develop and shape the illusion of directly experienced life. This is done, of course, not by the laws of reason, producing discursive symbols called words. It is done rather according to the laws of the imagination from which words flow as articulate but non-discursive symbols.

Those of us who speak in ritual events need to become more proficient in such non-discursive language. We must understand that ritual speech is not for the sake of information but "to articulate knowledge that cannot be rendered discursively because it concerns experiences that are not *formally* amenable to the discursive projection. Such experiences are the rhythms of life, organic, emotional and mental—which are not simply periodic, but endlessly complex, and sensitive to every sort of influence. All together they compose the dynamic pattern of feeling. It is this pattern that only non-discursive symbolic forms can present, and that is the point and purpose of artistic construction."[8]

When a presider in ritual presents words, an experience of insight into feeling should take place in the participants. The words should not be finely reasoned but rather they should flow from the poetic principle of ambivalence. In this way they can be open to several felt meanings. The precision of the languages of philosophy and theology is not needed here. This ambivalence allows the words to engage the imaginations of people whose lives may be presently scattered over a broad spectrum. Image words can draw their lives together. Condensing rather than expanding verbal expressions is more effective for this purpose.

Words must be created by those who speak in ritual with a kind of inventing and contemplation. Never should they be organized as just a spontaneous association of images, words, situations and emotions. Every word needs careful selection "to create the poetic primary illusion, hold the [participant] to it, and develop the image of reality so it has emotional significance above the suggested emotions which are elements in it. . . ."[9]

To be words disclosive of the Mystery in life, they must unveil more than meets the eye. Words become transformed in poetry and ritual. They start a vision and impose a rhythm. They make one aware of the qualities of ordinary experience, not of life's practical concerns. They must be materials totally taken up into artistic use so that they lead not away from the work but into it. Reality indeed furnishes the images, "but they are no

longer anything in reality; they are forms to be used by an excit-
ed imagination."[10] They give ritual the air of being "reality."
All untransformed words must be pared away. "Everything actual must be transformed by imagination into something purely
experiential; that is the principle of poesis."[11] All actual experience must be transposed into virtual experience of the semblance of life. "There is no trafficking with actualities in
poetry. . . ."[12] Ritual is *made*, not *reported*.

Anyone who must compose words to be taken up into ritual
such as presiders, preachers, and cantors would do well to medi-
tate on Langer's inspiring advice to poets.

> Where a theme comes from makes no difference; what
> matters is the excitement it begets, the importance it
> has for the poet. The imagination must be fed from the
> world—by new sights and sounds, actions and events—
> and the artist's interest in ways of human feeling must
> be kept up by actual living and feeling; that is, the art-
> ist must love his material and believe in his mission and
> his talent, otherwise art becomes frivolous, and degen-
> erates into luxury and fashion.[13]

Applying the principle of poesis to words integrated into
ritual does not mean that ritual scripts should be so tightly wo-
ven that no words inspired by the celebration itself would ever
be used. Surely not! As anyone knows who presides and preach-
es, there are unplanned happenings within a created ritual
which cannot, indeed should not, be ignored. They can be taken
into the ritual and help its flow. But never should we be satisfied with a spontaneous use of words which lapses into discursive and explanatory talk or ritual babble. Words are most
successful in furthering the rite when they are poetic in nature
and are subsumed into the rhythm of the ritual, losing themselves in its dominating art form.

In preaching, for example, an appreciation for lyric poetry
can be useful to the preacher. Here the power of words can
reach a zenith in performative utterance. "Their very sound can
influence one's feelings about what they are known to mean.

The relation between the length of rhythmic phrases and the length of chains of thought makes thinking easy or difficult, and may make the ideas involved seem more or less profound. . . . This rhythm of language is a mysterious trait that probably bespeaks biological unities of thought and feeling which are entirely unexplored as yet."[14]

Another form of poesis or word-weaving which can serve a preacher well is narrative. Here story becomes the primary focus and the illusion created is virtual memory. In the re-creation of past events, real or mythical, images and words serve the action. The tense changes from present to perfect, the tense characteristic of story. What shapes the story, this virtual history, is memory. The event remembered is experienced again but not in the same way as the first time. "Memory is a special kind of experience, because it is composed of selected impressions, whereas actual experience is a welter of sights, sounds, feelings, physical strains, expectations, and minute, undeveloped reactions. Memory sifts all this material and represents it in the form of distinguishable events."[15]

Those to whom we preach listen for the word that will engage their own memory of their experiences. They need that word which connects one memory with another disparate memory. The way we preach aesthetically can organize people's consciousnesses so that the nuggets of memory are sorted out and composed into units of personal knowledge. Preaching as virtual memory, then, is not actual history or a record of history, "the recognition of *the past* as a completely established (though not completely known) fabric of events, continuous in space and time, and causally connected throughout."[16]

Preaching, of course, is a verbal art which always connects the memory of our past experiences with that memorial event, the paschal mystery. By telling our story in the light of the Jesus story of dying and rising, all of our memories are held together under that one Easter symbol, that single over-arching root metaphor. It is within that victory over death, that completed event, that we ritually recall our own lives. What Jesus did once for all, in a completed past, needs to become virtual history in ritual so that we can enter into that lived experience again and again and make it our own. It is not an accident that the ritual of Eucharist flows from the command: "Do this in memory of me." The narrative memorial makes that past event present for participation.

So much for the aesthetic use of words in ritual. A consideration of the creation of poesis does indeed enlighten the ways in which we should compose and use words in ritual celebrations.

Liturgy Resembles Drama

The art of ritual resembles the dramatic arts more than poetry because ritual, like drama, is primarily action, not words. Both drama and ritual are enacted words. Like all poetic arts, drama and ritual create virtual history as their primary illusion. But, unlike poetry whose primary abstraction is words, drama and ritual have *act* as their primary abstraction. Whereas literature uses narrative to create the illusion of a life of past events completed, drama and ritual involve acting out history for the immediate and visible responses of human beings. Literature creates a virtual past; drama creates a virtual future. Act in drama springs from the past and is directed toward the future, "always great with things to come."[17]

This is an aesthetic description which approximates the theological teachings on the sacraments. They are present actions, drawing their power from the past action of Jesus' dying and rising, for the sake of a kingdom to come. This past–present–future dialectic is at the core of the dramatic illusion. It deals with the future, with commitments and consequences.

Whereas the literary mode is memory, the dramatic mode is destiny. It is the future grown out of the present. Theater is "virtual history in the mode of dramatic action."[18] Ritual is similar. There, in symbolic action reflecting the past, the future is made present before our eyes in proleptic realization. The kingdom is already present, but not yet in its fullness. It is the making of that future, from the human point of view, which organizes and unifies the rhythm of ritual, the dramatic action. It is this experience of the present, full of its own future, which is really dramatic and which is precisely the experience intended in ritual. The Eucharist is and should be experienced as a foretaste of the heavenly banquet.

All of this makes for a clear immediacy, a "now," a perpetual present in drama and in ritual. This "now" future is a product of the imagination. It "is always under the aegis of some historical vision which transcends it; and its poignancy derives not from any comparison with actuality, but from the fact that the two great realms of envisagement—past and future—intersect in the present, which consequently has not the pure imaginative form of either memory or prophecy, but a peculiar appearance of its own which we designate as 'immediacy' or 'now.' "[19]

As we live our ordinary lives, the future is only vaguely felt. We lack a whole vision of what will be out of past and present, except in very unusual moments of prescience. But in drama and ritual action, this sense of felt destiny is paramount. "It is what makes the present action seem like an integral part of the future, how best that future has not unfolded yet."[20] In other words, in dramatic and ritual act, the pie is not in the sky by and by but it is in the oven, baking now, for those who have noses to sniff it.

The dramatic quality which good ritual requires is this: every expression is determined by the total action of which it is a part and toward which it tends. Every ritual moment is contained in embryo in the very first unfolding of the action. The tension and resolution that is death and resurrection must be present from the entrance rite onward. It must not be experienced as an unrelated surprise at the moment of the words of institution. And the tension between the ritual's originating event in the paschal mystery to its fulfillment in the parousia as it is felt in the present is precisely what gives to ritual action that peculiar intensity called dramatic quality.

There must always be this sense of the whole—past, present, future—gathered into this present moment. This sense of anticipation of what will come must be energized in ritual if there is to be the appearance of form being fulfilled. "Dramatic action is a semblance of action so constricted that a whole, indivisible piece of virtual history is implicit in it, as a yet unrealized form, long before the presentation is completed."[21] The ritual whole, then, is a perpetual, progressive action toward fulfillment. Human destiny unfolds before us in ritual activity. "The future appears as already an entity, embryonic in the present. That is Destiny."[22] Destiny here is pure semblance. It does not exist in actual fact. The kingdom is not yet of this world, although breaking forth in this world. This sense of life as a continuum even beyond death is what holds life together for believers and what is reaffirmed for them experientially in ritual action.

Drama and ritual resemble one another in yet another way. They both depend not only upon authors but also upon actors. Before they are completed in articulate utterance, the created texts must be filtered through the imaginations of those who enact them, those who give them immediacy and vitality. This is a great risk. Great plays and well-composed rituals can collapse unless authors and actors are operating from the same vision, the same commanding form. This form must be so clearly articulated in the text that it can "govern the crisscross of many imaginative minds, and hold them ... to one essential conception, an inmistakable 'poetic core.' "[23]

This having been said, it must also be acknowledged that drama and ritual are more variable than any of the other occurrent or performing arts. Performers are given more latitude to enact the conceived and expressed action according to their own conceptions and expressions. The enactment of the same ritual, for example, will vary from one worshiping community to another.

Christmas eucharistic rituals are unique in each parish. The same ritual structure and texts are followed but the symbolic action takes on varied tones and lines, depending upon the insights and abilities of the varied assemblies and liturgical ministers. Rituals, therefore, must be created with sufficient flexibility for adaptation to and in the given assembly. Canned ritual, like a canned homily from a preaching service, can offer suggestions of images, symbols and rhythms. But the enactment, the articulate utterance, must be created locally.

In all cases, whatever is spoken and done in ritual must flow from a deep encounter between the ministers, the texts and the times. It should be "the overt issue of a greater emotional, mental, and bodily response, and its preparation in feeling and awareness or in the mounting intensity of thought is implicit in the words spoken."[24] Unprepared ritual is experienced like a recipe-reading. Ritual that flows from the encounter within the ministers, however, is Mystery enfleshed. It is "an utterance, motivated by visible and invisible other acts, and like them shaping the oncoming Future."[25] This ministerial interaction in ritual action is mutually nourishing. The sharing of vision and energy from one to another can make liturgy more alive—and the ministers more holy.

A liturgical minister resembles an actor in drama in some ways. In other ways, the resemblance ceases. By exploring the relationship between the actor and the dramatic text we can learn something of what a liturgical minister should be and do, as well as some things to avoid. By analogy, the ministers "perform" the rites.

With the actor as well as the minister, the body speaks louder than the mouth. An exciting line spoken with a relaxed body or a line of love spoken with clenched fists is a false and failed expression in a drama. So is a ritual's preface dialogue a visual lie when spoken with eyes in the book and no expression of warmth. We must look like what we say. The body must be connected with the words and not serve as their countersign.

How can we achieve this integrity of ritual word and gesture? What Langer says of the actor on this point applies as well to the minister:

> Since every utterance is the end of a process which began inside the speaker's body, an enacted utterance is part of a virtual act, apparently springing at the moment from thought and feeling; so the actor has to create the illusion of an inward activity issuing in spontaneous speech, if his words are to make a dramatic and not a rhetorical effect.[26]

These remarks raise again the issue of whether the liturgical minister is an actor, a performer. The answer must be yes—with qualifications. A presiding priest, for example, does not always feel like the words he must say in the Eucharist. This might be especially the case if he is required to celebrate the Eucharist many times in one day. He may feel like "saying Mass" rather than celebrating ritual. He says the words and, *ex opere operato*, it works. Or does it? On God's part, of course it does. He keeps his promise "where two or three are gathered," despite what we do. But our part of the covenant, *ex opere operantis*, is to do more than make the magic happen. It is our promise to "be there" too, and to be there with the imagination.

With imagination encountering texts and times, the minister expresses the import of the ritual in body gesture as well as words. The gesture, in fact, is the pacemaker for the verbal. It is the herald preparing the eye for what the ear will hear. "Anyone who starts with the words, and then hunts for the appropriate gesture to accompany them, lies to the face of art and nature both."[27] Every utterance by any liturgical minister needs to be prepared by some elements of expression and bearing that foreshadow it. It need not be that the expressions called for in ritual mirror the actual present inner life of the minister. Often the actual and the virtual will not coincide. But, in imagining oneself into the role, one can begin to actually feel what one is to represent. A minister, like an actor, must be guided by the ideas of emotion in the script. One does not express one's personal emotions but those of the role. "He does not undergo and vent emotions; he conceives them, to the smallest detail, and enacts them."[28] This, of course, calls for discipline and surrender—a dying in order to live—on the part of any effective minister in ritual. One must indeed lose oneself to find oneself in ritual activity!

Those who lead worship must create conditions of possibility for those in the assembly which are similar to that created by actors for their audience. Each creates a virtual image for the perceivers to enter, a world-out-of-time for the sake of a real world in the future. One difference, of course, is that in ritual there is a "performing" audience. They are as much the action as the ministers are. They create the image as well. These worshipers, like all who perceive art, must be lured away from the ordinary experience of life into the ritual world in order to perceive more profoundly what is really happening ordinarily. In art this is called the attitude of contemplation or the aesthetic attitude.

In ritual this attitude involves establishing a certain psychic distance for the assembly. The ritual artist's task is to elicit this attitude since one can hardly expect everyone stepping in from the parking lot to have it in the forefront of consciousness. Yet such an aesthetic and contemplative attitude is possible for all, and it is precisely what should be evoked, for example, by an entrance rite which gathers, opens and quiets the folks.

Of course the ritual and its artists don't bring this about themselves directly. You don't *tell* people to be aesthetic. You establish, rather, a relation between the ritual and its public. You invite them into ritual to participate in it, to be in relation to it as an assembly. The psychic distance, the attitude for perception and participation, is the by-product of this relation. This is exactly what actors do, and it is an adequate description of the way liturgical ministers should engage the imaginations of worshipers in the creating of ritual action. In this way ritual's virtual illusion of Presence is created as an expression which makes possible the experience of Mystery for the assembly.

Those who participate in ritual as art can experience a personal relation with Presence, with Mystery. It is often highly emotionally charged and of a peculiar character. Sometimes it is quiet and even routine. It is a relation in the imagination which filters out the practical and the concrete aspects of the ritual in order to experience it symbolically. This relation, Langer suggests, is "our natural relation to symbol that embodies an idea and presents it for our contemplation, not for practical action. . . . It is for the sake of this remove that art deals entirely in illusions, which, because of their lack of 'practical, concrete nature,' are readily distanced as symbolic forms."[29]

We must be aware that ritual illusion is the opposite of delusion. The former discloses and makes present truth; the latter, a lie. The latter aims not at distance but the greatest possible nearness. It makes illusion out to be the real.

Ritual resembles drama also in that it calls upon so many other art forms to assist in its task of creating virtual history in the mode of dramatic action. Drama's thrust into the future through enacted words is carried along sometimes by dance and music. Ritual uses these as well. But drama and ritual must not be hybrids of other forms. They must be arts unto themselves with their own abstraction from the ordinary and with their own image and illusion. Both are poetry in the mode of action. Any other arts used must become swallowed up in the action, losing themselves to another commanding form to create that semblance, that illusion, that image unique to dramatic and ritual art.

We must be extremely careful in creating, composing and choreographing ritual that we do not create a "start-stop" experience. Now we speak, now we sing, now we dance, etc. It must not be a hybrid of drama, dance and music. It must be an art in itself. To do so, according to Langer's philosophy of art, it must have its own primary abstraction and its own virtual image. Let me risk stating what these might be.

Ritual grows out of that very ordinary natural entity called action. It takes action with its native tensions and resolutions out of its practical, concrete setting. Action is then filtered through the creative imagination to become something utterly new and more than itself. It becomes *symbolic* action. Action no longer simply goes somewhere. That somewhere is created. It bears the import of something beyond itself. It no longer merely *points toward* its consummation in the future. Like all symbols, it points to a reality beyond itself and *makes that reality present* without being identical to it. There is an apparition of destiny, of kingdom come. In terms of Christian ritual, the actions symbolize the presence of the risen Christ. They signify what they contain and contain what they signify—*in modo sacramenti* is like *in modo artis!*

The primary abstraction of symbolic action creates the expression of the virtual image of the art of ritual which is Presence. As the poetry creates the virtual image of life, as literature creates virtual memory, as drama creates virtual future, so ritual creates virtual Presence. In Christian liturgy, for example, the future fullness of risen life is made present as is the past saving death of Jesus. This paschal mystery, the dying and rising, is in and with the assembly as Presence.

In this aesthetic way, the Mystery is expressed and experienced as Presence in the assembly—and the description of liturgy from paragraph 2 of the *Constitution on the Sacred Liturgy* of Vatican II becomes real. It is an expression and an experience of the Mystery of Christ and the nature of the Church. The Word is made flesh—and dwells among us.

Ritual, like drama, is not just another slice of the pie of life. Both are "other," aloof from the actual but for the sake of the actual. All of the elements of "play" which constitute both art forms make the action convincing by holding it aloof from actuality in the realm of the virtual. Distance is established so that participants do not consider this as just another piece of natural behavior. It is in but not of this world.

Creating the dramatic illusion in ritual, where a virtual future is unfolding before us, involves attention to every detail of the action. Liturgy is, indeed, about a lot of little things, and *everything* matters. "The import of every little act is heightened, because even the smallest act is oriented toward that future. What we see, therefore, is not behavior, but the self-realization of people in action and passion; and as every act has exaggerated importance, so the emotional responses of people in a play are intensified. Even indifference is a concentrated and significant attitude."[30] My, but isn't that the truth in our liturgical assemblies! Liturgy really is about a lot of little things—as is anything that truly matters—like love, like life.

In conclusion, it does seem that ritual resembles drama in many notable ways. No doubt ritual is dissimilar from drama in some dramatic ways as well. But I leave the fuller exploration of the differences to critics and others more skilled in analysis than I. Let it be said, however, that this comparison at least seriously opens or furthers the conversation on ritual as a species of dramatic art.

Ritual Resembles Dance

It may be obvious that creating poetry and drama resembles the creation of ritual. Ritual's words should be poetic, and ritual is, more than words, enactment. It is undoubtedly a more far-fetched claim to assert that ritual also resembles the very physical art of dance and that ritual should be choreographed.

To begin with, dance itself is an art not easy to pin down. As Martha Graham is supposed to have said, "My dears, if I could explain my dance I wouldn't have to dance it." Words are especially inadequate for defining dance, and no other art suffers more misunderstanding. Is it musical rhythm expressed in bodily motion? Does the dancer merely express the emotional content of the music which undergirds and causes the gesture? Or is dance one of the plastic arts, shifting pictures and designs? Some have suggested that dance is one of the dramatic arts like pantomime, telling a story without words but with gestures.

Dance fits none of these definitions according to Langer. She bores through to that creative core which makes dance an art unto itself, borrowing energy from but different than music and drama. Dance abstracts the reality of movement or gesticulation from ordinary experience, making this its primary abstraction. Dance removes it from any practical or discursive purpose. It is not actual but virtual behavior. The choreographer and the dancer filter gesticulation through the creative imagination and it becomes dance's primary illusion, gesture, i.e., motion motivated by the semblance of an expressive movement, a movement containing an insight into feeling. It is indeed *vital* movement. By being imagined, the gesticulation ceases to be actual behavior and becomes aesthetic expression containing an understanding of feeling. It is, then, a free symbolic form all its own.

What is created by dance's gestures? What is this art's unique image or illusion? The virtual realm of power, "not actual, physically exerted power, but appearances of influence and agency created by virtual gesture."[31] The motion springs from something beyond the dancers, and the relation between them is more than spatial. It is a relation of unseen forces made present in symbolic gesture. These are dance forces, virtual powers. They are not like the forces of physics but more like the powers we experience in our free willing of things. It is power from deep within the person. It is the *feeling* of power we have to make things happen, vital power. And, of course, this feeling is imagined, not actual. It is the conception of feeling which is expressed in dance's gestures.

I once attended an open rehearsal of the Stuttgart Ballet at the Kennedy Center in Washington, D.C. Marcia Haydee and Richard Cragun, the principal dancers of the company, were being instructed by their choreographer in their roles in the ballet, "Daphnis and Apollo." Several female dancers were being asked to form a "forest," created by their posed bodies, as Apollo pursued Daphnis through the woods. The choreographer told the dancers to imagine themselves as trees, to let "treeness" into their imaginations and to let those images flow into their bodies so that the illusion of tree was created. They were to feel the power of becoming trees and they did. Each one assumed a unique position which was recognized unquestionably as "tree." This subjective experience of volition and free agency on their part brought to gesture the idea of the feeling of the realm of powers. It was, of course, not real but virtual gesture. It was "the final articulation of *imagined* feeling in its appropriate physical form. The conception of a feeling disposes the dancer's body to symbolize it."[32] The movement was real enough, but what made it emotive gesture was illusory. It was virtual self-expression, emotional experience expressing itself through movement under the aegis of an imagined vision, a commanding form.

This illusion of powers creates for performer and perceiver a non-physical but symbolically convincing realm or world. Curt Sachs calls it "the vivid representation of a world seen and imagined."[33] Motion becomes gesture under the power of a symbol-making imagination and more than meets the eye is disclosed.

Now, how, you may ask, does this resemble ritual? Ritual is action, symbolic action. Unlike dance, it uses words. But, like dance, non-verbal movement is a significant part of it. The body "speaks." Like dance, ritual addresses the imagination through the sense of sight. At times the gestures of the ministers are unaccompanied by words, as in processions and in the laying on of hands. The whole burden of expression is borne by the body, by what is seen rather than what is heard. The way one moves must express more than meets the eye.

The minister's body needs to be ready for rhythm. It must create the virtual image of Presence in a way analogous to dance's creation of the virtual realm of power. The manner in which ministers live and move and have their being in the ritual realm expresses a deep, inner sense of feeling of Presence which emanates from a center of living power, the will filtered through the imagination. "In a body so disposed, no movement is automatic; if any action goes forward spontaneously, it is induced by the rhythm set up in imagination. . . ."[34]

Ministers' concept of Presence which they embody is an idea of something utterly real and actual. We even capitalize Real Presence for emphasis in our liturgical jargon. But the symbols of Presence, the gestures of ritual, are illusory in order to articulate and reveal an import that is indeed actual, namely Mystery. "Everything illusory and every imagined factor (such as a feeling we imagine ourselves to have) which supports the illusion belongs to the symbolic form; the feeling of the whole work is the 'meaning' of the symbol, the reality which the artist has found in the world and of which he wants to give his fellow men a clear conception."[35]

Again, it must be stressed that the feelings represented in ritual, like those expressed in dance, are created by the imagination. The minister may actually feel the opposite of what he or she is called to embody. But ritual roles require the *appearance* of feeling in the body, not the *showing* of feelings that are immediate to the minister. For the ritual moment one must lay down one's life of feeling for those who are to be loved in the assembly. Ritual is an art form, not actual behavior. To grasp this one must distinguish between feelings *experienced* and feelings *perceived*. The latter are to be expressed in dance and ritual. Movement *seems* to spring from feeling but is, in reality, a created element. With some imaginative surrender, however, these two may even coincide.

Part of the power of an entrance procession, a Gospel procession, the procession with gifts and a Communion procession lies in the illusion of the image of the realm of powers. In the gathering of the assembly, we move from the ordinary realm, graced always but not so explicitly seen as graced, into the realm of Presence. All—both those in the procession and those who participate by perceiving the gestures—can feel human beings as tension in space, moving toward a resolution in the sacred. The entrance rite, then, is not just a coming into another space in the world. It is entering a realm of Presence and requires a heightening of tension to which processions contribute.

This heightening of tension is also the whole point of the Gospel procession. The discharge of energy in that gesture seeks resolution in the Gospel proclamation, the realm of the Presence of the Word made flesh.

After hearing the word, the gesture of gift preparation follows. A new tension in space is created as a preparation for the resolution in praise which follows in the Eucharistic Prayer. Again, this is not just a practical, nuts-and-bolts carrying of bread and wine from the back of the space to the front. It is not for the sake of getting from here to there. This is symbolic gesture. It bears more than meets the eye. It gathers up in those simple gifts the very complex actualities of ordinary existence. It extracts them from life's normal strains and makes of gifts and bearers symbols which make us present for Presence in our great prayer of thanksgiving. For this to happen the human beings involved must imagine the tension of ordinary and extraordinary, secular and sacred. The two must become one in their metaphorical movement, tension expressed and resolved in space.

The Communion procession, in which the whole assembly participates in the gesture, is not so much a movement from the world to the kingdom. The realm of ritual has already expressed and created the possibility of experiencing the sacred. In the procession the image of virtual Presence finds consummation in sharing in the meal which is one symbol of that Presence. The illusion created by the energy of the ritual to the point of the Communion procession must be forwarded toward that consummation by the words and the music which accompany the gestures. It is my experience that the placement of the greeting of peace at this point in the ritual usually disrupts rather than forwards the ritual energy. Surely this can be a very expressive gesture. It is one that has a long history in our tradition even though it has only recently been restored as a gesture for the assembly. Nevertheless it might more effectively be located elsewhere in the ritual in order to avoid disrupting the rite of Communion. History may place it before Communion but experience may suggest otherwise.

What Langer says of dance is true, by analogy, of all the gestures in ritual. Dance is "the oscillation of a human being between two external poles of tension, thus transplanting the dancing body from the sensually existing sphere of materialism and real space into the symbolic supersphere of tension."[36] Processions, then, must never appear as simply a matter of getting from here to there. Ministers' gestures must not be mechanical. These are not actual but virtual events helping to create the virtual image of Presence. Ritual, by resembling dance, can transform the vision of its participants by engaging the imaginations through these virtual elements, these centers of force, which express the realm of powers made visible.

In addition to ritual action resembling dance action, it is also possible to integrate the art of dance itself into the art of ritual. Dance has, in most cultures in history, always been intimately related to religion and worship. Dance, of course, must become a ritual element if it is not to be an intrusion and an interruption of the ritual's rhythm. It must never appear that the ritual has stopped and the dance started. The ritual prepares for dance so that the dance gesture flows perfectly and aesthetically from what preceded and rhythms into what follows. Dance in ritual, if used judiciously and not too frequently, can heighten and intensify ritual's expressive powers. It can, indeed, be used to create the virtual image of Presence which is the primary illusion of ritual art. If dance only creates its own virtual expression of the realm of powers, however, it has failed to be swallowed up in ritual; it has not been integrated into another commanding form. If, however, it is integrated, it helps to create the experience of ecstasy, of communing with the Presence, which is the peak liturgical experience. It aids in breaking the beholder's sense of actuality by setting up the virtual image of a different world—the kingdom, in but not of this world. It creates a play of forces that confronts the perceiver with that kingdom's imploding in the world.

Some may fear that the introduction of dance into worship will return the assembly to the pre-conciliar role of spectators. No such thing is intended, nor need such be the case if dance is taken up into and becomes an element of ritual. Indeed, some simple bodily movements by the assembly can effectively be used to more fully express the meaning and feeling of some spoken or sung texts.

A problem reflected in this protest may lie in an inadequate understanding of *actuosa participatio*, that active participation in liturgy which is the right and duty of all believers. As I have mentioned previously in this work, active participation in ritual is primarily internal. All ritual elements create the conditions of possibility for the inner experience of Mystery. Some of these elements involve speaking and moving. Others involve silence with no sensual stimulation. But active watching and listening should also be seen as valid and valuable participation in ritual. In this sense ritual dance, as the bodily expression of the dance minister's insight into faith with feeling, can have the unique and magnetic power of drawing participants into the Mystery which is expressed and experienced by the artists of gesture.

Ritual Resembles Music

The dancer's body and that of the minister should always be ready for rhythm. This leads us to that art which undergirds dance by helping to create its rhythm: music. As Langer points out: "The rhythm that is to turn every movement into gesture,

and the dancer himself into a creature liberated from the usual
bonds of gravitation and muscular inertia, is most readily established by music."[37]

Our consideration of the resemblance between ritual and
dance leads, then, quite naturally and logically to ritual's resemblance to music. It may seem surprising that that art most frequently associated with ritual, namely music, should be
considered last among these parables of ritual. Music, after all,
was described by Vatican II as "a treasure of inestimable value,
greater even than that of any other art. The main reason for this
pre-eminence is that, as a combination of sacred music and
words, it forms a necessary or integral part of the solemn liturgy."[38] Indeed, music has a direct *munus ministeriale*, a ministerial
function, in liturgy. Music enters traditionally into the very fabric of ritual expression. This has not been said of any of the other arts.

It remains now to explore the creative core of that eminent
art used in ritual in order to grasp more fully what it means to
compose and perform ritual.

In one sense, this is a case of the last being first since music
is the most spiritual of the arts. Its primary abstraction from the
ordinary world is not material. It is vibrating air, breath, spirit.
It is sound. This takes us furthest away from the realm of conventional verbal symbols and non-verbal gestures. Music's significance is not contained in words, born at least in their
inception from reason. It has no vocabulary in the sense of poetry, drama and dance. Music is, rather, "an unconsummated symbol"[39] in that its import, its expression of insight into feeling, is
more ambivalent than the other occurrent arts. It is, if you will,
more readily of the imagination and open to the Spirit.

Music as art creates its illusion out of sounds. Sounds are
related to one another as significant form. They contain and express insight into life. Like all of the primary abstractions of the
arts, they are not important as literal sounds. Like all artistic elements, they take on artistic import. They become music only
when they become virtual, illusory expressions. Music's illusion
is that of an experience of virtual time created by the primary
abstraction of "sounding forms in motion." "Such motion is the

essence of music, a motion of forms that are not visible, but are given to the ear instead of the eye."[40]

Music's tonal entities move in pure duration. It is a kind of time taken out of time. It is the semblance of time. This is not a measuring of a succession of disconnected moments. It is not pure sequence. It is rather lived or experienced time—time as a passage in which the moments are connected. One moment is the outcome of the last and prepares for the next. "This semblance of this vital, experiential time is the primary illusion of music," according to Langer. "All music creates an order of virtual time, in which its sonorous forms move in relation to each other—always and only to each other, for nothing else exists there. . . . *Music makes time audible, and its form and continuity sensible.*"[41]

Something of this experience of the suspension of ordinary time should be the effect of the art of ritual. It takes us out of time in order to let us experience time as not just a succession of unrelated moments measured by a clock and the turn of the sun. Such an experience of virtual time lets the perceiver feel the pulse of eternity, present in lived and experienced time. It is time connected by eternity. This inward sense of duration which is the essence of music and which resembles ritual must be grasped intuitively.

To experience this, those who compose ritual need to create and enact forms in such a way that our temporal continuity is lost in that of ritual's sounding forms in motion much as music demands the absorption of the whole of our time-consciousness. Both should be, at their best, a passing over and out of time in order to return to it enlightened and enriched.

The creative task of the musician and that of the artist of ritual becomes one of solving the problem of symbolizing the knowledge of experienced time in virtual forms. How does one create an expressive form of the direct experience of time as passage, the sense not of mere change but of connected transience?

Such time symbols are not simple. It is not "length" or "intervals" between moments. Passage has volume. It is not only long or short but great or small. Time experienced is "a big time," "an exciting time," or "a sad time."

As such, this direct experience of time is an indivisible unit filled with tensions and resolutions, rising and falling. Ritual, insofar as it resembles music's forms, must also contain and be an experience of such volume, indivisibility and tension. This is "the illusion of flowing time in its passage, an audible passage filled with motion that is just as illusory as the time it is measuring."[42] As such, music and ritual require a definite time of perception. There must be a clear beginning, development and closing recapitulation. There is, in these two occurrent art forms, "a growth from the first imagination of its general movement to its complete, physical presentation, its occurrence."[43] For music, the occurrence is performance; for ritual, it is celebration.

The composition of music resembles in significant ways the composing of rituals. The first stage of composing musical forms is the conception of the fundamental idea, the commanding form of the work. The artist fiddles with tunes and rhythms until one idea takes over and a structure emerges from the wandering sounds. The ritual maker plays with the words and gestures of the given ritual structure as they relate to the times until some idea, some impulse or insight into life, begins to emerge and dominate the imagination's creative forces. It could be a dominant feeling of hope as the artist creates the liturgies of Advent's four Sundays. This motif then begins to control the creative drive of the imagination as it searches to create symbolic action that expresses the lived experience of hope and its opposites—discouragement, despair, loneliness, etc. Once that commanding form is found, the entire liturgy or series of rituals exists in embryo. In that germ, the general symbolic possibilities are present to be ferreted out by the imagination. Its final form will flow from the aesthetic choices the artist will make to bring the motif to complete ritual articulation—choices of ornamentation, elaboration or simplification. This commanding form unfolds to full expression in processions and rest, song and silence, word and gesture. All are carefully rhythmed "by a sort of implicit logic that all conscious artistry serves to make explicit."[44]

This commanding form is the matrix of the music and the ritual. It exerts a kind of pressure on the creative imagination which is not essentially restrictive but, rather, is fecund. It gives life. There will be a certain rightness and necessity about the idea conceived, a rightness which guides all the artist's judgments about the elements to be used in the expressive form, a rightness to the unified relationships among all the selected elements.

The devices used by composers to establish the primary illusion of time in music are many: recognition of related tones in melodies and harmonies, the intonation of speech patterns, etc. But the most characteristic is rhythm. This is the principle of all vital activity.

Life is rhythmic, organic movement. And art exists to express the highest organic movement, the inner rhythms of the emotional truth of human life. Music does this through rhythm, the same principle that makes our physical existence into a biological design in breathing and heartbeats.

Ritual must be created with these innate rhythms as well. Each new word or gesture is prepared by the ending of the preceding one. This is the essence of rhythm, "the setting up of new tensions by the resolution of former ones. . . . The situation that begets the new crisis must be inherent in the denouement of its forerunner."[45] The fundamental rhythm of life which is to be perceived in the Christian ritual symbols is that of the paschal mystery. Living comes through dying, and death is the door to life. This root metaphor of the Christian faith has its own rhythm which needs expression in the ritual forms of word and sacrament. In this way ritual gives insight into faith with feeling.

The commanding form, or idea, which is born in the ritual artist's imagination as he or she encounters the worlds of texts and times, contains its own organic rhythm as its source of unity. The work unfolds like a flower from its seed. The germination calls for a surrendering as it discloses its inner rhythm, the relation between the tensions. This innate vital rhythm of subjective time, as it unfolds in the composing process, prepares a future, creates expectations and moves the sounding forms to a resolution which relates liturgy intimately to life. Like music, ritual as an art communicates the truth of the Gospel through the forms created out of the attitude of the ritual's artist. This is "an attitude taken up by the artist consequent upon his perceptions. . . . It is characteristic of great art that the attitude it communicates to us is felt by us to be valid, to be the reaction to a more subtle and comprehensive contact with reality than we can normally make."[46] In this sense the art of ritual is in no way superfluous to life. Rather it conveys what cannot otherwise be conveyed. Art is an expressive form appropriate to Mystery.

Liturgy, like music and the other arts, must be composed in an organic way and possess an intrinsic, living unity. It contains the very core of the experience of life which is what Langer calls permanence in change. What is constant in life is change, growth, and development in an organic fashion. Even the change that is death leads to new life.

This paschal mystery is conceived artistically in its many moods of the seasons of the liturgical year and in the modalities of diverse occasions. This mystery becomes the commanding form for the creation and celebration of Christian ritual activity. It is the leit-motif of all liturgy.

What Langer says of a composer of music can be applied analogically to one who composes ritual:

> The "commanding form" . . . controls its entire subsequent development. It is the comprehension of this organic unity and individuality that enables a composer to carry out a protracted piece of work on the strength of one initial "inspiration," and make the product more and more integral, instead of less and less so, by the constant importation of new ideas—sometimes even themes that occurred to him long ago, developments he has used elsewhere, traditional preparations—all to be assimilated and transfigured by the unique composition. As long as he can keep the musical organism alive in his imagination he needs no other rule or goal.[47]

There is another way in which ritual resembles music. Once each has been conceived and given an organic significant form, that form must be created anew in its performance and its celebration. The "piece" of music and the "piece" of ritual need actualization for their completion. They can't be perceived just by reading them. This means that, in one sense, "the piece" does not exist. What does fully come into being as "an organically developed illusion of time in audible passage"[48] is *this particular concrete realization* of the composition. The peril of composers is their dependence on performers in both music and ritual. But performance can also be the composer's fulfillment.

Both musical performance and liturgical celebration call for an intense and consuming encounter with the "composition." It must be studied until understood and practiced until it becomes personally expressive of the truth contained in it, filtered through the performer's/minister's imagination. Without this attention and involvement the composition exists only as so many isolated elements. In music these are pitch, duration, timbre, volume, consonance or dissonance and stress. In ritual these would be ritual pieces—words, gestures and music of the entrance rite, liturgy of the word, liturgy of the Eucharist, etc.— which are not rhythmed and correlated to one another. What is missed is the logical and imaginal connectedness of the tonal or ritual sequence. What Langer says of sound which is not music can be true of ritual as well: "We have no clear awareness of what has passed, and therefore no impression of melodic or harmonic development, nor definite expectation of what is to come.... We hear succession rather than progression...."[49] Ritual involves such progression rather than succession.

In a truly artistic performance or celebration, the created piece is carried to a definite stage of completion. It becomes available for perception and participation. Such performance/ celebration is just as creative an act as composition. The musician and the minister have an aesthetic sensitivity which is stimulated by the composition. They begin to imagine the experience of sounding forms in motion which they are to create in the living work. For them, a "feeling of utterance" sets in. This is not just a subjective gush of emotion, however. This artistic utterance "strives to create as complete and transparent a symbol as possible, whereas personal utterance, under the stress of actual emotion, usually contents itself with half-articulated symbols, just enough to explain the symptoms of inward pressure."[50]

Those who celebrate must walk the thin line between a cold and impersonal robot-rubricism and a personal display of emotion similar to the intimacy called for in an encounter group. This is not an easy balance for the liturgical minister to achieve. As in any performing, occurrent art, it takes patient practice and participant feedback. The goal is to be natural within the limit that is the liturgical context. As has been pointed out above, true creativity always involves the pressure of limitations including the limitation of restraint on personal emotion in ritual. This balance is artistic utterance. It is inspired by the rhythm of the ritual itself and flows from its commanding form.

This balance calls for a kind of imagined, inward seeing and hearing of what the ritual should be like in experience. This is what Aaron Copland calls "the sonorous image."[51] In music and in ritual, beautiful sound cannot be produced without first hearing the imagined sound in the inner ear. This "muscular imagination,"[52] as Langer calls it, conditions the final stage of communicating and communing in the ritual which is the articulate utterance.

Participation in ritual is similar to the experiencing of listening to music. It involves the intelligent engagement of the ears with the expressive form of the ritual. Like musical listening, ritual hearing develops with practice. One can no more appreciate the full depth of an aesthetic worship experience on a first hearing than one can grasp the full import of one of Beethoven's complex last string quartets the first time around.

The first principle in hearing music or ritual is to experience the piece not analytically but synthetically. Listening for separate elements is not what is needed. The participant should strive to feel the work as a whole, to experience the primary illusion which is virtual time, "to feel the consistent movement and recognize at once the commanding form."[53]

In one very notable way, active participation in ritual differs from active listening to music. In ritual, the audience or the assembly is the performer. Participation includes their own words, gestures and music. Those who minister in the ritual do so to energize the audience into ritual performance as well. The congregation is always a performing audience. The artist-ministers must know the techniques which draw people from being spectators into being performers.

Ritual as art must not be done *for* but rather *with* the assembly which is, in a very real sense, a *community* of believers, not merely isolated individuals. Ritual art comes alive when it expresses the real and experienced unity which exists in a faith community. This does not necessarily mean that everyone must know one another. It does mean people who come together with the common attitude of faith to share in *some* common means for the attainment of *some* common ends. As Gabe Huck has said, ritual needs community needs ritual. The two stand in a relationship of reciprocity. Yet the goal of performing participation remains similar to the goal of musical listening, "the perception of feeling through a purely apparent flow of life existing only in time."[54]

One other dimension of musical creation can throw light on the process of creating ritual and that is vocal music. Just as in the composition of song, the words must be transformed from merely verbal material with their sound and meaning into musical material, so in composing ritual, words give up their purely literary status and take on a ritual function. Any expressive form used in ritual must, in fact, become a ritual element. This is exactly what should happen when vocal and choral music are sung during rituals. The words often become only the semblance of speech. The words are assimilated into the illusion created by ritual. They lose themselves insofar as they affect the image of virtual time, dissociated from actual time. They become virtual elements in a realm of purely ritual imagination. Ritual swallows the words and music just as music swallows words in a song. Neither is a hybrid of two or more arts. Each is a complete unified aesthetic expression which every element must serve to create, support and develop. Whatever words are used in ritual must be such that they fit the ritual's flow. To excite the imagination of an artist creating or celebrating ritual, they must be composable ideas which suggest centers of feeling and lines of connection. Words drawn from an historical, theological or scientific vocabulary are not directly composable in ritual. Neither is the verbiage of signal-giving, page-calling, and number-announcing. Such throw-away language interrupts ritual flow. It is not assimilable but stands out as foreign to ritual.

In order to strengthen the case for ritual being similar to music, the creative experience of an American composer will be called upon as a witness—Aaron Copland.

Copland states clearly that music is born in the imagination. In fact, he says that an imaginative mind is essential to the creation of any art. This would include ritual. The creative process for Copland is similar to that described in the previous chapter on creativity in ritual. A germinal idea comes which defies rational explanation. It possesses and inspires the artist as a form of superconsciousness or subconsciousness. "The inspired moment," he says, "may sometimes be described as a kind of hallucinatory state of mind: one half of the personality emotes and dictates while the other half listens and notates."[55] The task in this process is that of extending the germ idea into a whole so that it adds up to a rounded experience. This task of the composer of music resembles that of a ritual maker.

Copland balances the "hallucinatory" with the rational in his description of composition. The creative imagination must also be critical. This means not merely to be aware but also to be "aware of being aware."[56] This is a kind of being both inside and outside the work being created.

When the piece is completed, the composer realizes that, although his creative mind "is very much alive to the component parts of the finished work, it cannot know everything that the work may mean to others. There is an unconscious part in each work—an element that Andre Gide called *la part de Dieu*."[57]

This openness to Spirit must always be kept in mind as rituals are composed. They should never be so tightly organized that nothing "of the moment" can happen since the Spirit blows where it will. As Aidan Kavanaugh has said, liturgy needs to be a little septic. Copland would surely agree since he wrote:

Nothing is so boring as a merely well-rehearsed performance, well-rehearsed in the sense that nothing can be

expected to happen except what was studiously prepared in advance. This has vitiated more than one
tasteful and careful performance. It is as if the musician, during the execution, had stopped listening to
himself, and was simply performing a duty rather than
a piece. It is axiomatic that unless the hearing of the
music first stirs the executant it is unlikely to move an
audience. A live performance should be just that—live
to all the incidents that happen along the way, colored
by the subtle nuances of momentary emotion, inspired
by the sudden insights of public communication.[58]

That is a perfect description of what should be happening
when liturgical ministers lead an assembly in ritual.

Summary

This exploration of the creative core of the four arts of poetry, drama, dance and music has yielded insight into the creative
composing and choreographing of rituals. If one can understand
and has experienced creativity in any one of these occurrent
arts, that person has the aesthetic wherewithal to create ritual.

Such aesthetic sensitivity needs to be complemented by an
understanding of liturgy both historically and theologically. It
goes without saying, I suppose, that a full ritual artist must also
be an intensely committed believer.

Since it is unlikely that many individuals would possess all
of the historical, theological and aesthetic knowledge and gifts
to create rituals alone, it would be optimum for a team of persons with these complementary skills to function together. They
would, of course, function in close union with representatives of
the assembly with and for whom the rituals are being created
and celebrated.

All of this may seem intelligible but unlikely to occur in the
real world of today's Church. But if the thesis is accurate that
ritual as an expressive form is art, then those who care about
worship's effectiveness should begin to pave the way for greater

aesthetic sensitivity in our people and in those who create and lead the celebrations of our ritual events. The final chapter explores one direction in which to proceed.

Notes

1. Susanne K. Langer, *Feeling and Form* (N.Y.: Charles Scribner's Sons, 1953).
2. *Ibid.*, p. 31.
3. *Ibid.*, p. 40.
4. *Ibid.*, p. 46.
5. *Ibid.*, p. 24.
6. *Ibid.*, p. 220.
7. *Ibid.*, p. 228.
8. *Ibid.*, pp. 240–241.
9. *Ibid.*, p. 253.
10. *Ibid.*
11. *Ibid.*, p. 258.
12. *Ibid.*, p. 257.
13. *Ibid.*, p. 254.
14. *Ibid.*, p. 258.
15. *Ibid.*, p. 263.
16. *Ibid.*
17. *Ibid.*, p. 306.
18. *Ibid.*, p. 307.
19. *Ibid.*, p. 308.
20. *Ibid.*
21. *Ibid.*, p. 310.
22. *Ibid.*, p. 311.
23. *Ibid.*, p. 314.
24. *Ibid.*
25. *Ibid.*, p. 315.
26. *Ibid.*, pp. 315–316.
27. *Ibid.*, p. 316.
28. *Ibid.*, p. 323.
29. *Ibid.*, p. 319.
30. *Ibid.*, p. 324.
31. *Ibid.*, p. 175.
32. *Ibid.*, p. 181.
33. *Ibid.*, p. 178.

34. *Ibid.*, p. 203.

35. *Ibid.*, p. 182.

36. *Ibid.*, p. 185.

37. *Ibid.*, p. 203.

38. *Vatican Council II* (Northport, N.Y.: Costello Publishing Co., 1975), quoted from *Constitution on the Sacred Liturgy*, n. 112.

39. Langer, *op. cit.*, p. 31.

40. *Ibid.*, p. 107.

41. *Ibid.*, pp. 109–110.

42. *Ibid.*, p. 120.

43. *Ibid.*, p. 121.

44. *Ibid.*, p. 122.

45. *Ibid.*, p. 127.

46. J.W.N. Sullivan, *Beethoven: His Spiritual Development* (N.Y.: Vintage Books, 1927), p. 16.

47. Langer, *op. cit.*, p. 130.

48. *Ibid.*, p. 134.

49. *Ibid.*, p. 136.

50. *Ibid.*, p. 139.

51. Aaron Copland, *Music and the Imagination* (Cambridge, Mass.: Harvard University Press, 1952), p. 22.

52. Langer, *op. cit.*, p. 140.

53. *Ibid.*, p. 147.

54. *Ibid.*, p. 148.

55. Copland, *op. cit.*, p. 43.

56. *Ibid.*, p. 45.

57. *Ibid.*, p. 46.

58. *Ibid.*, pp. 52–53.

Chapter VII
If Ritual Is Art, How Do We Get There?

In January 1982, at the North American Academy of Liturgy meeting, I made an informal presentation of the thesis that liturgy *is* art. My colleagues were quite taken by this idea and found themselves substantially in agreement with my insight. Many, however, indicated that they felt somewhat inadequate to flesh it out in scholarship and, particularly, in practice. They said they had been schooled more as scientists of liturgy than as its artists. They understood what I was saying but they were not sure what should be done about it, or what *they* could do about it.

One participant in the workshop was a homiletics professor at Colgate University. He urged me to include a chapter in this book on how persons can be educated toward the aesthetic. If all that this book says about ritual as an aesthetic expression is true, then, he suggested, we must raise some radical questions about both liturgical methodology and the education of those who will be the ministers in worship.

This concluding chapter is a response to this man's more than reasonable request to treat of education toward the aesthetic. To raise this issue is, of course, to fly in the face of much that passes as education in our own culture in the United States. It is to propose an alternative consciousness about what it means to learn, indeed, what it means to be human.

I

Another Dimension and Direction for Learning

The arts in this country seem to be going down the tubes. The current budget cuts that affect the position of the arts in our educational system present, in my judgment, a symptom of a serious crisis in contemporary culture. I call it a crisis of the starved imagination. The so-called *quality* of life in a culture with a starved imagination is perverted into a *quantity* of life for hollow consumers. This leads to the belief that more is better and biggest is best. But has this materialism-gone-mad made Americans happy?

If the quality of life in a terribly complex society is to be more than superficial, learning must be more than superficial, according to educator Bennett Reimer.[1] Education must explore the depths of the human spirit; while teaching the sciences and technology, it must not neglect the *human meaning* of these proved scientific facts and the products of technology.

I read too many of the present products of all the educative forces in this country as largely superficial people. Television and the lived values at home counteract any serious efforts in our schools to counteract the sterile and quantitative scientific-technological values which primarily permeate our educational systems. Such values turn out producers and consumers of *things*. But where is the ability to appreciate and enjoy life?

Watch us eat our fast food, or even our fine food, and tell me how advanced are our appreciative powers over those who feed at the trough! Watch us as tourists skim over the surface of what we see, boasting "I saw more than you did during our two hour tour of the Louvre!" Listen to a nation boast of a bomb that will only kill people yet preserve property! For God's sake, what values are we teaching?

I ask you—where's the depth, what are the values, what is the meaning of such an existence? However, in general, the intellectual and moral climate of our times seems agreeable to the proposition that man does not live by bread alone but by adventures at the highest level of human intuition, aspiration and understanding. This, of course, is the level of the arts.

We are a people trapped in our own progress—a folk duped by the dream that bigger is better. Yet the truth is that less is more and more may be less. Outside us we seem to teeter on the brink of annihilation, and inside we feel helpless.

I repeat: "If the quality of life in a terribly complex society is to be more than superficial, learning must be more than superficial."[2] To plumb the depths of human existence, to see more in life than meets the eye demands the sensitizing of the human imagination—that power of *knowing* in us which is beyond logic, science, history and philosophy—imagination, the crossroads of all our faculties where new visions are disclosed and deeper commitments energized.

To speak of the education of the imagination is, of course, to speak of the arts, or, better yet, the aesthetic dimension of all our experience. But to mention the arts in our educational systems may be like speaking of the dead, i.e., it is done in reverent tones yet with a knowledge that life can indeed go on without them. They were, after all, peripheral to education anyway!

But *can* life go on without arts? *Should* it? Well, I suppose the answer to that question will depend upon your understanding of the nature and function of the arts in a culture, a society.

If you share the view of the majority of Americans that art is a fringe factor in the human enterprise, then you can quietly accept the disappearance of the arts from the mainstream of education. And if you equate arts with frivolous entertainment, there to distract us from the main working business of life, then you can acquiesce in the budget cuts for the arts in our society. If you understand the arts as a nice luxury for the elite, mere frosting on the cake of life, then you will not protest the excision of the aesthetic line from your school's budget—at least not with the vigor with which you might protest the reduction of funds for sports programs in that same budget.

Could this mean that we Americans understand life as a game to be won at all costs, a problem to be solved more than a mystery to be lived? Are our violent, competitive sports the major American ritual, reviewing and renewing our self-identity?

If, however, you understand art to be not an extra but an essential in life, indeed that which gives the quality of feeling to our experience, and if you see art as a way of participating profoundly in all experience, then you must speak a prophetic "No" to those who would casually eliminate the arts from our educational curriculum, saying in all charity: "Father, forgive them for they know not what they do."

For surely they cannot know they are shortchanging our learning beings in that area of life which makes life most worth living, that creative part of us, the part that makes us most like our Creator. Surely those in fiscal power cannot mean to turn us into machines who can neither value nor appreciate the beauty, depth, mystery of ordinary existence! Yet as I watch the young and restless—and those not so young who remain restless in their reluctance to release their youth—I wonder if such a shallow civilization can long survive its own superficiality.

It is learning to appreciate the aesthetic qualities, not only in the arts, but in ordinary experience itself which enables us to enjoy the art of living. In this way, value and meaning transcend production and consumer-oriented boredom. The human transcends the mechanical.

Now isn't that precisely what seems to be missing in our current American way of life: significance, meaning, value? We skim the surface of all our experiences without the sensitivity to savor and appreciate the aesthetic qualities of feeling and beauty. We miss life's golden moments because of our compulsive, learned behavior.

Art can develop in us a savoring of significance whether in listening to music rather than being bombarded with incessant sound or in dining rather than in gulping food. The deeper the experience of the aesthetic qualities, the deeper the sense of significance gained from any human experience. Dewey says it well: "The residue of sharing the significant qualities of the art work is a deeper sense of the nature of human life."[3]

We talk today of "life-styles" and "the quality of life." From what I can observe, our society educates us not into a *quality* of life but into a *quantity* of life in which we nearly strangle ourselves in consuming goods—and consuming people as though they were goods for consumption as well. This is what one often discovers to be the meaning of free alternate life-styles—styles of living which deal with all reality, including ourselves, as objects, as things to possess and manipulate without the feeling of subjective, committed responsiveness. In our restless quest for more and more, we may be losing our feeling for life itself.

Without the arts, a major part of human reality would be closed off to comprehension: namely, human feeling. The arts are not superfluous. They exist to convey that which cannot be otherwise conveyed. Mere words cannot reflect the subjective, feeling level of existence.

The arts are the means for exploring and understanding subjective responsiveness. A discerning sensitivity to the aesthetic qualities in a work of art can arouse feelings, meanings and values which far transcend mere information about feeling, information conveyed by the sciences, history, and philosophy. "Science has been able to provide knowledge of matter . . . but not of its essence."[4] The arts allow us to experience immediately the organic feeling of life itself with its rhythms of tension and resolution. In his philosophy of music education, Bennett Reimer tells us: "The arts are the most powerful tools available for refining and deepening . . . experiences of feeling."[5]

Art, then, is simply a heightened and intensified experience of the aesthetic meaning present in all experience—for those with eyes to see and ears to hear, to paraphrase the man Jesus who was the art of the incarnate God. All experience is art in germ because experience is what art is, namely an organism's struggles in an environment to make order and meaning out of chaos and absurdity.

The commitment demanded of educators in this society of starved imagination is staggering. To a great extent, upon our educational efforts may depend the survival of the human race. As long as art remains merely the beauty parlor of civilization, civilization is not secure. An education which relies primarily upon analytic and discursive reason greatly reduces the possibility and the extent of human knowing. " 'Reason' at its height,"

Dewey warns us, "cannot attain complete grasp and a self-contained assurance. It must fall back upon imagination—upon the embodiment of ideas in an emotionally charged sense."[6]

Without the arts as the expression of imagination, we teach facts without human meaning, and share information without human insight. What is truly *human* in reality cannot be *pointed to* but must be *embodied* in the shapes, patterns and forms of the arts.

A retrieval of the arts in our academic enterprise is, I submit, a major factor in educating beyond the superficial, in leading out into the deep streams of human living. We must not limit ourselves in education to methods so literal as to exclude the imagination, methods not touching the desires and emotions of the learners and teachers as well.

All who teach must learn that art separated from life separates us from life's fullness. We need to know that "instruction in the arts of life is something other than conveying information about them. It is a matter of communication and participation in values of life by means of the imagination, and works of art are the most intimate and energetic means of aiding individuals to share in the arts of living."[7]

If we are to prepare generations of the future to create a civilization beyond that bomb which is the triumph of a bankrupt scientific-technological culture, we must neither eliminate nor reduce our commitment to aesthetic education. A movement toward a better world will involve aesthetic sensitivity in persons who would make peace, not war. As Dewey has remarked, a person to be greatly good must imagine intensely and comprehensively.[8] The kingdom of justice and peace proclaimed in liturgy will only be enfleshed in history if imaginations become energized to envision that just world which is God's gift but in a shape of our imagining.

For the sake of a future full of hopeful significance rather than hopeless superficiality, we educators need to take to heart John Dewey's insight into the relation between art and civilization: "The final measure of the quality of that culture is the arts which flourish. Compared with their influence, things directly taught by word and precept are pale and ineffectual."[9]

II
Education Toward the Aesthetic for the Sake of Ritual

Ritual creators must be persons who are aesthetically aware. They should be exposed to good art from the earliest years of life. They also should be helped to be aware of and perceive the aesthetic dimension and quality in all human experience. In this way people's imaginations become energized to see the world in new ways. The important but limited objective view of reality which is given by the sciences of reason is complemented by a vision of the truly human dimension of existence, the realm of the subjective, the deep river of human feelingfulness.

With such an activated imagination as a principle of knowing underlying even reason, a person can quite naturally experience creativity in everyday life simply by making meaning out of his or her relationship to all that happens. Such an aesthetically alive being will be also conditioned to perceive the aesthetic qualities in the refined works of art. This, in turn, can prepare that person to create and celebrate the art of ritual.

Plato has given a wise chart to follow in introducing one to the aesthetic:

> For he who would proceed aright in this manner should begin in youth to visit beautiful forms; and first, if he be guided by his instructor aright, to love one such form only—out of that he should create fair thoughts; and soon he will of himself perceive that the beauty of one form is akin to the beauty of another, and that beauty in every form is one and the same.[10]

Exposure to and experience with aesthetic forms is an indispensable element in educating persons to be ritual artists. They must know drama, music, dance and poetry by studying it and experiencing it. Unfortunately, this has not been a sufficiently significant part of seminary formation. And clergy are not notable in their participation in their own community's aesthetic activities. Their training did not show this to be important either for ministry or humanity.

Yet, if the thesis of this book is correct, and if John Henry Newman is right in asserting that faith begins and grows in the imagination, then we who preside and preach at faith celebrations neglect the arts to our personal and professional peril. The responsiveness to forms of feeling, i.e., aesthetic awareness, may be missing in us. Our recited rituals and our pat preaching can disclose our imaginations' poverty.

But whose fault is it? Aren't we simply doing unto others as was done unto us? Aren't we using the only form of communication with which we are most familiar and comfortable, namely the didactic lecture approach? Surely, blame is not the issue. Conversion is.

If there is to be a change it may come from some few who seek to fill the gap in their learning by reading and sharing in aesthetic experiences. Some may risk experimenting with expressive forms in ritual which prepare for communing rather than communicating. For the majority, however, a more radical redirection may be required. A more substantial change in educational philosophy and curriculum will be required of schools of ministerial education if such aesthetic sensitivity is to be brought forth from the many who are called to minister in worship.

First, the prejudice against the arts as frivolous, froth, or frosting on the cake must be overcome in our society. We must come to value what is apparently non-productive and non-consumed. As one poet, W. H. Auden, notes:

> ... poetry makes nothing happen; it survives
> In the valley of its saying where executives
> Would never want to tamper.[11]

We must treasure not just the disciplines of reason and science which make things happen. We need to develop a natural appreciation for those disciplines of the imagination which give meaning, value and feeling to all that is made to happen and even that which happens without our making. The arts must be accepted as ways of knowing through expression and perception, equal partners with the sciences in the venture of human cognition. Only then will they be valued enough to hold a central place in curricula.

A challenging and exciting proposal in this direction has been made recently by that noted humanist educator, Mortimer J. Adler. In his book, *The Paideia Proposal: An Educational Manifesto*, Adler insists that America's young need to receive a general and liberal education. The present multitrack system, based upon early specialization and vocational training, is the besetting sin of our time. His radical reform proposal would aim at "enabling the young to become better human beings and better citizens, not just better at some particular line of work."[12]

He proposes three columns in a curriculum which would continue simultaneously for the twelve years of schooling. The first is the acquisition of fundamental knowledge in all areas of learning. This would be taught didactically by lectures and the like. The second develops basic skills: reading, writing, mathematical and unscientific methods. These are taught through practice and coaching. The third column serves to enlarge understanding. It is the aesthetic appreciation of art and critical and evaluative thought. This would be done by the Socratic method with teachers and pupils engaged in experiences and discussions as equals. Paideia thus becomes "the general learning that should be the possession of all human beings."[13] Models are being experimented with at high schools in Chicago and Oakland, California. Catholic educators might do well to consider such a comprehensive curriculum as a way of educating the whole person.

A curriculum at any educational level which takes aesthetic knowing seriously would have students both participating in the creation of art and in perception of works of art. Attendance at dramatic performances, ballet, opera, and concerts should be credited and connected to a class which involves both sharing information and background about the works and post-reflection on the aesthetic experience which each participant had. Such aesthetic experience must be more than entertainment. It must be learning.

In this process of direct engagement with aesthetic forms, students could come, by experience, to an appreciation of what it means to create and to appreciate art. The principles of creativity could be articulated and the imagination energized by experience and reflection upon that experience. Gradually the aesthetic dimension of all experience would become an active part of their normal perceptions of life. This spirit communicated in our educational systems can change the shape of the liturgical minister's personal life as well as his or her creating of worship experiences. A new wide-awakeness in the ritual artist will surely keep the folks in the pews awake and lead them to fuller, active, interior participation.

With regard to investing this heightened aesthetic awareness into ritual-making, students preparing for liturgical ministry and artistry should engage regularly in the creative process outlined in Chapters V and VI. Having learned the ways that drama, music, dance and poetry are created, they should ply their imaginations in the creative composing of religious rituals. This encounter with the texts and the times which constitutes ritual creativity will allow them to create and critique within a learning environment. They will then not face their first Mass, or whatever, with cold, simplistic questions like "What songs will we sing?" and "Who should bring up the gifts?" Instead the newly trained liturgical artist will engage in a creative process for his or her initial public ritual which will produce a through-composed unified experience for the entire assembly. Regrettably, candidates for ordination to the priesthood today are rarely prepared for ritual as art.

One problem in preparing persons for liturgical ministry lies with those who teach the subject. Seminarians are usually taught liturgy by persons schooled in liturgy-as-history and liturgy-as-theology. Their methodologies were learned in Paris or Mainz or Trier or the spin-offs of those academic institutions in the United States such as the University of Notre Dame and The Catholic University of America. I taught in both of these latter places briefly and learned to respect the contribution these scholars have made to the long twilight struggle of liturgical renewal. Their awareness of structures and texts of the past have been valuable contributions to the restoration of our rituals. But theirs is only one part of the liturgical task.

If liturgy's language is aesthetic and if liturgy's principal appeal is to the human imaginative system, then liturgical studies must review its methodologies. To date it seems that this discipline, or constellation of disciplines, has resembled the first seven functional specialties of Bernard Lonergan's *Method in Theology:* research, interpretation, history, dialectic, foundations, doctrines and systematics.[14] Now is the time to engage in Lonergan's eighth functional specialty as well: communications. Here, according to Lonergan, is where "theological reflection bears fruit. Without the first seven stages, of course, there is no fruit to be borne. But without the last the first seven are in vain, for they fail to mature."[15] Lonergan states that all eight specialties are tasks for the theologian. "Communications is concerned with theology in its external relations."[16] He mentions interdisciplinary relations with art, language and literature.

Method in liturgical studies must include that eighth specialty as well. Through the interactions of theologians and artists, we will come to understand not only the history of our rites but also the rhythms of the forms of imagination which can move the soul.

Imagination has not been the dominant motif of Western Christianity or of our theological education since the Aristotelian movement provided a fairly clear *terminus ad quem* for the earlier Latin theology of the image. Many have feared the ambiguity of this older stress in Scripture, the Fathers and the Latin monastic tradition. This may be the day to retrieve that ancient tradition.

Academic institutions preparing liturgists must not be satisfied merely with graduates who know history and theology. Graduate programs must prepare people to *do* liturgy, not just *know about* liturgy. In my experience those who profess great knowledge of the subject are not infrequently unable to create and celebrate effectively. This is not to criticize them personally. It is rather to point out that gifts other than those of liturgical scholarship are required to make liturgy live. Artists of ritual are needed who can be like the performers who complete the musical composition in an articulate utterance. Graduate schools of liturgical studies, seminaries and ministry training programs must incorporate this dimension into their curricula. To paraphrase Aristotle, knowledge about liturgy does not make the good liturgist. But a ritual maker who works aesthetically can create the conditions of possibility for perceiving the mystery many claim to miss in the modern Mass. As Herbert Marcuse says: "Art makes the petrified world speak, sing, perhaps dance."[17] Is it pure fantasy to suppose that future priests be required to possess a certain aesthetic sensitivity so that the world of faith can speak, sing and dance?

Educating toward the aesthetic in liturgy needs to take place not only in higher liturgical education, in ministerial education and in general education. It must also happen for the persons in our pews on the Lord's Day. The average parishioner must not be confused by a new breed of tyrannical liturgical reformer called the aesthete. Inflicting novelties upon unsuspecting believers would be anything but beautiful. If it is truly beautiful, it persuades to its own truth and validity.

Some explanation is called for to prepare the people to understand and participate in liturgy as art. But it is my conviction that the best education at this level is experience. If ritual is created and celebrated as an art form rather than a communal recipe-reading, the people will be educated by the experience. The proof of the pudding is in the eating.

A few years ago I proposed to Bishop Edward W. O'Rourke of Peoria that we invite the eighteen members of our Civic Ballet to be among the artists of the ritual of the Vigil of Easter. They were to dance during the Light Service, the Exultet, the Exodus reading and the Alleluia. He reluctantly agreed to try it—once! But he feared more negative than positive reactions.

When the vigil ended, the bishop came up to me and said, "I take it all back. That was Easter." Later, in the rectory, he told one of the Knights of Columbus, "If someone told you they danced in the cathedral at Easter you would think it was wrong. But, if you were there, you would know it was right." The "proof of the pudding" for parishioners is largely in the experience of exploration more than in an exhaustive explanation.

Don't misunderstand this example, please. I am not saying that ritual requires dance or any extravagant addenda in order to be expressed and experienced as art. As a matter of fact, doing ritual as art does not necessarily require changes in the present ritual texts and structures. They are not perfect, of course, but they can be made to flow if done with aesthetic sensitivity. Our present problem is not primarily textual or structural but aesthetic. The change called for is more in the imagination of the liturgical ministers who are creating the rhythm of the rite with the assembly. If an art work of public prayer is expressed, people will perceive it and participate in it prayerfully. When it's over, they'll know the difference. Mystery will have been experienced as Presence.

Parishes must begin to consider hiring or training a ritual artist to coordinate the local ritual events. At budget time, that parish activity which touches most people, most often, and possibly most profoundly must be given a larger share of the fiscal pie. If we are serious about our ritual as art rather than merely as texts, then someone trained in the art of worship must be part of the parish staff.

The ritual maker in a parish would be ideally someone who is part of that worshiping assembly, hopefully a deeply committed person of faith as well as a formally trained ritual artist. Such a staff member would not replace the liturgy committee but would work closely with that body.

For example, the liturgy committee would meet in September to create, compose and choreograph the Advent and Christmas celebrations for the parish. They might pray over the scriptural and ritual texts at home, making notes on what connections their imaginations made between the texts and the times. These personal reflections would be shared in the committee meeting. The artist, of course, would be a committee member. Previous images, symbols, stories, myths and ritual actions connected with that assembly's celebrations would be reviewed. Goals and directions are thus given to the artist by the committee. The artist would participate in all this, especially by careful listening and imaging.

After the meeting ends the artist goes away to his privacy to create the ritual on paper. The process may be one very much like that of a composer of music. It may resemble what happened for Arthur Honegger, the twentieth century French composer. He called it "a secret operation, mysterious and untransmittable."[18] It begins always, he claims, in the imagination. A lengthy quotation describing the compositional process pursued by Honegger offers some sense of how creation can happen.

> Like all the arts, we have rules which we have learned, and which have come down to us from the masters. But over and beyond the studied, consciously willed, inherited "craft" of the profession, three remains a kind of compulsion for which we are not, so to speak, responsible. It is a drive from our subconscious which resists explanation.[19]

> I first seek the contour, the general aspect of the work. Let us say, for example, that I see taking form a sort of palace in a very opaque fog. Reflection progressively dissipates this fog and permits me to see a bit more clearly into it. Sometimes a beam of sunlight appears to illumine a wing of the palace as it grows: this fragment then becomes my model. When this phenomenon spreads, I begin my search for my materials for construction. I prospect in my notebooks. . . .

> When a motif, a rhythm, an entire phrase comes to me, I jot it down. . . . So I check my notebooks of sketches in the hope of uncovering there some melodic design, a rhythmic plan, or some sequence of chords susceptible of being useful. Sometimes I think I have found what I am looking for, and I set to work. Often I start off on a false scent.

> Then, like a ragman, I take up my basket and set forth in quest of more appropriate fragments. I try again. I permit a melodic line to ripen, I project the different

paths it opens to me. What disillusionment! One needs the courage to start again three, four, five times. Such, for those who ask, is the definition of talent: "The courage to begin again." Sometimes, a very secondary element will yield the key to the problem. This rhythm or this motif, which had seemed so banal to me, I suddenly perceive in its true light; it interests me passionately, and I will not abandon it for an instant.[20]

Honegger's description of "the secret operation" gives some insight into the way one could approach the composition of ritual expressions. Creativity, which Honegger calls "an uncommon use of ordinary materials,"[21] will call for the artist of ritual to find time and space for fruitful reflection without interruption. For this reason it may be difficult for a pastor of a large parish to function as the community's liturgical creator. A parish liturgist may be needed to give something of the kind of attention to composing ritual which Honegger says he gives to composing music. Of course, ritual creativity begins with much more already given than a musical composition, namely the texts and the times. Nevertheless, a ritual maker can learn from a composer's experience. Honegger writes:

I am shut up in my studio. I try not to hear the doorbell or the telephone. Anyone who watched me without seeing me would undoubtedly get the impression of a man on a holiday. I come and go, I take a book from the shelf, I reread a favorite passage, I open a score. I offer, indeed, the picture of a man completely at leisure.

Nevertheless, I am unable to apply myself definitely to reading or to any other distraction, because I discover within me an urge for expression trying to seek the light of day. Sometimes the day and night pass without my writing a note. Or I take a pencil and try to recover the points of departure which I had thought I had found and have lost. I am a steam engine; I need to be stoked up; it takes me a long time to get ready for genuine work. If I relax for the duration of a month, I need days or weeks to get the machine in motion. This getting started becomes more and more painful with age. Nevertheless, the motor runs true only directly in gear.[22]

Honegger's creative goal is similar to that of the creator of ritual expressions. Both choose to compose forms "which would be comprehensible to the great mass of listeners and at the same time sufficiently free of banality to interest"[23] the more sophisticated. This underlines the claim made earlier that ritual is an expression somewhere between folk and fine art, somewhere between absolute programmed activity and utter spontaneity.

After this period of incubation and creativity, the ritual artist may go back to the committee for feedback before completing the work. Such completion means bringing created form to articulate utterance in celebration. It means selecting and training the various ministers much in the way a director of a drama would function. Each minister must understand the ritual as a whole as well as his or her part. The artist or perhaps another "director" coordinates the preparations and choreographs the ritual toward its enactment. In this way the action flows faithfully from the commanding form created by the artist.

After a season or a special celebration has been completed, the committee functions again to give feedback to the artist on the strengths and weaknesses of the ritual art work. In this way of both guiding and critiquing the artist and the work, the committee fulfills its function. The committee should be composed not only of representatives of all the various liturgical ministries but also of several persons in the pew and the priests.

This, it seems to me, is a more challenging and also realistic role for the liturgical committee than that assumed by many such groups, namely liturgy "planning" or picking songs. If a ritual is "planned" by a committee it may become a filling-of-the-slots in an outline. We give and take on who gets to choose which songs and rituals. It is scarcely a through-composed piece with unity and integrity.

This reminds me of the story about the origin of the camel. It is a horse created by a committee. A committee that commissions a sculptor for a piece to adorn the new Civic Center gives directions, makes suggestions and sets policies to guide the artist. They do not participate directly in creating the work. Later they give feedback and critique—and retain or fire the artist. An analogical role should be served by a liturgy committee vis-à-vis its ritual artist.

Conclusion

We who are artists must now take up the torch in that long twilight struggle which is liturgical renewal. In our hands and imaginations, more than those of scholars, will rest the greatest share of this burden for the remainder of the century. Choreographing liturgy toward the imagination will be, I submit, our prime agenda.

The task of making ritual an art which allows assemblies to experience Presence and Mystery is breathtaking. No one says it more imaginatively than James Carroll in his novel, *Madonna Red*. This was cited earlier and can serve here as an effective conclusion to these reflections. The scene is Washington, D.C. Father Tierney is preparing the daughter of the British ambassador for her First Communion. The ambassador anxiously says to the priest:

> "Perhaps you'd understand what I mean, Father, if you had a daughter. Frankly I do not think Catholicism as it is now will engage her imagination sufficiently to survive into adulthood with her."
> "I think I do understand what you mean, frankly." Tierney's voice too had a sudden edge to it. "In a small way I do have a daughter. Yours. And the challenge of nurturing in her a religious, a Catholic imagination leaves me winded."[24]

Perhaps it will be only after we are sufficiently winded, that is, out of the hot air of our explanations, that we can truly *do* ritual. Only when our wind becomes taken up into the Spirit, which breathes where it will, can we create liturgy as an expression and an experience of the Mystery of Christ present in the assembly. Perhaps it will be when engaged artistic imaginations make liturgy what it truly is—an art—that believers' imaginations can know the faith that survives into adulthood.

Serious art has never grown from theories, even the theory of this book. It grows organically in its expression and experience. "Its carriers and supporters have been those few creative natures for whom a path of work has been determined by destiny."[25]

So, come on, artists! Our time is now! Stop *talking* about it! *Do* it!

Notes

1. Bennett Reimer, *A Philosophy of Music Education* (Englewood Cliffs, N.J.: Prentice Hall, 1970), p. 8.

2. *Ibid.*

3. John Dewey, *Art as Experience* (N.Y.: Minton, Balch & Co., 1934), p. 25.

4. *Ibid.*, p. 15.

5. Reimer, *op. cit.*, p. 38.

6. Dewey, *op. cit.*, p. 33.

7. *Ibid.*, p. 336.

8. *Ibid.*, p. 349.

9. *Ibid.*, p. 345.

10. *Plato, Symposium* in the *Portable Greek Reader*, ed. W.H. Auden (N.Y.: Vintage Books, 1948), p. 496.

11. W.H. Auden, "In Memory of W. B. Yeats," in *Selected Poetry of W.H. Auden* (N.Y.: Vintage Books, 1970), p. 52.

12. Mortimer J. Adler, *The Paideia Proposal: An Educational Manifesto* (N.Y.: Macmillan, 1982).

13. *Time*, September 6, 1982, p. 59.

14. Bernard Lonergan, *Method in Theology* (N.Y.: Herder and Herder, 1972), p. 127.

15. *Ibid.*, p. 355.

16. *Ibid.*, p. 132.

17. Herbert Marcuse, *The Aesthetic Dimension* (Boston: Beacon Press, 1978), p. 72.

18. Arthur Honegger, *I Am a Composer* (N.Y.: St. Martin's Press, 1966), p. 74.

19. *Ibid.*

20. *Ibid.*, pp. 64–82.

21. *Ibid.*, pp. 71–72.

22. *Ibid.*, pp. 84–85.

23. *Ibid.*, p. 92.

24. James Carroll, *Madonna Red* (N.Y.: Little, Brown and Co., 1976), p. 81.

25. Mary Wigman, "The New German Dance," in *Modern Dance*, p. 20, quoted in Susanne K. Langer's *Feeling and Form* (N.Y.: Charles Scribner's Sons, 1953), p. 206.